KAS THOMAS
PERSONAL AIRCRAFT MAINTENANCE

A Do-It-Yourself Guide for Owners and Pilots

McGRAW-HILL BOOK COMPANY

New York   St. Louis   San Francisco   Auckland   Bogotá
Hamburg   Johannesburg   London   Madrid   Mexico
Montreal   New Delhi   Panama   Paris   São Paulo
Singapore   Sydney   Tokyo   Toronto

Library of Congress Cataloging in Publication Data

Thomas, Kasman.
Personal aircraft maintenance.

  (McGraw-Hill series in aviation)
  Includes index.
  1. Airplanes—Maintenance and repair. I. Title.
II. Series.
TL671.9.T48   629.134'6   79-29721
ISBN 0-07-064241-9

1 2 3 4 5 6 7 8 9 0 VHVH 8 9 8 7 6 5 4 3 2 1

The editors for this book were Jeremy Robinson and Joan Zseleczky,
the designer was Elliot Epstein, and the production supervisor was
Paul A. Malchow. It was set in Electra by Waldman Graphics, Inc.

Printed and bound by Von Hoffman Press, Inc.

Quotation: p. ix, from Richard Bach's *A Gift of Wings*, p. 111,
copyright © 1974 by Creature Enterprises, Inc. Reprinted by
permission of Delacorte Press/Eleanor Friede.

Frontispiece: Beechcraft Skipper. (*Beech Aircraft Corporation*)

CONTENTS

PREFACE

When it comes to performing maintenance on their own planes, pilots stand confronted (as Pogo said) by insurmountable opportunities. The opportunities are many, but pilots see mainly the roadblocks that stand between them and the opportunities. "I don't know how to do any maintenance," some aviators say. "I don't feel safe doing my own work," others admit. "The FARs won't let me do the things I need to do," many pilots complain.

Actually, pilots are not nearly as hog-tied by the Federal Aviation Regulations as they think. (FAR Part 43 allows pilots to perform practically all the maintenance checks required for an average 100-hr inspection; with appropriate supervision, a pilot can do much more.) The most serious impediment to pilot involvement in maintenance is not the rulebook or the FAA, but the present lack of well-illustrated, up-to-date service literature dealing with routine lightplane maintenance. It is true that pilots have always been able to avail themselves of manufacturers' service manuals; however, these ponderous tomes (which vie with insurance policies for their lack of readability) offer the inexperienced pilot–mechanic surprisingly little in the way of usable "here's how it's done" information, particularly when it comes to small jobs, such as pulling an engine's oil screen. The FAA's handbooks for mechanics, with their case-hardened prose and their heavy emphasis on theory, are not much better. (The government handbooks do a good job of explaining how jet engines work. They don't say anything about how to reline Cleveland brakes.)

This book is an attempt to fill in the gaps left by the manufacturers' manuals and FAA handbooks and to provide pilots with a truly *practical* guide to the performance of routine maintenance. It is written from the pilot's point of view. Included in this volume are discussions of all the most commonly performed maintenance checks from spark-plug cleaning to brake-pad replacement, preceded by discussions of the legalities, tool requirements, and special safety precautions that make aircraft maintenance unique and followed by troubleshooting charts designed to help the reader make an intelligent judgment concerning when (and when *not*) to take the plane to the shop.

If you have ever wanted to reline your brakes, clean and gap your spark plugs, service an oleo strut, replace cockpit windows, add soundproofing, install a new battery, change a flat tire, fix a cracked fairing, lubricate your control system, clean your fuel strainer, change your oil filter, bleed your brakes, or troubleshoot your starter, this book will tell you how. You'll learn what tools to use and where to get them, which procedures to follow, what common errors to avoid—and even how to get longer service life out of new parts, in many instances.

The emphasis in this book is on *how to*; the text only occasionally ascends into the rarefied air of theory, and then only where absolutely necessary. I have made every attempt to concentrate on specifics, where actual maintenance procedures are being discussed. Nonetheless, there are some areas (upholstery, for example) in which airplanes differ so drastically in hardware usage and component design that I have been forced to offer only general advice. In these areas, the reader should be guided by the aircraft service manual. (It goes without saying that the aircraft service manual should be consulted before maintenance task is begun. This book is meant to *supplement*, not replace, the service manual.)

Naturally, no volume of this scope can truly be considered the product of one person working alone. In preparing this book, I have drawn on the collective wisdom and experience of many, many people. Although there is not space enough here to mention by name all the individuals responsible (directly or indirectly) for the genesis of this book, I would like to offer my profound gratitude to at least the following persons:

To Thomas A. Bishop and his co-workers at Cleveland Wheels and Brakes, who graciously proofread and commented on the wheel and brake chapters, and without whose help those chapters might have suffered in breadth and depth.

To William R. McFall—airline transport pilot, airframe and powerplant rated mechanic, corporate jet jockey, and long-time friend—who kindly read and offered helpful suggestions regarding much of the manuscript during its preparation.

To the mechanics at Asheville (North Carolina) Flying Service, who patiently answered questions, demonstrated procedures, and held still for photographs.

To my parents, who as always offered encouragement whenever it was needed. (In addition, my father, Robert E. Thomas, offered a good deal of solid technical advice which found its way into many parts of the book; for this, I am very grateful.)

And finally, to my wife Karen, who did so much more than I had any right to ask.

Kas Thomas

It was all there in the hangar to see, the moment I opened my eyes, like an exhibit in a museum when the light is turned on . . . . Like a new art student who in one day first sees the work of Vincent Van Gogh and Auguste Rodin and Alexander Calder, so I suddenly noticed the work of Snap-On and Craftsman and the Crescent Tool Company, gleaming silent and waiting in battered toolbox trays.

RICHARD BACH,
A *Gift of Wings*

Suppose that during the course of your next biennial flight review you are asked to take a short test. Furthermore, suppose that this short test consists of the following 10 multiple-choice questions. (You have two minutes to finish.)

1. Your plane's nose-strut oleo is low. You rock the plane's nose up and down; when you let go of the plane, the nose continues to oscillate for several seconds. From this, you know that the strut is in need of
   a. oil
   b. air
   c. water

2. An aircraft spark plug must be replaced when its electrodes are worn
   a. to a gap of 0.030 in.
   b. to a gap of 0.020 in.
   c. to less than 50 percent of their original size

3. When an aircraft engine's cylinders are painted green around the base, you know that the cylinders are
   a. chrome-walled
   b. nitrided
   c. 0.010 in. oversize in bore

4. Cleveland organic brake linings must be replaced when
   a. the brake pedals begin to feel spongy
   b. the pads have worn to a thickness of 0.100 in. or less
   c. the pads have worn to a thickness of 0.010 in. or less

5. To lubricate an aileron piano hinge, you would use
   a. lightweight engine oil
   b. dry graphite
   c. any high-quality bearing grease

6. An air-oil separator is normally used in conjunction with
   a. a dry-type vacuum pump
   b. a wet-type vacuum pump
   c. a rear-mounted prop governor

7. Aircraft batteries are normally
   a. 18 or 36 V, grounded negatively
   b. 12 or 24 V, grounded positively
   c. 12 or 24 V, grounded negatively

8. A much smaller than normal rpm drop on single-mag operation is cause to suspect
   a. water in the fuel
   b. improperly advanced magneto-to-engine timing
   c. failure of the magneto impulse couplings

ONE
PREVENTIVE MAINTENANCE AND YOU

9. An rpm increase of 150 to 200 rpm during engine shutdown indicates an idle-mixture setting that is
   a. too lean
   b. too rich
   c. just right

10. A pilot can legally do all but which of the following to a plane (without the aid of a mechanic):
    a. replace the cockpit windshield
    b. replace cockpit side windows
    c. troubleshoot landing light circuitry.

Now that you're finished, score yourself. (The answers to the test appear on the last page of this chapter.) Considering that this quiz covers pretty basic material—material that every pilot should know—you really should have gotten nothing less than a perfect score. But in any event, you can consider a score of 8 or 9 out of 10 good, and 7 fair; any score of less than 7 right answers is ample reason for you to buy this book.

If you scored somewhat low on this quickie quiz, don't feel bad. (Most pilots would not fare well on *any* test of maintenance knowledge.) It's actually not your fault that you didn't do better. The fact is, an overwhelming confluence of forces and events has acted to virtually guarantee that today's pilot remains ignorant in the area of maintenance.

One reason pilots are less "maintenance proficient" than they should be is that the Federal Aviation Administration (FAA) no longer requires—as the old Civil Aeronautics Administration did—that applicants for private and commercial licenses study maintenance *per se* before being allowed to take written and practical tests. Today's student pilot is a walking encyclopedia of meteorological lore, a master of Federal Aviation Regulations (FARs), and an expert in radio navigation, dead reckoning, and half a dozen other subjects. Yet this same person generally knows little or nothing about aircraft maintenance. It's not on the FAA tests.

Along with the FAA, the large general aviation manufacturers have done their share to discourage pilot involvement in maintenance by, among other things, peppering owner's manuals with admonishments to the effect that all routine maintenance (even the simplest oil or filter change) should be carried out by factory-authorized service personnel. (Auto manufacturers do the same thing: General Motors urges its customers to leave routine maintenance to authorized GM dealers. The dealers, after all, lose money if you change your car's oil yourself.) Nowhere do the manufacturers tell you that it is, in fact, perfectly legal for you to do most of the actual work involved in a 100-hr. inspection.

Perhaps nothing discourages pilots from becoming involved in maintenance, however, as much as the FARs. So sternly worded are the FARs pertaining to the performance of aircraft maintenance that many pilots hesitate even to change their oil, for fear of imprisonment. The imposing language and Byzantine complexity of the FARs have understandably caused a large number of otherwise rational pilots to fear personal involvement in aircraft maintenance, to the extent that most owners would rather have a mechanic put air in their tires or add water to the battery than do it themselves.

The net effect of all this has been to convince pilots that (1) there is not a great deal in the way of meaningful maintenance that an owner can legally do to a plane, and (2) consequently, there is no real reason for pilots to become personally involved in maintenance on a dirt-under-the-fingernails level. "Why should I get involved in maintenance?" many pilots ask themselves. "After all, there's nothing *I* can do."

Of course, that's sheer nonsense. There happens to be a great deal you can legally do to your plane in the way of minor maintenance (minor in terms of the labor involved, not minor in significance). And there happen to be many good reasons why you should be doing these things—why you should consider personal involvement in aircraft maintenance not only desirable, but essential.

For starters, consider the fact that lightplane mechanics are becoming frighteningly scarce. In 1977, according to Labor Department statistics, there were approximately 0.73 general aviation mechanics for every 1000 airplane-hours flown by the general aviation fleet. In 1985, there will be only 0.54 mechanics per 1000 hours flown. From 1977 to 1985, the fleet size will have increased some 47 percent, and hours flown will have climbed 53 percent—but the mechanic population will have grown only 13 percent. Obviously, if this trend continues, something's got to give: Either general aviation aircraft are going to have to become easier to maintain (possible, but not likely); or a great many more lightplane mechanics are going to have to join the work force (also not likely, since the airlines are hiring mechanics away from general aviation at a record rate); or we're all going to have to fly fewer hours and pay more for maintenance. Or—there's a fourth option—we're all going to have to learn to do our own routine maintenance (i.e., the oil and filter changes, spark-plug rotations, and other mundane tasks that currently take up about one-quarter of the average mechanic's time).

Even if the prospect of a serious mechanic shortage doesn't worry you, there are some very sound economic reasons for you to become personally involved in the servicing of your plane. Let's face it: Maintenance is expensive and rapidly becoming more so. Mechanics' wages, kept pitifully low for many years, have finally begun to rise to realistic levels (meaning that mechanics are now on an equal wage footing with garbage collectors), and shop rates around the country have begun to reflect this. (No longer is it possible to have your Cessna worked on for an hourly rate below what you'd pay to have your car serviced.) Shop rates of $35 to $40 per hour are just around the corner. In some cases, they're already here.

The choice is yours: Pay $50 for an oil change ($100 if you own a twin), or unbuckle the cowling and do it yourself. Spend $50 to $100 every 100 hours to have someone else service your spark plugs, or pull, clean, gap, and rotate them yourself. Pay a mechanic $40 or $50 or more to reline your brakes for you, or learn how to do the job yourself at a total parts cost of $10 or $12.

If you can afford to spend $2000 a year to have somebody else do all the minor maintenance on your light single (twice that figure for a light twin), that's great—you probably don't need this book. If not, you need to learn as much as you can as fast as you can about aircraft maintenance, so that you will be able to (1) do as much of your own work as you can. (2) know how to get a good deal on the work you can't do yourself, and (3) understand how to operate your plane so as to avoid costly repairs. (This book will help you in all three areas.)

Even if you're not worried about the impending mechanic shortage (and you have the money to afford professional maintenance 100 percent of the time), there are still valid reasons for you to become much more maintenance proficient. One of the most pressing is FAR 91.163(a). This regulation (in case you haven't studied your FARs in a while) puts the responsibility for maintaining a plane in flyable condition squarely on the owner's or operator's shoulders. It states: "The owner or operator of an aircraft is primarily responsible for maintaining that aircraft in an airworthy condition." In other words, if anything mechanical goes wrong with your plane, and you have an accident because of it, the first person the FAA is going to want to talk to is you, not your mechanic. *Legally, you are responsible for your plane's maintenance.*

Legal and economic considerations aside, there is still another very important reason for you to want to become personally involved in your plane's maintenance—personal satisfaction. That's the feeling of reassurance, of confidence—of triumph—that comes from knowing that *you* did the work and did it right. It's a feeling totally unknown to most plane owners.

The aesthetic rewards of doing your own maintenance may not seem particularly important to you now, if you're not now performing much of your own maintenance (and if you bought this book mainly with the idea of saving money). Eventually, however, you may find that the aesthetic benefits completely eclipse any financial ones. As you begin to perform more and more of your own maintenance, you will find your attitude toward your plane changing. You'll begin to understand—*really* understand—how your plane's systems work. You'll start to notice things you would have overlooked earlier (a dripping pushrod seal, perhaps, or a frayed ignition lead). Where once you dreaded having to take off the cowling for any reason, you'll actually find yourself looking for excuses to remove it. (In fact, you'll soon start to wonder how you could ever have gone *two whole months* without looking under the cowl.) Instead of regarding every low oleo strut, every hard start, every worn-out brake lining as an assault on your sanity, you'll come to regard these and other contingencies as minor annoyances—opportunities, really. Opportunities to learn.

Maintenance self-sufficiency can mean the difference between saving money and spending it; between being grounded during a mechanic shortage and flying often; between meeting the requirements of the FARs and not meeting them. More important, it can mean the difference between fully understanding how your plane works and remaining (in one sense, at least) isolated and alienated from it.

Many—if not most—pilots have come to see their role in the maintenance process as that of a helpless spectator, someone who is (like the expectant father waiting outside the delivery room) simply barred from the proceedings.

What many of us seem to have forgotten (or what some of us never knew in the first place) is that a pilot's certificate—*any* pilot's certificate—is not only a license to fly, but a license to perform limited maintenance. As stated in FAR 43.3 (h), "The holder of a pilot certificate issued under Part 61 may perform preventive maintenance on any aircraft owned or operated by him that is not used in air carrier service." (Air carrier service merely means the hauling of people or freight for money.) If you own or operate a plane and you have any level of pilot's certificate, you may legally perform preventive maintenance on your plane. (Not anyone else's plane—just *your* plane.)

What is preventive maintenance? According to FAR Part 1, preventive maintenance "means simple or minor preservation operations and the replacement of small standard parts not involving complex assembly operations." (Read that again, slowly.)

As it turns out, this definition covers a lot of ground. Some idea of exactly how much territory is involved can be gained from a portion of Appendix A of FAR Part 43, which lists some 25 categories of work considered by the FAA to be preventive maintenance. These 25 categories are as follows (and I quote):

1. Removal, installation, and repair of landing gear tires

2. Replacing elastic shock absorber cords on landing gear

3. Servicing landing gear shock struts by adding oil, air, or both

4. Servicing landing gear wheel bearings, such as cleaning and greasing

5. Replacing defective safety wiring or cotter keys

6. Lubrication not requiring disassembly other than removal of nonstructural items such as cover plates, cowlings, and fairings

7. Making simple fabric patches not requiring rib stitching or the removal of structural parts or control surfaces

8. Replenishing hydraulic fluid in the hydraulic reservoir

9. Refinishing decorative coating of fuselage, wings, tail group surfaces (excluding balanced control surfaces), fairings, cowling, landing gear, cabin, or cockpit interior when removal or disassembly of any primary structure or operating system is not required

10. Applying preservative or protective material to components where no disassembly of any primary structure or operating system is involved and where such coating is not prohibited or is not contrary to good practices

11. Repairing upholstery and decorative furnishings of the cabin or cockpit interior when the repairing does not require disassembly of any primary structure or operating system or interfere with an operating system or affect primary structure of the aircraft

12. Making small simple repairs to fairings, nonstructural cover plates, cowlings, and small patches and reinforcements not changing the contour so as to interfere with proper airflow

13. Replacing side windows where that work does not interfere with the structure of any operating system such as controls, electrical equipment, etc.

14. Replacing safety belts

15. Replacing seats or seat parts with replacement parts approved for the aircraft, not involving disassembly of any primary structure or operating system

16. Troubleshooting and repairing broken circuits in landing light wiring circuits

17. Replacing bulbs, reflectors, and lenses of position and landing lights

18. Replacing wheels and skis where no weight and balance computation is involved

19. Replacing any cowling not requiring removal of the propeller or disconnection of flight controls

20. Replacing or cleaning spark plugs and setting of spark plug gap clearance

21. Replacing any hose connection except hydraulic connections

22. Replacing prefabricated fuel lines

23. Cleaning fuel and oil strainers

24. Replacing batteries and checking fluid level and specific gravity

25. Removing and installing glider wings and tail surfaces that are specifically designed for quick removal and installation and when such removal and installation can be accomplished by the pilot

It should be noted that while the above list is taken by FAA officials in Washington to be an exhaustive, definitive list of all the things a pilot may do in the name of preventive maintenance (as of this writing), pilots have for years engaged in certain *additional* routine-maintenance tasks (not mentioned in the foregoing list) with the full consent and blessing of local FAA inspectors. For example, pilots have for many years been changing their oil and oil filters without supervision from A&Ps, despite the fact that these operations are not specifically permitted under Appendix A to Part 43. The same goes for replacement of induction air filters, vacuum system filters, etc.

It should also be pointed out that not even the 25 items listed in Appendix A of Part 43 can be considered preventive maintenance all the time, in all situations. For some airplanes, some of the 25 procedures listed may be too complicated to qualify as preventive maintenance. (For instance, on certain light twins the replacement of prefabricated fuel lines—as allowed in item 22—might call for some rather complex assembly operations.)

The only sure way to find out whether a certain procedure that you'd like to perform does or does not qualify as preventive maintenance is to call your nearest FAA General Aviation District Office or Flight Standards District Office and ask for an official opinion. (Look in the white pages of your phone book under U. S.

TABLE 1-1   RECURRENT MAINTENANCE ITEMS (Light aircraft)

Item or procedure	Frequency of recurrence (hr)			Can pilot perform?
	50	100/1*	300/2†	
1. Change oil	X			Yes
2. Change oil filter		X		Yes
3. Rotate spark plugs	X			Yes
4. Replace spark plugs			X	Yes
5. Test compression		X		Yes‡
6. Set magneto timing		X		No§
7. Replace ELT battery			X	Yes
8. Replace aircraft battery			X	Yes
9. Adjust idle mixture		X		No§
10. Change tires		X		Yes
11. Grease wheel bearings		X		Yes
12. Service oleo struts		X		Yes
13. Inspect exhaust stacks		X		No§
14. Replace induction air filter		X		Yes
15. Replace vacuum air filters			X	Yes
16. Service hydraulic reservoirs	X			Yes
17. Dress propeller		X		No§
18. Lubricate control hinges		X		Yes
19. Clean, inspect fuel strainers		X		Yes
20. Clean, inspect oil screens		X		Yes

*100 hr or 1 year, whichever comes first.

†300 hr or 2 years, whichever comes first.

‡Pilot cannot perform this or any other operation in lieu of annual-inspection requirements.

§Pilot may legally perform this operation under a mechanic's supervision. Mechanic must make log entry approving the aircraft for return to service before aircraft can be flown.

Government, Department of Transportation, Federal Aviation Administration.) If possible, try to get that opinion in writing.

It should be fairly evident by now that, contrary to prevailing hangar mythology, the FAA has by no means reduced pilots to disenfranchised bystanders where maintenance is concerned. (If you still think that pilots can do little in the way of meaningful maintenance, take a look at Table 1-1. The 20 recurrent maintenance items listed in this chart account for roughly two-thirds of the total routine maintenance requirements of an average light single-engine aircraft; and of the 20 items, all but four may legally be accomplished by any licensed pilot.) So far, however, we have only mentioned the kinds of maintenance a pilot may perform *unassisted* and *unsupervised*. It turns out that with a little help from a mechanic, a pilot can do just about anything, including engine overhauls.

According to FAR 43.3 (d):

> A person working under the supervision of a holder of a mechanic or repairman certificate may perform the maintenance, preventive maintenance, and alterations that his supervisor is authorized to perform, if the supervisor personally observes the work being done to the extent necessary to ensure that it is being done properly and if the supervisor is readily available, in person, for consultation. However, this paragraph does not authorize the performance of 100-hour or annual inspections, nor inspections performed after a major repair or alteration.

Needless to say, this regulation covers a lot of ground. Under this provision of FAR Part 43, it is entirely legal for you to rebuild your engine, repair or replace damaged fuel tanks, overhaul oleopneumatic shock struts, etc., so long as you are being supervised by a qualified individual. (Incidentally, this is the regulation that makes it legal for engine overhaul shops to hire non-A&P-rated personnel to assemble engines. It is also the regulation that makes it possible for mechanic-school trainees to obtain on-the-job experience while working toward their A&P certificates.)

If FAR 43.3(d) sounds like a good deal, it is. The only catch is this: While you can indeed do the work, under supervision, you *cannot* legally return the plane to service when you're done with it. The holder of the mechanic's (or repairman's) certificate must approve the aircraft for return to service, and this is something that can be done legally only if (among other things) a thorough maintenance record entry is made listing a description of the work, the date of completion, the name of the person who performed the work, and the signature and certificate number of the person approving the aircraft for return to service. (This requirement is spelled out in FAR 43.5.) In other words, a mechanic's imprimatur must be put on your work; a mechanic must "sign it off" in the plane's logbooks. Unfortunately, for liability reasons, many mechanics are unwilling to sign other people's work off.

It should be pointed out that all the legalities we've discussed so far apply only to factory-built (i.e., non-homebuilt) aircraft; the provisions of FAR Part 43 do not apply at all to sport aircraft licensed in the experimental category. According to FAR 43.1(b): "This Part does not apply to any aircraft for which an experimental airworthiness certificate has been issued, unless a different kind of airworthiness certificate had previously been issued for that aircraft." This, of course, only makes sense. Requiring the builder of a sport aircraft to hire out all its maintenance would be like telling dirt farmers to hire Ph.D. agronomists to fertilize their crops. Fortunately, neither farming nor sport flying has gotten to that stage yet.

PREVENTIVE MAINTENANCE GROUND RULES

The fact that pilots are allowed to perform preventive maintenance with impunity does not mean that the performance standards that apply to professional mechanics do not also apply to pilots. Whether you knew it or not, the same standards *do* apply. FAR 43.13(a) states:

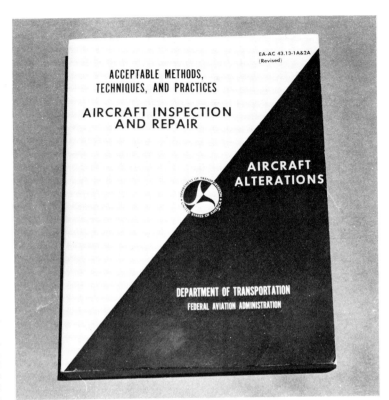

FIGURE 1-1 The aircraft mechanic's bible: AC 43.13-1A & 2A. All aircraft maintenance— including preventive maintenance—must be performed in accordance with the "approved procedures" given in this volume.

Each person maintaining or altering, or performing preventive maintenance, shall use methods, techniques, and practices acceptable to the Administrator. He shall use the tools, equipment, and test apparatus necessary to assure completion of the work in accordance with accepted industry practices. If special equipment or test apparatus is recommended by the manufacturer involved, he must use that equipment or apparatus or its equivalent acceptable to the Administrator.

The question of what constitutes "methods, techniques, and practices accept-able to the Administrator" (the Administrator here meaning the FAA's top official) has been answered in encyclopedic detail in a mammoth, two-part FAA Advisory Circular known as AC No. 43.13-1A&2A: *Acceptable Methods, Techniques, and Practices: Aircraft Inspection and Repair, Aircraft Alterations* (Figure 1-1). This formidable document, which comprises some 417 pages in all in its current edition, prescribes acceptable techniques relating to the repair and/or adjustment of just about every aircraft component, system, or subsystem imaginable. In addition, considerable background information on such subjects as corrosion protection, nondestructive testing, and aircraft hardware is presented, complete with charts, drawings, and photographs. (Old-timers will recognize AC No. 43.13-1A&2A as an updated version of the now-defunct CAM 18, a similar handbook issued decades ago by the Civil Aeronautics Administration.) Certainly, anyone who is contemplating the performance of preventive maintenance on a U. S. registered aircraft ought to consider AC No. 43.13-1A&2A required reading. Even if you're not contemplating doing your own maintenance, it's worth having as a reference. (For information on how to obtain AC No. 43.13-1A&2A and other FAA publications, please refer to Appendix B.)

Besides prescribing the methods to be used in *performing* aircraft maintenance (including preventive maintenance), the FAA has a few noteworthy things to say about the *end results* that must be achieved by those methods. In particular, FAR 43.13(b) states:

> Each person maintaining or altering, or performing preventive maintenance, shall do that work in such a manner and use materials of such a quality, that the condition of the aircraft, airframe, aircraft engine, propeller, or appliance worked on will be at least equal to its original or properly altered condition (with regard to aerodynamic function, structural strength, resistance to vibration and deterioration, and other qualities affecting airworthiness).

In other words, if you decide to clean and lubricate your plane's wheel bearings, you must perform the work in such a way (and use cleaning solvents and bearing grease of such a quality) that, when you're finished, the wheel bearings will be as good as new—or at least in as good condition as they would be if a professional maintenance technician had done the work. Also, in keeping with the requirements set forth in FAR 43.13(a), you would have to do the job using the same kinds of tools (i.e., wrenches, jacks and jackstands, etc.) that a mechanic would use; and these tools, in turn, would have to be used in accordance with the recommendations given in AC No. 43.13-1A&2A. Furthermore, if any "special equipment" (such as a jacking adapter) is recommended by the airframe or wheel manufacturer, you would have to use that equipment. All these things are required by FAR 43.13 (a) and (b).

A question naturally arises: Given the vast number of different makes and models of airframes, engines, and appliances in common use, how can one be entirely sure what the "properly altered condition" of a given piece of equipment is? (For instance, how can one know in advance exactly what type of bearing grease should be used on a 1962 Skyhawk's wheel bearings?) The answer is that it is necessary in most cases to consult the appropriate manufacturer's service manual to obtain this information.

While service manuals (or shop manuals) are available for practically every aircraft accessory (or appliance) in common use—including tires, wheels, brakes, spark plugs, avionics, magnetos, and carburetors—the airplane service manual published by the airframe manufacturer constitutes the single most useful source of maintenance information for the amateur *or* professional mechanic. Almost everything a person needs to know to comply with FAR 43.13 while performing preventive maintenance can be found in the airframe manufacturer's service manual. Under FAR 23.1529, aircraft manufacturers are required to include the following types of information in their service manuals:

1. A description of the aircraft's main systems (electrical, hydraulic, fuel, etc.)

2. Lubrication instructions setting forth the recommended lubrication intervals for various systems, as well as the specific lubricants, fluids, etc. to be used in those systems

3. Pressures and electrical loads applicable to the various systems

4. Tolerances and adjustments necessary for proper functioning of the airplane

5. Recommended methods of leveling, jacking, and towing the aircraft

6. Procedures for balancing the control surfaces

7. Identification of the aircraft's primary and secondary structures

8. Frequency and extent of inspections considered necessary for proper maintenance of the airplane

9. Special repair methods (if any) applicable to the airplane

10. Recommendations regarding special inspection techniques, such as x-ray, ultrasonic, and magnetic particle, that might be required for various aircraft systems

11. A list of special tools required for routine maintenance.

In addition to all this information, airframe manufacturers' service manuals generally contain an entire section devoted to engine servicing operations (i.e., information regarding magneto timing, exhaust system inspection, oil-change intervals, carburetor adjustment, and so forth). Indeed, the airplane service manual is the primary source of such information; minor engine maintenance is generally not covered in engine manufacturers' manuals (which are devoted primarily to overhaul procedures), since exhaust system design, ignition system design, the choice of a carburetor or fuel injection system, etc., are determined by the *airframe* manufacturer, rather than the engine manufacturer.

Obviously, an airplane service manual is a handy thing to have around if you have any intention of performing preventive maintenance on your aircraft. Your owner's manual may tell you how often your control system should be lubricated; but only in the aircraft service manual will you learn exactly which inspection plates need to be removed and where they're located, which bellcranks and hinge points need to receive lubrication, and exactly what kinds of lubricants to use (dry graphite vs. oil vs. silicone spray, for example). Likewise, while your owner's manual may offer general advice on battery, tire, brake, propeller, and engine maintenance, only your aircraft service manual will give you the specific how-to/when-to/why-to information you'll need to accomplish that maintenance in accordance with FAR 43.13.

Suffice it to say, if you haven't already obtained a copy of the service manual

FIGURE 1-2 The aircraft service manual is the final authority on the particular servicing requirements and repair procedures applicable to a given airplane model. No maintenance procedure should be attempted without first consulting the aircraft service manual.

for your plane, you should do so now. (And don't let the fact that some manufacturers have begun offering microfiche manuals in lieu of paper versions deter you; NCR Corporation offers a low-cost, lightweight, hand-held microfiche viewer that will allow you to read any fiche-format manual with ease.) FAA Advisory Circulars, manufacturers' operating handbooks, and how-to books (such as this one) will provide you with much good general advice on the performance of maintenance, but for obtaining specific information on *your plane's systems*, there is no substitute for a factory service manual. (For information on where and how to order service manuals, see Appendix B.)

RULES GOVERNING REPLACEMENT PARTS

It is important to realize (before you become involved in performing your own preventive maintenance) that the FAA requires all maintenance personnel—including pilots—to use not only approved methods, but approved *materials* as well. In particular, FAR 43.13(b) requires persons performing preventive maintenance to use materials "of such a quality that the condition of the aircraft, airframe, aircraft engine, propeller, or appliance worked on will be at least equal to its original or properly altered condition."

Since any airplane in its original or properly altered condition contains only FAA-approved "aircraft quality" parts and materials, FAR 43.13(b) in effect requires you to use only FAA-approved replacement parts in your airplane when you perform preventive maintenance. This means, among other things, that if a bulb burns out in your cockpit overhead light, you must replace it with an FAA-approved bulb of identical part number. Likewise, if your battery conks out on you, you've got to shop for an FAA-approved replacement; you can't simply buy a Sears DieHard® and put it in your plane. The same goes for oil filters, spark plugs, seat belts, dopes and paints, nuts, bolts, safety wire, etc.

How can you be sure that a given replacement part is legal for installation in your plane under FAR 43.13? One fairly easy way to ensure compliance with FAR 43.13 is to order replacement parts for your plane directly from the airframe manufacturer, using the part numbers given in your plane's factory-approved parts catalog. Every airframe manufacturer issues, for each of its airplane models, an exhaustive parts catalog giving word descriptions, drawings, and part numbers for virtually all the parts employed in the airplane's construction, right down to the AN (Air Force/Navy) numbers of the cotter pins used in the smallest bolts. (In addition, detailed information on airframe serial-number applicability and parts interchangeability is usually given.) Thus, if it becomes necessary for you to order a new rotating beacon bulb for your plane—and you have (or have access to) your plane's parts catalog—obtaining a "legal" bulb for the beacon is a simple matter of flipping to the "rotating beacon" section of the catalog, looking up the appropriate bulb part number, and ordering the part through your local Cessna (or Beech, or Piper, or whatever) dealer. When the replacement bulb arrives, you'll know it's legal for your plane under FAR 43.13.

In many instances, ordering a replacement part from the airframe manufacturer via the parts catalog is the easiest, most practical way to obtain a legal replacement part. (This is particularly true of cockpit windows, wheel pants, fairings, cowlings, and other parts that, because of limited interchangeability among different aircraft models, are not likely to be stocked by anyone except the original manufacturer.) Sometimes, however—especially when the part in question is widely available—it makes more sense, from the standpoint of thrift and/or convenience, to shop around. Why go to the trouble of ordering a vacuum air filter from Cessna if you can obtain an identical unit, instantly and at a reasonable price, from your local FBO?

Unfortunately, obtaining a replacement part from anyone other than the original equipment manufacturer (OEM) entails a certain amount of risk, and you should be aware of this risk if you intend to do much shopping around for parts. Like it or not, a brisk business is done in this country in "unused" and "like new" aircraft replacement parts that are represented as being of aircraft quality but lack any evidence of having been manufactured (or overhauled) to FAA standards.

How can you tell whether a given replacement part is legal for installation on your plane? You should look for one of the following:

1. An FAA Form 8130-3 (i.e., an airworthiness approval tag). This tag identifies a part or group of parts that has been approved by an authorized FAA representative.

FIGURE 1-3 What makes an "aircraft part" a bona fide aircraft part? In many cases, it's the letters FAA-PMA (which, according to present FARs, must be "permanently and legibly" imprinted on any and all parts made under the Parts Manufacturer Approval provisions of FAR Part 21). The mere use of the word "aviation" on the box doesn't make what's inside an approved aircraft part; it's the FAA-PMA imprint that counts.

2. A Technical Standard Order (TSO) number and identification mark. Under FAR 21.607, any aircraft part that is manufactured under the Technical Standard Order system must be "permanently and legibly" marked with the name of the manufacturer, the applicable TSO number, the part's serial number and/or date of manufacture, its model designation, and its approximate weight.

3. An FAA-PMA symbol. According to FAR 45.15, any aircraft part that is manufactured under a Parts Manufacturer Approval (PMA) per FAR 21.303 must be "permanently and legibly" marked with the name or symbol of the PMA holder, the appropriate part number, the letters *FAA-PMA*, and the name of each type of certificated product on which the part is eligible for installation. (See Figure 1-3.) Alternatively, if the part is too small to be marked in this fashion, the part or its container must have attached to it a tag bearing the above information.

4. A shipping ticket, invoice, or other document which provides evidence that the part was produced by a manufacturer working under either an Aproved Production Inspection System (per FAR Part 21, Subpart F) or an FAA Production Certificate (per FAR Part 21, Subpart G).

All aircraft parts except for nuts, bolts, and other small hardware items (which are manufactured under their own systems of classification; see Chapter 3) are manufactured either under an Approved Production Inspection System, a Production Certificate, a TSO authorization, or a PMA; thus, every bona fide aircraft quality replacement part will carry one of the above types of identification marks or tags. If you come across a part that is not so identified, don't install it in your airplane. Instead, ask for your money back—and notify the FAA.

It should be emphasized that even if you *can* identify a part as having been manufactured under FAA approval, you should not automatically assume that the part is in an airworthy condition. It could be that the part is too old to be used; such items as rubber hose, aircraft fabric, and dry-cell batteries have very definite shelf lives. Alternatively, the part in question may have been damaged through rough handling or improper storage, and often such damage is not easily visible from the outside. Then, too, it's possible that the part may be subject to one or more outstanding airworthiness directives. All these possibilities must be checked before a replacement part—even an FAA-approved part—is installed on an aircraft.

If you have purchased (or are considering purchasing) *salvaged* parts, still other possibilities must be considered. Many times, aircraft components come to the salvage market by way of "donor" airplanes that have been involved in accidents. Thus, it becomes necessary for the purchaser to consider whether the component in question was subjected to heat or fire (or smoke), sudden acceleration or deceleration, immersion in salt water, or other conditions that would render it unairworthy.

Needless to say, shopping for aircraft replacement parts is not the simple, risk-free task that shopping for auto parts usually is. The FAA requires that all aircraft replacement parts quite literally carry the FAA's stamp of approval, but beyond that the parts must be airworthy. The willful or even unwillful installation of an unairworthy part on a United States certificated aircraft places the owner or operator of that aircraft in violation of FAR 91.163, which states that "the owner or operator of an aircraft is primarily responsible for maintaining that aircraft in an airworthy condition." Thus, it behooves you to exercise great care in the selection of replacement parts for your plane. In many instances, the cheapest part will not be the least expensive one available.

RECORD KEEPING When a certificated mechanic makes a repair or adjustment to an aircraft, the work is not legally "complete" (nor may the aircraft be returned to service) until the mechanic makes an entry in the plane's logs including (1) the nature of the work performed, (2) the date of completion, (3) the name of the person performing the work, and (4) the signature and certificate number of the person approving the aircraft for return to service. (Under FAR 91.165, it is the duty of the aircraft's owner or operator to ensure that maintenance personnel make such log entries.) Any item of maintenance, no matter how minor, must, if it is performed by a certificated mechanic, be recorded in the plane's logs.

At this writing, there is no parallel requirement for pilots; unlike mechanics, pilots may (according to the provisions of FAR 43.5) perform preventive maintenance on their aircraft, and return the aircraft to service, without entering the work in the aircraft logs. (There is, however, a move afoot to rewrite FAR 43.5 to require pilots to make these log entries.) Nonetheless, there are several good reasons why you *should* record your work in the plane's logs, even though you may not be required to. First, detailed log entries will serve to remind you of exactly how many days or flight hours ago you changed oil, added battery water, changed tires, cleaned your spark plugs, etc. Such information is all too easily forgotten if it isn't recorded in a permanent record somewhere. (If you should ever need to know how many quarts of oil, or sets of tires, or spark plugs you've gone through in the past 300 hours of operation, a well-kept set of logs will tell you. A poorly kept set of logs will not.) Second, detailed log entries will aid mechanics and potential buyers of your aircraft in determining what kind of maintenance the plane has been receiving, so that work will not have to be needlessly repeated. (When you are ready to sell your plane, you may find that copious maintenance records add measurably to its resale value.)

Still another reason for religiously entering all maintenance work, no matter how minor or seemingly unimportant, in your plane's logs is that it will serve to absolve innocent individuals (namely, the mechanics whose names appear before yours in the logbooks) of any responsibility for the quality of your work. If you do not "sign off" your own work in the plane's logs, you are, in effect, holding another person (perhaps several persons) liable for your work; in the event of an accident, the FAA, the National Transportation Safety Board, and indeed the courts (if litigation ensues) will look to the person whose name last appears in the logs for an explanation of what happened. From the standpoint of fair play, it is your duty to enter your own work in the aircraft logs. (Look at it another way: If you have no second thoughts about the quality of your work, you should have no second thoughts about making the necessary log entries.)

Actually, there are at least two types of maintenance for which you *must* make detailed log entries, whether you had planned on making such entries or not. One is any maintenance performed for the purpose of *complying with an airworthiness directive* (AD). Most AD notes involve alterations or repairs of such complexity that a mechanic or repair person is required to do the work; however, some AD notes specify compliance procedures that may be undertaken by a pilot working under the preventive maintenance provisions of FAR Part 43. (For instance, some ADs require a relatively simple one-time inspection of an airframe or engine component.) In this case, a pilot who elects to perform the work must make a logbook entry, since (according to FAR 91.173) an airplane's permanent maintenance records must contain information on "the current status of applicable airworthiness directives, including the method of compliance."

Another type of pilot-performed maintenance for which a logbook entry is required is any preventive maintenance operation which *could conceivably change the flight characteristics* of the aircraft. According to FAR 91.167(a),

> No person may carry any person (other than crewmembers) in an aircraft that has been repaired or altered in a manner that may have appreciably changed its flight charac-
> teristics, or substantially affected its operation in flight, until it has been approved for

return to service in accordance with Part 43 and an appropriately rated pilot, with at least a private pilot's certificate, flies the aircraft, makes an operational check of the repaired or altered part, *and logs the flight in the aircraft's records.* [Emphasis added]

This means that if, for instance, you were to replace your plane's wheel pants with pants of a different design, you would not be able (legally) to carry passengers in the plane until you had test flown it and logged the results of the flight in the aircraft logs.

The decision whether to enter every single spark-plug change and every last lube job in the aircraft logs is up to you; as the FARs are presently written, you don't have to log every bit of preventive maintenance you perform on your plane. However, logging every repair certainly can't hurt; in fact, in the long run it can only pay substantial dividends. My own advice is to keep as complete a set of maintenance records as you possibly can.

*   *   *

In this chapter, I have attempted to address such questions as these: Should pilots play a more active role in the maintenance process? Can pilots legally accomplish very much maintenance on their own? What methods and materials must pilots employ when performing their own preventive maintenance? What are the record-keeping requirements that apply specifically to pilot-performed maintenance?

In answering these questions, I hope I have managed to convince skeptics that: (1) Greater pilot involvement in maintenance is desirable from many standpoints, not the least important of which is that of increased operator knowledge (and therefore safety). (2) Greater pilot participation in maintenance is *essential* if general aviation is to weather the impending mechanic shortage. (3) Pilots can do more maintenance than is commonly imagined. (4) There is indeed money to be saved by doing your own preventive maintenance, folklore to the contrary notwithstanding. (5) The FARs pertaining to pilot-performed maintenance—imposing though they may be—are amenable to human interpretation, and in fact are not as restrictive as many pilots suppose.

I also hope I have succeeded in conveying the impression that (6) it is a good idea always to enter any work you do in the aircraft logs, and (7) anyone who attempts to perform preventive or other maintenance without the aid of a manufacturer's service manual is (to say the least) acting foolishly. I'll say it again: If you don't already have a factory service manual for your plane, and if you intend to start performing your own preventive maintenance, *get one now.* This book, by itself, will not tell you everything you need to know.

Above all, I hope I have—if nothing else—set in motion a consciousness raising process that will cause you to want to broaden your maintenance knowledge, for no other purpose than to become a more well-rounded pilot. There is, after all, something intrinsically satisfying about knowing how a magneto or a prop governor or an oleopneumatic shock strut works; to know these things is, in some small way, to know Truth. Mechanics have long understood this feeling. It is time pilots learned their secret.

TEST ANSWERS: 1-a, 2-c, 3-c, 4-b, 5-a, 6-b, 7-c, 8-b, 9-b, 10-a

Before you make up your mind to return this book because you aren't ready to invest a fortune in special aircraft tools that might be used once and never again, let me assure you of three things:

First, you must buy certain tools if you intend to do any work on your plane; borrowing tools is not the answer. You would have better success borrowing jewels from Tiffany's than borrowing wrenches from an A&P. This is as it should be; your mechanic, after all, has probably spent many years and several thousand dollars accumulating a set of high-quality instruments. Lending them out would be risking damage to or loss of this investment.

Second, we're not discussing a very big investment as far as your personal tool collection goes. In fact, you probably already own most of the implements you'll need to carry out preventive aircraft maintenance. It's true that if you wanted to, you could invest thousands of dollars in heavy-duty jacks, air compressors, spark-plug test stands, drills, hoists, and assorted doodads—but you certainly don't have to. For preventive maintenance purposes, one or two hundred dollars' worth of tools (mostly wrenches, pliers, and other items that you should already have anyway) will do.

Third, aircraft tools are actually a very good investment. For every dollar you invest in tools, you'll get back somewhere between $3 and $10 over the life of the tool—not just in savings on aircraft repairs, but also on auto repairs, lawn mower maintenance, etc. (Some tools, of course, are better investments than others; a $1.98 tire pressure gauge, for example, may return $100 to $150 in reduced tire maintenance over a period of several years, if used properly.)

Granted, good tools can be, and usually are, expensive. A good ratcheting torque wrench, for example, now costs from $60 to $70, minus sockets (which cost an extra $3 apiece). But look at it this way: Why hesitate to sink $200 into quality tools when you've already spent $10,000 to $100,000 (or a good deal more) on the airplane itself? Besides, if you put off buying needed tools for another year or two, you'll only be paying that much more for the implements when you *do* finally decide to buy them (tool prices have been increasing steadily for more than a decade). And in the meantime, you will have paid dearly to have someone else do your spark-plug rotations, filter changes, etc., while you were "saving money" by going without tools.

In this chapter, we'll discuss three types of tools: (1) *essential* tools, (2) special-purpose gadgets and tools that are essential

TWO
THE PILOT'S TOOL KIT

for certain tasks only, and (3) time savers that fall into the "nice to own but you don't absolutely need one" category. By the end of this chapter, you'll see how really few in number, and relatively low in cost, those "essential" implements are.

TOOL-BUYING TIPS   Fortunately for us all, the FAA—while very strict on requiring that all aircraft parts carry its approval—does not require that the tools used in aircraft maintenance be manufactured to any government specification. The only FAA requirement regarding tools is that given in FAR 43.13(a), which states (in part), "Each person . . . performing preventive maintenance . . . shall use the tools, equipment, and test apparatus necessary to assure completion of the work in accordance with accepted industry practices." For all practical purposes, this means that any ordinary hand tool that can get the job done is acceptable for use in preventive maintenance. Thus, you are free to do your tool shopping at Sears, Western Auto, your local hardware or auto parts store, or wherever you choose.

A couple of caveats before you actually begin to go shopping: First, beware of so-called bargain tools; for instance, the super-cheap screwdrivers, pliers, etc., that you see so often in the 98-cent jumble basket at local hardware stores. After you've ruined your share of screws and spent some time nursing a few badly bruised knuckles, you'll come to realize that there is no such thing as a bargain tool. Cheap tools can be hard on equipment (placing you in direct violation of FAR 43.13); more often than not, they won't hold up long enough in service to make their "low" price a good deal. Use this kind of junk on a wheelbarrow, perhaps —but not on an airplane.

Second, don't waste your time buying any tool that is sold without a money-back guarantee. If the maker or seller of the tool doesn't think highly enough of the product to guarantee it unconditionally, that fact by itself should tell you something—namely, to do your shopping elsewhere.

Where special-purpose aircraft tools (such as differential cylinder compression testers or strut pumps) are concerned, you'll no doubt find it convenient and/or essential in some cases to shop by mail. All the well-known mail-order pilot's supply houses do a brisk business in such tools. The key thing to realize here is that pricing policies and shipping charges vary significantly from one firm to the next; consequently, it is possible to save substantial amounts of money by shopping around. Compare catalog prices and shipping charges carefully before buying tools by mail, and again, be sure that anything you buy comes with a money-back guarantee.

With these few general pointers out of the way, let us consider the tool and equipment items you'll be needing.

SCREWDRIVERS   Inspection plates, access panels, fairings, and cowlings are, in most cases, held down by slotted fasteners of one description or another. To deal with them, you'll need a variety of screwdrivers.

Phillips
screw and driver

FIGURE 2-1 The Phillips screw and driver design differs from the Reed & Prince screw and driver design; the two types of drivers are not interchangeable. Notice how the Reed & Prince driver tapers to a sharp point, in contrast to the Phillips tip, which is blunt.

Reed & Prince
screw and driver

You probably don't have to be reminded that screwdrivers come in two basic types: standard slot screwdrivers and the four-blade-tip variety commonly called Phillips screwdrivers. What you may not know, however, is that not all four-bladed screwdrivers are Phillips drivers. There are actually two separate kinds of screwdrivers with a cross-slotted tip. One is called the Reed & Prince, while the other is the true Phillips.

The Reed & Prince driver differs from the Phillips primarily in that its tip is pointed, whereas the tip of the Phillips is distinctly blunt (Figure 2-1). This may seem a trivial difference, but in fact the two tools are made for use with two different types of screws (the true Phillips-head screw, which has an open center, and the Reed & Prince screw, whose slots form a perfect cross). The use of a Phillips screwdriver on a Reed & Prince screw will very likely result in irreparable damage to screwhead, tool, or both. Accordingly, you'll want to keep both types of cross-slotted screwdrivers in your toolbox and examine every screwhead carefully, before you begin work, to determine which type of screwdriver you need.

Likewise, you'll want to carry a good assortment of standard slotted screwdrivers (long, short, big handle, small handle, fat tip, narrow tip) in your tool collection so you'll be equipped to handle a wide variety of slotted screws. A good rule of thumb to remember when choosing a standard screwdriver for a particular application is that *the tip of the driver should fill at least 75 percent of the screw slot.* (This holds for the blade's thickness as well as its width. Both are important.) If the blade isn't wide enough to fill the slot, you'll risk damaging the screw; or, worse, the blade may slip and damage the structure you are working on.

Regardless of the type of screwdriver you're working with, it's generally wise to select a tool with a fairly large handle and, space permitting, a fairly long shaft. The reason for this is that the heftier the handle (and the longer the shaft, in most cases), the greater your mechanical advantage over the screw and the less twisting force you'll have to supply to get the job done.

Rather than carry an assortment of screwdrivers around everywhere, many professional (and amateur) mechanics prefer to cut down on toolbox clutter by carrying a single open-ended screwdriver handle and an assortment of tips (slot,

Reed & Prince, Phillips) that can be used with the handle. Sears sells a magnetic screwdriver kit of this type consisting of one screwdriver/nutdriver handle and four magnetic bits for about $6; you may well want to investigate this option before you decide to invest in a closetful of screwdrivers. (See Figure 2-2.)

Before we leave the topic of screwdrivers, here are some tips for dealing with hard-to-budge screws. (Consider this information carefully; you're going to need it someday.)

1. The very first thing to do when a screw refuses to turn is try a different screw-

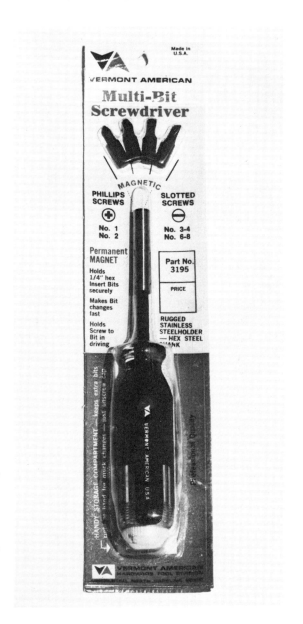

FIGURE 2-2 Vermont American, Craftsman, and others offer versatile multibit screwdriver kits that eliminate the need to carry dozens of full-size screwdrivers in your toolbox. By substituting different bits (which are available in Phillips, Reed & Prince, slot, Allen, square-recess, and other styles) in the end of the handle, one tool can be made to do the work of several screwdrivers and nut drivers. Some manufacturers even offer ratcheting handles.

driver, preferably one with a much longer shaft and a much bigger grip. You'll be surprised at the difference that this change of tools can make.

2. Be sure the tip of the screwdriver fills most (or all) of the screw-head slot.

3. Give the offending fastener a shot or two of penetrating oil. This will (in most cases) help to free up rusted threads. Then wait a couple of minutes before going back at it with your screwdriver.

4. If need be, try to gain extra leverage by closing the jaw of an adjustable-end wrench down onto the blade of the screwdriver. Use the wrench to turn the screwdriver blade tip (but be careful not to let the blade slip and damage the screw).

5. Try giving the screw a momentary twist in the *tightening* direction, and then unscrew it.

6. Tap the head of the screw smartly with a mallet, being careful not to damage the underlying structure. (Use this method as a last resort and, even then, exercise extreme care.)

If you still can't get a screw started after trying all of the above, by all means call for help. And remember to keep your cool. If you decide to "really lay into" the screw, you could easily strip it, and ultimately cause yourself even more grief.

WRENCHES Obviously, you can't expect to be able to remove seats from your plane, rotate your spark plugs, or tighten wheel through bolts without a good set of wrenches. And it goes without saying that at least one of your wrenches will have to be of the torque-measuring kind. Without a torque wrench, you're nowhere as far as preventive maintenance is concerned.

If you don't already own a good torque wrench, plan on getting one soon. The main things to look for are (1) a slim profile (you'll be using the tool in some awfully tight spaces); (2) a working torque range of 5 to 50 ft-lb, and (3) a money-back guarantee. Any high quality deflecting-beam or dial-type torque wrench will do for starters, but if you can afford it I strongly recommend that you opt for an adjustable, ratcheting, ⅜-in. square-drive torque wrench such as AC Spark Plug's ST-110 (Figure 2-3), which sells for about $60. The dial- and beam-type torque wrenches are less expensive (at around $15) but are hard to read and use in tight spaces (the bottom plug on the number four cylinder of a Continental O-300 in an older Skyhawk, for instance). The torque-limiting feature and flexible head of the ST-110 do away with such problems.

If you've never used a ratcheting-type torque wrench before, you'll find it's truly a pleasure to work with. To use one, all you do is (1) unlock the grip and adjust the handle to the desired torque setting on the micrometer-type scale; (2) relock the grip; (3) set the ratcheting adjustment in the "tightening" mode; (4) snap a socket onto the wrench; and (5) start tightening your bolt or nut. The important thing to remember when using one of these wrenches is to move the handle slowly

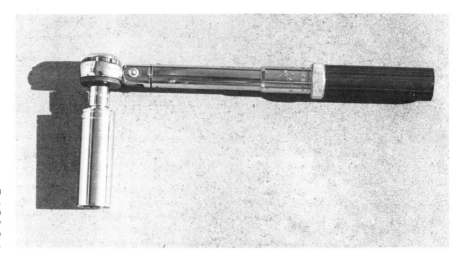

FIGURE 2-3 AC makes a ratcheting, microadjustable, ⅜-in. square-drive torque wrench (the ST-110, shown here) that's ideally suited to aircraft maintenance work. The cost is around $60.

and smoothly; if you yank on the handle at all, you won't torque the nut or bolt properly. When the nut or bolt reaches the proper torque, the handle will automatically "break," or move freely. (The release of friction at this point is easily felt and heard; there will be no doubt in your mind that the proper torque has been reached.) At any time during the torque procedure, if you encounter chattering or a jerking handle motion, loosen the nut and begin again. You were probably turning the wrench too fast.

That's basically all there is to operating a ratchet-type torque wrench. The dial- and beam-type wrenches are used in much the same manner as the ratcheting version, except that you must read the wrench's torque *while the tool is moving.* You cannot stop just before reaching the desired torque and then start up again; if you do, you'll get an erroneous torque reading.

Incidentally, the FAA advises (in its various publications for mechanics) that all torque wrenches, regardless of design, be tested for accuracy on a regular basis. So plan on having your wrench calibrated by a certified repair station or by the wrench's manufacturer at least a couple of times each year. In addition, be sure to have the wrench checked any time it has been dropped or otherwise subjected to rough treatment.

Of course, torque wrenches, as the name implies, are made mainly for tightening nuts and bolts. To loosen nuts and bolts, you'll need an assortment of ordinary box, open-end, or socket wrenches. (One thing you definitely do *not* want to do is use your torque wrench as a breaker bar; if you do, you'll ruin the tool's calibration.) Chances are good you've already got enough "everyday" wrenches in your tool collection to get you by as far as the operations in this book are concerned. If not, you should immediately invest in a good socket/ratchet set (such as you often find on sale in department stores for $25 or so).

The reasons for choosing a socket/ratchet set over, say, a set of combination wrenches are manifold. First, you'll be needing those sockets to use with your torque wrench anyway, so investing in some square-drive handles and sockets is probably the least expensive way to round out your wrench collection (if your collection is small to begin with). Second, sockets are enormously versatile—not only because the sockets themselves come in both six- and twelve-point styles (the six-pointers being more reliable on rusted or rounded-off nuts and bolts), but owing to the variety of special handles and extensions that can be used with them. (By utilizing various extensions and flexdrives, you can often gain access to "difficult" nuts and bolts that may not be reachable with an ordinary wrench.) And on top of everything else, a socket/ratchet combination is faster working than any other kind of wrench.

When working with wrenches, remember that the principal limitation of the open-end wrench is strength. Because it *is* open, an open-end wrench just isn't as strong as a box wrench. Thus, if you use an open-end wrench to try to loosen a very tight nut, you may well find (as you really lay into it) that the jaws of the wrench will actually spread apart, while the unbudging nut stands still. In the end, you may find that you've ruined your wrench, rounded off the nut, or both.

Therefore, when you need to loosen an exceedingly tight nut, the instrument of choice is the box wrench, preferably a twelve-point model. Alternatively, you should plan on using a six-point socket coupled with a nonratcheting square-drive handle. (The ratcheting mechanism may fail if you attempt to budge the nut with a socket/ratchet combination.) If you opt for the socket, be sure to stabilize the handle by planting your free hand firmly atop the drive end of the wrench (do not grab the socket itself); otherwise the socket may cock over, damaging the nut. And always be in a position to *pull*, not push, on the wrench's handle. That way, if anything suddenly lets go, you'll fly backward, away from the work, rather than headlong into it.

The rule about pulling, rather than pushing, on a wrench really applies to all types of wrenches in all situations. Also, where an open-end wrench (or its even weaker counterpart, the adjustable-end wrench), is involved, it's important to remember that the pulling force should be exerted on the side of the handle to which the longer, stronger jaw is attached (see Figure 2-4).

PLIERS   Pliers are made primarily for grabbing things, and sometimes for cutting things. In the context of aircraft maintenance, pliers find their most frequent use in safety-wiring.

When we discuss safety-wiring, we're usually implying duckbill pliers. But rather than buy a pair of duckbills just for safety-wiring, it might be a better idea (especially if you are not well practiced in the art of safety-wiring) to buy one of the screwdriverlike "safety-wire tools" sold by pilot's supply houses for around $6. (Alternatively, you may want to splurge on one of those $30 plierlike devices that not only twist wire, but grab like duckbills and cut like dikes.) An experienced mechanic can do an artful job of safety-wiring a hard-to-reach nut or bolt with a pair of duckbills—and so can you, with enough practice. For now, though, you should probably go with a special wire-twisting tool of some sort, rather than pliers,

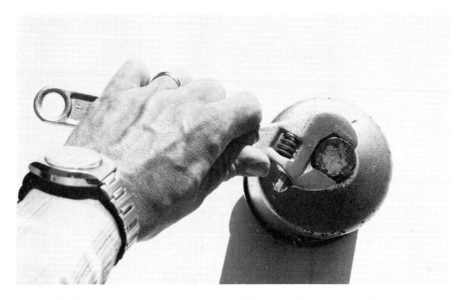

FIGURE 2-4 In using any open-end wrench, the proper procedure is to wrap your fingers around the side of the wrench to which the longer, stronger jaw is attached, and then pull—not push. The right way of doing this is shown at top.

for all safety-wiring jobs; see, for example, Figure 2-5. It'll make your life easier in the short run.

In addition to a safety-wire twister of some sort, you'll need a tool with which to cut the wire, and this usually means diagonal cutting pliers, or dikes. Plan on obtaining a pair of dikes if you don't already have one.

To hold onto fairly large pieces of work, you'll want a pair of pliers whose jaws can be adjusted to be parallel to one another, rather than opening at an angle as do needle-nose pliers. Here, you can get by with the usual combination slip-joint pliers, although a better choice would probably be a set of Vise-Grip pliers, made by Petersen Manufacturing Company (Figure 2-6). In contrast to slip-joints, Vise-Grips are infinitely adjustable through a wide range of jaw openings and will actually clamp onto whatever you're working on. (It's like having a third hand.) Once you get used to working with Vise-Grips, you'll never want to be without a pair on any job—they're that handy. Consider buying a large pair for large jobs and a small pair for working in tight spaces.

BRAKE TOOLS   If your aircraft is equipped with either Cleveland or McCauley brakes, as most planes are, a brake-riveting tool of the kind shown in Figure 2-7 should be considered an essential part of your tool kit. The $12 or so that you spend on this gadget will repay you at least 10 times over in the course of several years' flying. (Depending on how rusty your brake discs are, the payback period could be as short as 2 months!)

   This rivet-setting tool is a small clamplike device that consists of a jig, a knockout punch, a rivet-clinching punch, and a small circular plug of metal (often called the anvil). The tool is designed to facilitate the removal of the old rivets from your worn-out brake linings and the installation of new rivets on new linings. Any number of suppliers offer this brake tool; all the major airframe manufacturers carry the device for sale to the aftermarket, as do most of the big mail-order aviation

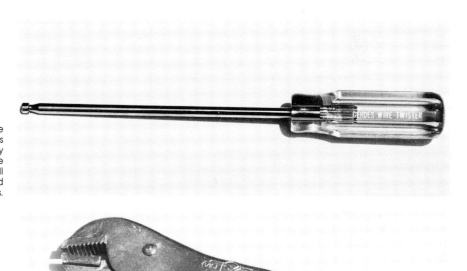

FIGURE 2-5 The Gerdes wire twister reaches into tight places and makes easy work of any safety-wiring job, yet is no more expensive than a set of duckbill pliers. Every pilot-mechanic should own one of these tools.

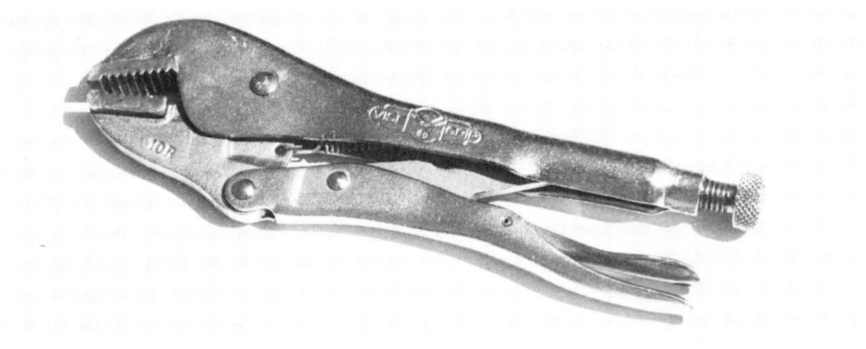

FIGURE 2-6 Vise-Grip pliers are infinitely adjustable through a wide range of jaw angles (in contrast to the more familiar slip-joint pliers) and will actually *clamp onto* the work. It's one of the handiest hand tools around.

FIGURE 2-7 If you intend to reline your own Cleveland brakes, you'll need a ball-peen hammer, a small bag of brass 4-4 rivets, a special brake-riveting tool (consisting of a small clamplike jig, two punches, and a support plug), and of course some new linings (lower right). The riveting tool is widely available from aircraft supply firms.

supply houses (Aircraft Components, Wag-Aero, and so on). In any given issue of *Trade-A-Plane*, you can usually spot three or four ads that feature this particular tool.

In conjunction with the rivet-setting tool, you'll be using a hammer (preferably of the ball-peen variety), a vise (to hold the riveting jig steady), brake linings, and brake rivets. Plan on obtaining these items if you don't already have them. (Again, any large aircraft parts supplier will be able to help you out.) Note that the rivets you'll be using are special aircraft-quality brass rivets, not the dime-a-truckload hardware-store variety. Be sure you get none other than the real thing where these rivets are concerned. (Refer to Chapter 6 for more information on the general subject of brake maintenance.)

SPARK-PLUG TOOLS   Even if you plan on doing no more than occasionally pulling and then reinstalling your engine's spark plugs, you're going to need a handful of special spark-plug tools, including (for starters): (1) a ⅞-in. deep socket that will fit aviation plugs, (2) a plug tray, (3) a thread clean-out tool, and (4) wire-type feeler gauges for measuring electrode gaps. In addition, you'll probably want to get some new 18-mm copper plug gaskets, along with a bottle of thread antiseize compound. (We'll discuss these items more fully in Chapter 10, but it wouldn't hurt to get them now.)

Obviously, a torque wrench isn't much good for spark-plug work without a deep socket to go with it. But don't let all the catalog ads mislead you into thinking that you have no choice except to buy one of the $20 aircraft spark-plug sockets made by Champion and AC. A ⅞-in. deep socket obtained through a hardware or auto-parts store will do just as well as one of the $20 aircraft versions and cost about $17 less. Champion's CT-430 deep socket, it's true, *is* magnetic and, as such, *may* keep you from accidentally dropping a plug on the ground someday. However, a nonmagnetic socket, properly used, will do just as good a job at a much lower cost.

The trick in buying a hardware-store-type deep socket is in finding a socket that is deep enough to accommodate aircraft plugs; many so-called deep sockets aren't. (Obviously, you'll want to take an old plug with you when you go shopping.) If you run into problems finding a ⅞-in. deep socket with ⅜-in. square drive, opt for ½-in. drive and a ⅜-to-½-in. adapter. The most you should have to pay, even with an adapter, is $7 or $8. (Of course, you could avoid the adapter problem altogether simply by opting for a torque wrench with ½-in. square drive instead of ⅜-in. drive. But the ⅜-in. drive is handier to have for non-spark-plug types of maintenance. Either way, it's a tradeoff.)

Incidentally, if it comes to choosing between a twelve-point ⅞-in. deep socket and a six-point (hex) version of the same thing, go with the six-pointer. A six-point socket is less apt to slip (and round off the corners of the shell hex) than a twelve-point socket.

Pilots who are just getting into preventive maintenance often ask if it is really necessary to have a plug tray. The answer is, you only need a plug tray if (1) you wish to be able to cart a lot of plugs around in one hand without fear of dropping and thus ruining them; (2) you want to keep your spark plugs arranged by cylinder and by position in the cylinder, so that they can be reinstalled in the proper holes, and (3) you would like to be able to judge engine health at a glance by comparing the properly arranged plug electrodes. If such things are important to you, you should look into buying a plug tray. (Champion's CT-446 tray can be purchased through any Champion dealer for around $6.) If these things don't interest you, forget about buying a plug tray.

Spark-plug bushings in cylinders tend to accumulate a great deal of carbon and grit between servicing periods, as you'll find out when you remove the plugs from your engine for the first time. Some of this grit will be forced directly into the combustion chamber as you reinstall each plug, leading to possible cylinder-wall abrasion damage—*unless* you buy a bushing clean-out tool (Figure 2-8) and use it to remove grit from the threads. In fact, the carbon buildup in your engine's spark-plug bushings may be so bad that you won't be able to screw your spark plugs back into their holes once you've taken them out. Even worse, you may find—after trying to screw a plug back into a carbon-encrusted bushing—that you've inflicted damage on the bushing's threads, necessitating expensive cylinder repair work. A $7.50 thread chaser will prevent this from ever happening.

Champion and AC both offer thread clean-out tools for aircraft-engine spark-plug bushings; both companies' tools are in the $6 and $9 range and can be bought through local dealers. A word of caution before you go shopping, however: These thread-cleaning devices are meant to be used only on cylinders with *brass* or *steel* bushings. If your cylinders have Heli-Coil inserts rather than machined bushings, you should not use a thread clean-out tool, since such a tool can cause damage to (or backing out of) the Heli-Coil inserts in your cylinders. Instead, clean the Heli-Coil inserts with a stiff-bristled toothbrush coated with bearing grease.

While you have your plugs out for servicing, you'll definitely want (among other things) to check their electrode gaps, so buy a set of wire-type feeler gauges. *Be sure the gauges you buy cover the 0.015- to 0.022-in. range of gaps.* If you can find a $1.98 set of automotive feelers that adequately covers this gap range (not all

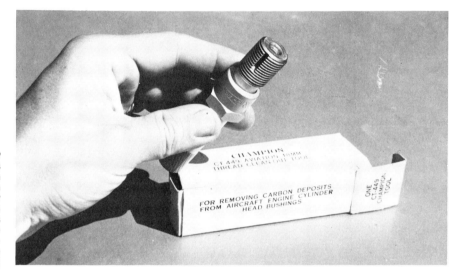

FIGURE 2-8 Champion's CT-449 thread clean-out tool (AC makes a similar one). Once the slots in the side of the tool have been coated with grease, the CT-449 can be screwed into—and then unscrewed from—steel or brass spark-plug bushings to remove carbon and dirt. (Thread clean-out tools of this sort are *not* to be used with Heli-Coil inserts.)

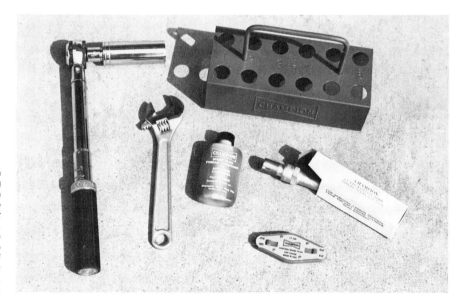

FIGURE 2-9 To do your own spark-plug rotations, you're going to need at least the tools shown here (except, possibly, for the thread clean-out tool, which is not to be used with Heli-Coil inserts). Automotive feeler gauges may be substituted for the Champion gap gauge shown in the lower part of the picture—*if* you can find any that read in the 0.015- to 0.022-in. range.

FIGURE 2-10 A portable air tank (such as you can buy through almost any auto-parts store) will give you quite a bit of capability when it comes to inflating tires, cleaning air filters, air drying parts, etc. A tank of this sort can even be used to pump up nose struts, since most nose-gear oleos require only 40 to 60 psi of air pressure (unloaded). The dial on the front of the tank is no substitute for an accurate tire-pressure gauge, however.

do), buy it. Otherwise, invest $5 or $6 in one of the feeler-gauge sets made for the aviation market by Champion or AC.

In this section, we've limited our discussion to just the four or five most basic, most essential tools for performing spark-plug maintenance (Figure 2-9). There are actually scores of other tools and gadgets you could buy to make spark-plug servicing easier. Some of these other tools and devices are covered in Chapter 10. For now, suffice it to say that the limitless Antarctica of spark-plug maintenance paraphernalia contains a tremendous amount of ground—and in these few paragraphs we've only briefly danced on the tip of one iceberg.

PORTABLE AIR TANK Some pilots might consider a portable air tank to be something of a needless extravagance as far as maintenance-related equipment goes. However, if you get very deep into preventive maintenance, you'll find that it is actually an exceedingly handy device to have around. With an air tank (and here, I'm not talking about a high-pressure gas bottle such as used in welding shops, but a small, 100-psi, hand-carried tank such as can be bought in most large auto-parts and department stores), you can pump up a low tire any time of day or night, right on the ramp, without taxiing the plane to an air hose (and possibly damaging a flat or almost-flat tire in the process). You can also inflate your nose-strut oleo whenever it looks low, and save the $7 to $10 it would otherwise have cost you to get a mechanic to do it. You can use your portable air supply to blast dirt off dusty parts, speed-dry solvent-coated hardware, operate a portable spark-plug sandblaster, etc. And,

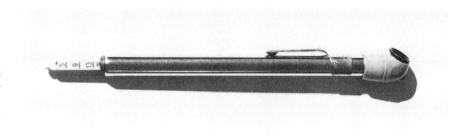

of course, you can keep your car's tires inflated properly at all times (since you'll probably want to carry the tank in the trunk of your auto).

"If I owned a plane," a mechanic once told me knowingly, "the first thing I'd do is get myself an air tank and take it with me whenever I go to the airport." To which I can only add, "Amen, brother."

TIRE GAUGE

Whether or not you decide to invest in an air tank, you should *at least* buy a tire pressure gauge (Figure 2-11) to carry with you on preflight inspections. (A more cost-effective piece of maintenance advice will not be found anywhere in this book.) Any $1.29 automotive-type gauge will do. The cheapest penlight-type gauge is better than none at all, but if possible you should invest an extra dollar or two in a dial-readout-type unit, for greater accuracy. Regardless of which type you buy, be sure the gauge reads over the proper range of pressures; if your nosewheel tire requires 55 psi air pressure, don't buy a gauge that reads only from 5 to 50 psi.

Once you've bought a tire gauge for the plane, keep it in the plane. That way, you won't face the occasional (and inevitable) irritation of having forgotten to bring the gauge with you to the airport on a day when one of your tires looks underinflated. And you won't have to worry about the gauge ever getting lost. (Like pencils, pens, and radioactive iodine, tire gauges seem to disappear with a half-life of about 8 days.)

Another suggestion: Have your tire gauge checked for accuracy any time it has been exposed to water, solvents, droppage, or pressures for which it was not designed, or at least once a year in any case. Tire gauges do go out of calibration eventually, and it's essential to know whether (and when, and by how much) a gauge is off.

BATTERY HYDROMETER

An aircraft battery hydrometer (Figure 2-12) is another one of those little gadgets that you should consider a must. You can get by with an inexpensive automotive-type hydrometer, if you can find one small enough; otherwise, you might just as well spend the extra couple of dollars and buy one of the aircraft battery hydrometers offered by the big mail-order houses. The so-called aircraft versions of this tool are no different from their automotive counterparts, except that they're designed for use in tight spaces (which is where aircraft batteries are invariably located). In addition, aircraft-type hydrometers are made for use with relatively small amounts of electrolyte, which is all you're going to get out of most airplane batteries. (Whatever you do, don't buy one of those giant "calf feeders" you see so often at auto-parts stores; they'll suck your battery dry.)

LUBRICATION TOOLS   If you don't already have one, pick up a $2.98 oil squirt can the next time you're at the hardware or auto-parts store. Keep it in the trunk of your car, or whatever you drive to the airport. Better yet, buy two squirt cans: Fill a small one with lightweight engine oil, and use it to lubricate your plane's control hinges (except Teflon-coated hinges). In a larger can, keep handy a small amount of MIL-H-5606 hydraulic fluid. Use the latter can to add small make-up quantities of MIL-H-5606 to your oleo struts, various hydraulic reservoirs, etc. Slip a short length of clear plastic tubing over the can's snout, and you've got a dandy brake-bleeding device; just hook the other end of the tube to the bleed fitting on your brake, and

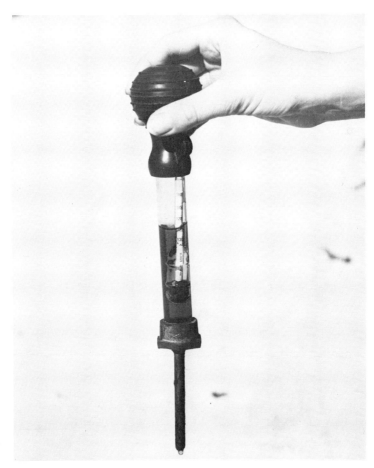

FIGURE 2-12 A battery hydrometer is another must. Be sure to get one that reads out in numbers (as shown here) rather than colors or words.

away you go. (And you can forget about ever having to buy a $50 pressure pot.)

Maybe you've never thought about it before, but most light aircraft have at least two or three zerk fittings or grease nipples located at various points on the airframe, usually in and around the landing gear. If you intend to get serious about doing your own airframe lube jobs, you'd do well to find out where the grease fittings are on your plane, and buy a grease gun with which to service them. Your airplane service manual (or, possibly, your owner's manual) will tell you where the grease points are on your airframe, and how often to lube them. If you need a grease gun, any auto-parts store can fix you up for anywhere from $3 to $30, depending on how fancy you want to get.

Actually, even if you already have a grease gun for your car, it's probably best to buy a second one for your plane; otherwise, it'll be necessary to empty and completely clean your auto's grease gun before filling it with aircraft grease to use on your plane. Rather than clean the grease gun every time you switch from plane grease to car grease (to keep from contaminating a car or plane grease point with the wrong type of grease), it's best to simply buy a second "airplane only" tool—and clearly label it as such. Check your service manual for the exact type of aircraft grease to use.

While we're on the subject of lubrication, it should be mentioned that a can of good quality penetrating oil (Figure 2-13) is virtually a must for any pilot's tool kit. This stuff has a zillion uses, not the least important of which is freeing up frozen nuts, bolts, screws, door latches, etc. I've never met an A&P who didn't use the stuff daily.

FIGURE 2-13 A spray can of penetrant oil is indispensable for freeing frozen fasteners, lubricating and rustproofing hinges, etc. WD-40, LPS 1, and Mouse Milk are probably the most widely used penetrating oils in general aviation.

FIGURE 2-14 Jeweler's screwdriver set.

Teledyne Continental Motors, in service bulletin M71-21, lists the following products as being "approved penetrating oils":

1. Crown Penetrating and Cleaning Oil (Crown Industrial Products Co., 100 State Line Rd., Hebron, IL 60034)

2. Kano Aerokroil (Kano Laboratories, 1000 S. Thompson Lane, Nashville, TN 37211)

3. Mouse Milk Penetrating Oil (Worldwide Aircraft Filter Corp., 1685 Abram Ct., San Leandro, CA 94577)

4. Sprayon No. 203 Penetrating Oil (Sprayon Products, Industrial Supply Div., 26300 Fargo Ave., Bedford Heights, OH 44146)

5. WD40 (Rocket Chemical Co., 5390 Napa St., San Diego, CA 92110).

KEEP-IN-THE-COCKPIT TOOLS

With the exception of the tire pressure gauge, most of the tools we've discussed so far have been the kind of items that (for reasons of size or weight) you probably wouldn't want to store inside your airplane. There are, though, certain tools that have a very favorable handiness-to-weight ratio and that you really ought to consider storing in your cockpit glove compartment on a permanent basis.

One example is a set of jeweler's screwdrivers (Figure 2-14), to use on the innumerable tiny screws that plane makers invariably scatter about the cabin. Sooner or later—in the course of removing an instrument-panel component, changing a cockpit night light, or replacing a piece of Royalite trim—you're going to have a close encounter with one of these tiny fasteners, and suddenly all your standard screwdrivers (even the smallest ones) will be thoroughly useless. At this point, your continued sanity may hinge on having a set of jeweler's screwdrivers in the plane.

Another nice thing to have in your cockpit glove compartment is an inexpen-

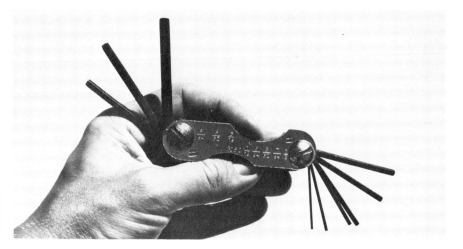

FIGURE 2-15 A miniature Allen-wrench set can come in handy for adjusting instrument-knob setscrews, gauging the thickness of brake linings, etc.

sive set of hex keys (or Allen wrenches). Various instrument knobs, seat parts, etc., may be held in place by internal-wrenching-type setscrews which can only be adjusted by means of the appropriate size of hex key. In addition to being useful as wrenches, however, your miniature hex keys will come in quite handy for gauging thicknesses. (On a walkaround inspection, for instance, you can hold various sizes of keys next to your plane's brake linings, to determine whether your linings have worn thin enough to need replacing.) For $1.98, you'll be hard pressed to buy a more versatile set of tools (Figure 2-15).

Still another item that I strongly recommend you carry in your plane is a Swiss army knife (Figure 2-16). These all-purpose knives, while certainly not cheap, do tend to pay for themselves again and again in the course of a year's flying. Their various screwdriver blades, knife blades, reamers, scissor attachments, etc. (some even have stowable tweezers) make them incredibly handy devices for making spot adjustments to seat mechanisms, door latches, fuel caps, visors, radios, cowling, inspection plates, and so on. You can even use the knife to open oil cans, in a pinch. Buying a Swiss army knife is arguably the smartest tool investment you'll ever make.

TOOLS OF THE NICE-BUT-NOT-ESSENTIAL VARIETY

As you know if you've ever had occasion to peruse a copy of *Trade-A-Plane*, there's virtually no end to the number and variety of maintenance-related doodads available to the flying public. (People in aviation do seem to have a medieval fascination with mechanical contrivances.) A few of the more useful—if not essential—of these devices merit brief consideration here.

It would be hard to deny the usefulness, for preventive maintenance purposes, of a good set of aircraft jacks and a tail stand. The catch here is that one jack, for just one wing, can easily set you back $250, which is more than most pilots are willing to pay for the privilege of changing a tire now and then. Fortunately, in most cases it is not strictly necessary to jack more than one of a plane's wheels off the ground to perform routine maintenance operations. And there are easier means (for most airplane models) to get one wheel off terra firma than to round up a $250 jack. Owners of high-wing Cessnas, for instance, can raise one wheel by using a small $30 or $40 1,500-lb hydraulic jack coupled to a special jacking adapter that fits onto the spring-steel gear. (Cessna sells the adapter as part number 10004-98, or you can make one yourself, if you know how to use a welding torch.) Likewise, with the proper adapter, one wheel of a Beech Bonanza can be brought off the ground using a simple scissors jack. Some other low-wing aircraft models may be jacked this way *without* the use of an adapter; check with your mechanic about this.

A tail stand is nice to have if you are planning to raise the whole airplane off the ground (to perform a gear-retraction-cycle check, perhaps), but tail stands, like the jacks that are used with them, don't come cheap. The going price is around $60. Fortunately, there's an inexpensive alternative to the tail stand, if all you want to do is hold the tail down: sandbags and more sandbags, placed on the horizontal stabilizer's spar. (Also, of course, you can always loop a firmly anchored chain or rope through the plane's tail-mounted tiedown ring. Just be sure you secure the chain or rope in a fail-safe fashion before walking away from it.)

Another nice-if-you-can-afford-it item is a mag synchronizer or dual timing light (available from aircraft supply firms for $40 to $60). Unless you are a licensed mechanic, you cannot legally adjust your magnetos' timing—but you can certainly *check* your timing with one of these lights without violating any rules. Given the fact that the practice of bumping (or improperly advancing) mag timing to reduce the runup mag drop is still fairly widespread among shop personnel, it only makes good sense to check your timing now and then.

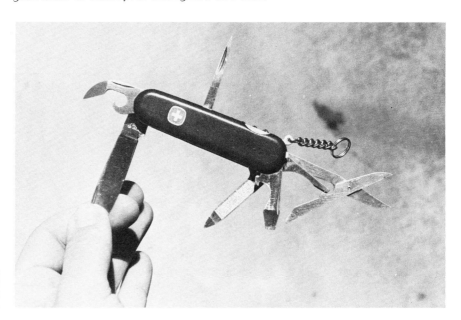

FIGURE 2-16 A Swiss Army knife can be among a pilot's most useful preventive maintenance tools.

FIGURE 2-17 A precision multimeter or voltmeter is essential for troubleshooting electrical systems, checking circuit continuity, etc. Unlike a tire gauge or a Swiss Army knife, however, a multimeter is unlikely to pay for itself quickly; it's strictly a "nice to have if you can afford it" item.

Like the dual timing light, a precision voltmeter (Figure 2-17) is a handy device to have around (for checking circuit continuity, testing battery output, troubleshooting broken microphones, etc.). Again, the initial cost ($40 to $60) is somewhat steep in relation to the total amount of use the device is likely to get.

Differential compression testers used to be fairly expensive, but a good unit can now be had for less than $35 if you're willing to shop around. With one of these instruments and a source of compressed air, you've got quite a bit of capability when it comes to diagnosing "top end" (i.e., cylinder and valve) problems. Check a recent issue of *Trade-A-Plane* for information regarding some of the more competitively priced compression testers.

If you intend to become very self-sufficient in the area of battery maintenance, a battery charger would be a good piece of equipment to have. Ideally, you want a constant-current charger that will deliver a current flow (in amperes) equal to 7 percent of the ampere-hour rating of your battery, or less. (For a 35-amp-hr battery, in other words, you'd want a charging current of about 2.5 amp, or somewhat less.) A good battery charger of this kind can set you back anywhere from $30 to $80, depending on how many optional features it has. Small, 0.5- to 1.0-amp trickle chargers, on the other hand, can be bought for as little as $10 (or less), if all you want to do is keep an already healthy battery fully charged. (J. C. Whitney's automotive accessories catalog usually lists a number of these inexpensive chargers.)

There is almost no end to the number of "nice to have" maintenance gadgets available to pilots. We've only considered a small sampling of such devices here (although we will have occasion to mention other, more specialized pieces of equipment at various times throughout this book). Suffice it to say, if a person had enough money, preventive maintenance could easily become a pretext for experimenting with sophisticated gadgetry.

Fortunately, just as one does not need an electric can opener to open a can, most preventive maintenance jobs can be carried to a successful conclusion with only a few very basic tools. And we've already discussed about 99 percent of those tools here.

Among mechanics, a frequently heard complaint regarding pilots who perform (or try to perform) their own routine maintenance is that most such pilots do not know enough about "aircraft methods" (or, as the FAA would say, "techniques acceptable to the Administrator"). Mainly, what mechanics are worried about is that pilots simply don't know enough about working with aircraft hardware.

As it turns out, there is a great deal of truth to this. Pilots, by and large, do *not* know as much as they should about the nuts and bolts that hold their aircraft together. Ask a pilot to explain the effects of air density changes on a plane's performance and you'll probably get a fairly detailed answer. Ask the same pilot why lock nuts are used on wheel through bolts but not on landing-gear torque link bolts, and you're likely to get a blank stare.

For whatever reasons, pilots have traditionally neglected to study the design, classification, and use of aircraft hardware. That is unfortunate, since a pilot who lacks a good working knowledge of AN, MS, and NAS hardware usage can never expect to understand such things as how to determine the proper torque range for a nut or bolt when the information is not given in the manufacturer's service manual; how to know when and where washers should be used (and what type); when to use a castle nut and cotter pin instead of a fiber locknut; when to use an all-metal locknut instead of a fiber locknut; what course of action to take when a castle nut fails to line up properly with the cotter-pin hole after the nut is installed at its recommended torque; and so on.

Needless to say, if you intend to perform any maintenance operations (even of a minor nature) on your plane, you'll eventually need to know this kind of information. To put it another way: If you think you can safely perform your own maintenance *without* knowing a lot about aircraft hardware and its proper use, you're only kidding yourself.

THREE
WORKING WITH AIRCRAFT HARDWARE

AIRCRAFT BOLTS

If you've spent any time looking through your airplane's parts catalog, you have probably noticed that most of the bolts used in aircraft structures carry either an AN, MS, or NAS number. These numbers correspond to the Air Force/Navy, Military Standard, and National Aircraft Standard specifications to which the bolts were manufactured. Of these three main types of bolts, AN bolts are the most common.

AN-type bolts can be identified by certain markings on the bolt head (Figure 3-1). Your standard, everyday cadmium-plated steel AN bolt will be marked with a raised asterisk or plus sign (+); corrosion-resistant steel is indicated by a single raised dash. Two raised dashes means the bolt is made of aluminum alloy. (You won't encounter many aluminum bolts, since they are not often used in places where they have to be removed frequently.)

It should be noted that not all AN bolts are of the usual hex-head design. Clevis and eyebolt styles are also available (Figure 3-2).

In addition to the above markings, AN bolt heads may also carry the manufacturer's name or initials. Sometimes, all you'll see is a number, an S or SPEC stamped on the bolt's head; this means the bolt is a *special* bolt made for a particular application. If you should have occasion to remove a special bolt for any reason, *remember not to replace it with anything but the identical item.*

Once in a long while you may come across a shiny-looking bolt having a raised or recessed triangle on its head. This is the NAS close-tolerance bolt. Bolts of this type are made slightly oversize and then ground to a very precise diameter;

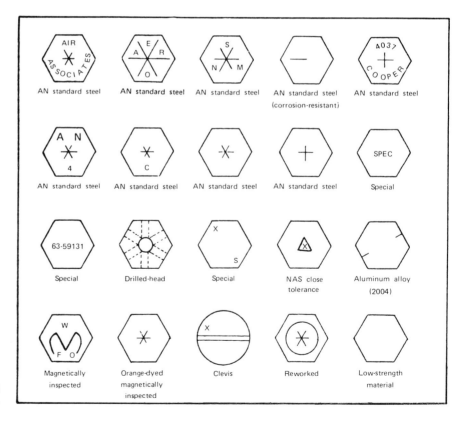

FIGURE 3-1 Typical bolt-head identification marks.

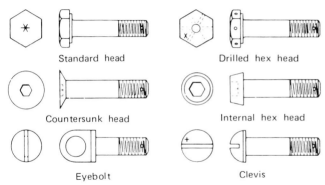

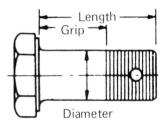

FIGURE 3-2 Aircraft bolts (AN, NAS, and MS) come in hex-head and numerous other styles.

FIGURE 3-3 In AN bolt nomenclature, length (or reach) and diameter refer to shank dimensions only.

they are made for applications in which a tight-drive fit is required (i.e., where the bolt will only go into its hole when struck with a 12 oz hammer). Handle NAS close-tolerance bolts with care; they cost up to $1 apiece (sometimes more) to replace.

So far, we've said nothing at all about the numbering system that is used for classifying AN bolts. (If you're thinking of skipping to another part of the book at this point, don't. The AN numbering system isn't as hard to learn as you think; it's actually quite simple.) Most of the AN bolts you'll have occasion to deal with will fall into the AN3 through AN20 series. These are hex-head bolts whose *shank diameter*, in sixteenths of an inch, corresponds to the AN number (see Figure 3-3). Thus, an AN3 bolt has a shank diameter of ³⁄₁₆ in.; an AN4 has a shank thickness of ¼ in. (that's ⁴⁄₁₆ in.); and so on.

In addition to the basic AN number (AN3, AN4, etc.), every aircraft bolt also has a dash number: for example, the 7 in AN5-7. This second number designates the *length* of the bolt in eighths of an inch. (This is the shank length, or *reach*, not the overall length. See Figure 3-3.) Obviously, then, an AN5-7 bolt would have a cross-sectional diameter of ⁵⁄₁₆ in. and a length of ⅞ in. Likewise, an AN4-6 bolt would have a shank diameter of ¼ in. and a reach of ¾ in.

If you've ever thumbed through an aircraft hardware catalog, you may have noticed that there are no AN bolts with a dash number of 8 or 9. The reason for this is that AN bolts are often several inches long, and to express such lengths in eighths of an inch would be confusing. It is much easier, and less confusing, simply to express bolt lengths (where necessary) in both whole inches *and* eighths. In other words, we simply let a dash number of 10 stand for one 1 in., let 20 stand for 2 in., etc., and use the second digit to express eighths of an inch as needed. Thus, an AN5-35 bolt is ⁵⁄₁₆ in. in diameter and 3⅜ in. long. An AN7-43 bolt would be ⁷⁄₁₆ in. in diameter and 4⅜ in. long. (Similarly, if you pulled a bolt from your plane and found that it was ½ in. across at the shank and 4½ in. long, you'd automatically know it's an AN8-44 bolt. Right?)

Up to this point, all the AN numbers we have discussed belong to AN bolts of the type that have drilled tails (for use with castle nuts and cotter pins, or safety wire). To indicate an *undrilled* bolt, such as would be used with a fiber locknut, it is necessary to add a capital Λ to the bolt's dash number. Thus, for example, the bolt used to hold a Piper Arrow's wheel halves together is an AN5-35A; it is ⁵⁄₁₆ in. in diameter, 3⅝ in. long, and undrilled (for locknut use).

The main thing to remember about AN bolts having drilled tails is that these bolts should never be used in conjunction with elastic locknuts. The minute burrs around the drill hole of such a bolt can tear up the nut's nylon insert, rendering the whole assembly unsafe. *Do not use an elastic locknut on a drilled shank.*

There's one more AN bolt designation you should be familiar with, and that's the H designation. Whenever you see the letter H between the AN number and the dash number (as, for example, in AN5H-10A), you should know that the bolt in question has a drilled head. You'll run across these bolts in blind holes where nuts can't be used and where, consequently, it is necessary to safety-wire the head of the bolt. Certain brake installations and prop flanges employ head-drilled bolts.

NUTS AND WASHERS   AN nuts are numbered somewhat differently from AN bolts. The principal difference is that the first number in a nut's AN designation does not tell you anything about the nut's size; rather, it tells you what *kind* of nut it is (see Figure 3-4). Thus, AN310 and AN320 are ordinary and shear-type castle nuts (for use with cotter pins or safety wire); AN364 and AN365 are thin and thick elastic stopnuts; AN363 is your all-steel stopnut; and AN350 is the aircraft-type wing nut (drilled for use with safety wire). There are also plain and light hex nuts (AN315 and AN340) having neither castellations nor self-locking features, and coarse-threaded versions of these same nuts (AN335 and AN345). Their use on aircraft is somewhat limited, however, so we won't deal with them here except to say that you're most likely to find them in the engine compartment, used with lockwashers.

Why, exactly, do castle nuts carry the numbers AN310 and 320, while locknuts carry the numbers AN363, 364, and 365? Only the Pentagon can answer that one. Castle nuts carry the number 310 (or 320) for the same reason that income-tax forms carry the number 1040. They just do.

Fortunately, the second part of a nut's full AN designation (namely, the dash number) is somewhat easier to fathom. The rule here is that the nut's *dash number* is the same as the AN *number* (or first number) of the bolt that the nut is designed to fit. In other words, an AN310-8 nut is designed to fit onto an AN8 bolt, an AN310-5 nut fits an AN5 bolt, and so forth. Notice that the nut's dash number does not represent the exact diameter of the threaded hole portion of the nut. The nut is several thousandths larger than the bolt (it has to be, or the nut wouldn't turn down onto the bolt). Whatever you do, don't try to tell a mechanic that an

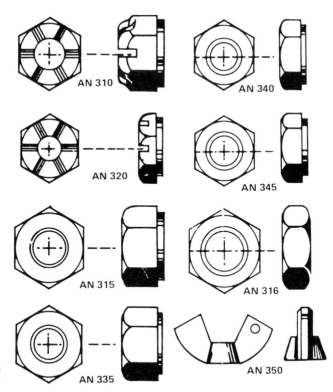

FIGURE 3-4 Non-self-locking aircraft nut designs.

AN310-6 nut has a ⅜-in. hole in it, or you're apt to find yourself the butt of a few jokes.

If you look through your plane's parts catalog, you'll notice that quite frequently a nut's AN designation is three or four digits long. In this case, the last two digits of the dash number specify the *number of turns of thread per inch* (or the thread pitch). The one or two preceding digits call out the nut size (or the bolt size, actually) in sixteenths of an inch. For example, you may find that the main wheel halves on your plane are held together by AN365-524 nuts on 4-in. through bolts. From what we've just described, you would know that a nut of this kind would go on an AN5 bolt (⁵⁄₁₆ in. in diameter) and have a thread pitch of 24 turns per inch. Simple.

Thread pitch is frequently called out in the dash number for the simple reason that there are four main thread types in common use: American National Fine, American National Coarse, American Standard Unified Fine, and American Standard Unified Coarse. Thread pitch is important because you have to know the exact pitch before you can look up the proper torque range of a given nut-bolt combination. (We'll say more about that in a minute.)

Earlier, we mentioned the fact that drilled-shank bolts are made to be used with castle nuts but not with fiber locknuts, while undrilled bolts, which carry the letter A, are made for use with locknuts but not with castle nuts. Nothing was said, however, about why castle nuts and drilled bolts are used where they are, or why locknuts and A bolts are used where they are (rather than vice versa). One might wonder, for instance, why—if the FAA allows locknuts to be used on wheel bolts and in other critical locations—locknuts can't be used *everywhere*, rendering castle nuts and drilled bolts obsolete.

To understand why castle nuts and safety wire (or cotter pins) are used in some places and locknuts in others, it is necessary to back up a bit and talk about the *design* of these nuts. (Form, after all, follows function.) Let us begin by considering elastic stopnuts.

The AN365 stopnut, as you can see from Figure 3-5, is basically nothing more than a standard hex nut that has been increased in height to accommodate a nylon (or fiber or elastic) insert. This insert (which, incidentally, is unthreaded) can be exposed to oil, gasoline, ether, carbon tetrachloride, and a variety of other solvents without ill effect (so you needn't rush out and buy a replacement if you happen to drop one of these jewels into a pail of Magic Clean-All). The insert is also quite stiff, although it won't hurt bolt threads or plating.

Nylon inserts come in a variety of colors, by the way; according to the Air Force, the different hues signify different heat-resistance qualities. For civilian purposes, you can forget about the color. It's not important.

The nylon insert is there, of course, to keep the load-carrying edges of the nut and bolt threads in positive contact at all times—even when the nut is not completely tightened down. You'll see how this works the first time you try to thread a fiber locknut onto a bolt. At first, you'll be able to spin the nut on with your fingers, but when the tip of the bolt reaches the nylon collar, you'll be forced to turn the nut the rest of the way down with a wrench. And as you do so, the steel threads of the bolt will slice into the nylon insert, creating extra friction and *forcing*

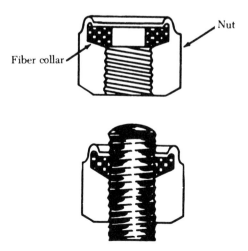

Nut

Fiber collar

FIGURE 3-5 Fiber locknut construction.

the insert upward; thereby placing a load on the bolt's threads. Once it is in place, no amount of vibration will cause the locknut to unscrew spontaneously.

So, where are elastic stopnuts commonly used? You guessed it: anyplace where there's vibration, which is to say all over the aircraft.

"But doesn't nylon become soft at high temperatures?" you may be asking. You're absolutely right; fiber-insert locknuts lose their locking quality at around 250°F, which is why you won't find many of these nuts forward of the firewall. For high-temperature applications, the people who make aircraft nuts offer something known as an all-steel, high-temperature self-locking nut (AN363), which comes in cadmium-plated and stainless steel (suffix C) versions. These nuts have a threaded *metal* insert that performs the same function as the nylon-type insert (although in a slightly different manner). They hold well at temperatures at which fiber locknuts won't do the job.

Vibration, as we've pointed out, cannot loosen a self-locking nut; however, it stands to reason that an applied torque could. Hence, it does not make sense to use a stopnut (of any kind) for any application in which either the nut or the bolt is subjected to rotational forces. What does make sense is a nut-bolt combination that can be secured with safety wire (which goes by the designation MS20995) or a cotter pin (MS24665). Hence the castle nut.

Take a good look at your plane's systems and you'll find that castle nuts are invariably used to secure drilled bolts wherever two parts meet that turn with respect to one another. Axles, control linkages, landing-gear torque links, and helicopter rotor hinges are examples of parts requiring castle nuts secured with lock wire or cotter pins.

Strange as it may sound, there's even such a thing as a self-locking castle nut (MS17825), which is just what it sounds like: a castle nut manufactured to standard specifications, but with a nylon insert added for extra safety. (Even if—FAA forbid—the cotter pin should break, this baby will *still* stay put!) Because these nuts cost several hundred dollars more per thousand than ordinary castle nuts and locknuts, you won't come across them very often. They're usually found only in areas that demand the absolute ultimate in fail-safe operation, such as the control system.

Before we leave the topic of nuts, let us be sure to get one thing straight: Castle nuts can be used and reused indefinitely (barring damage to the nut, of course), but *elastic stop nuts do wear out.* It is true that stop nuts may be reused many times, but there eventually comes a time when the fiber insert is so thoroughly "broken in" that it no longer provides sufficient thread compression to lock the nut. What's more, the FAA says that when this point is reached (that is, when you find you can spin the locknut all the way onto the bolt with only your fingers), the nut must be dispatched to hardware heaven. (You might want to make a mental note of where the most frequently disassembled stopnuts are on your aircraft and order some replacements now, so you won't be caught short when replacement time comes. It can be quite inconvenient to have to search for fresh wheel-bolt stopnuts while your plane is sitting atop jacks, minus wheels.)

About washers: you'll find some kind of washer—most likely an AN960 or AN970 flat washer—underneath almost every nut and bolt head you examine. (The FAA requires washers to be used on all nuts and bolts unless their omission is specified by manufacturers' service publications.) Usually, however, because aircraft nuts are either self-locking or externally secured in some fashion, lock washers are not used. In fact, the use of lock washers on aircraft primary and secondary structures is forbidden according to the FAA's bible on this subject, AC No. 43.13-1A (*Acceptable Methods, Techniques, and Practices: Aircraft Inspection and Repair*). When lock washers *are* used (as, for instance, in the installation of certain engine accessories), you'll generally find them sandwiched between a flat washer and a nut, to protect the accessory or underlying structure from the lock washer's sharp edges.) If you find a nut or bolt on your plane that has no washers on it at all, or that has lock washers instead of flat washers (or more than one flat washer under any one nut or bolt head), be suspicious. And notify your mechanic.

THE IMPORTANCE OF TORQUE

As you probably already know, the FAA is not content to let mechanics (or pilots, or anyone else) tighten aircraft nuts and bolts until they're simply good and tight, as is done in auto garages. Rather, the FAA makes it clear, in AC No. 43.13-1A and several other publications, that every nut-bolt combination in an aircraft must be *torqued* to its ideal tightness.

Proper torquing of nuts and bolts is more important than you may realize. Obviously, undertightening of nuts and bolts can cause unnecessary chattering, leading to premature failure of the structure and/or elongation of bolt holes and bushings. (This is a fairly frequent occurrence with wheel halves and brake parts.) Likewise, overtightening can cause permanent damage to nut and bolt threads, and/or deformation of the underlying structure.

But there's more going on here than simple under or overtightening. A more important consideration as far as the long-term health of the plane is concerned is the effect of uneven torque on load distributions. As the speed of an aircraft increases, the stresses placed on that aircraft's bolted structures increase substantially—often exponentially. It therefore becomes exceedingly important that each structural member carry no more (and no less) load than that for which it was designed. What may have started out as a small difference in load-bearing ability (i.e., bolt tightness) on the ground quickly turns into a *large* difference in stress distribution when the aircraft is cruising at 150 knots (and maybe pulling a couple of extra *g*'s, too). If the bolts are not torqued evenly, some portions of the affected structure are going to absorb more stress than others—leading, perhaps, to premature wear or outright failure.

The only way you can know for sure that the loads placed on your plane's bolted structures are being distributed evenly (the only way you can be reasonably certain that the nuts and bolts that are holding you up won't suddenly quit holding hands) is to see to it that all the nuts and bolts you touch are properly torqued.

In this connection, you should remember that *every nut and bolt you ever take apart will have a minimum and maximum recommended torque value for reassembly.* How do you find these torque values? The first place to check is the structure the bolt came from. Frequently, the proper torque value will be stamped or printed on the part or assembly that holds the bolt. (This is often true of wheel halves, for instance.) The next logical place to look is the airframe manufacturer's service manual. The aircraft service manual will usually contain both a general table of torque limits and (under the appropriate section heading) specific torquing instructions for the particular assembly under consideration.

Should you fail to find the appropriate torque limitations listed in the aircraft service manual or on the part or assembly itself, you can still find the proper torque values for your bolts by means of the FAA's Standard Torque Table (Table 3-1). To use this, all you need to know is the AN number of the bolt (the shank diameter in sixteenths of an inch, for most bolts), the AN number of the nut (see Figure 3-4), and the bolt's thread pitch in turns per inch (eyeball it). You'll also need to know whether the bolt and nut are made of steel or aluminum; most of the time, it will be steel. Of course, if you have the parts catalog for your plane (which you really ought to have), all this information will be at your fingertips.

Now, let's say you are putting your nose wheel back together after changing a tire, and you need to know how tight to torque the through bolts. The bolt torque is not given on the wheel halves, and you've forgotten to bring your plane's parts catalog with you. How do you determine the bolt's torque range? Well, first you grab a through bolt and measure its shank diameter. Finding that the diameter is ¼ in., you classify the bolt as an AN4. Next, you look at the nut that goes on the bolt and determine what kind of nut it is. You'll probably find that it is an ordinary locknut (AN365). You determine by visual inspection that both the bolt and nut are made of steel.

Now you get out your ruler once more and determine how many threads are on the end of the bolt for every inch of reach. A pitch of 28 threads per inch would put this particular nut-bolt combination in the fine-thread series. Now it's time for the Standard Torque Table. Starting at the top of the table, you put your finger on the column that lists the bolt series corresponding to your AN4 bolt (the top left); run your finger down the page to the nuts column containing your AN365 nut (that's the left-hand column); then move your finger straight down until, in the part of the table labeled Fine Thread Series you encounter the nut-bolt size of ¼-28. Directly across from the notation ¼-28, you read the numbers 50 and 70. Those are the *minimum* and *maximum* torque limits (in inch-pounds) for your nose-wheel through bolts. (To convert to foot-pounds, simply divide inch-pounds by 12. In this example, your lower torque limit would compute to 4.17 ft-lb; your upper limit, 5.83 ft-lb.)

Notice, incidentally, that the torques given in the Standard Torque Table are valid only for *unlubricated* nuts and bolts. The presence of grease, such solvents as kerosene, gasoline, or Stoddard solvent (each of which leaves a film residue when it dries), or freeing agents such as WD40, Mouse Milk, etc., will lead to improper torquing of the nut and bolt, thereby rendering the entire assembly

TABLE 3-1 FAA STANDARD TORQUE TABLE*

BOLTS

Steel tension	Aluminum
AN 3 to AN 20	AN 3DD to AN 20DD
AN 42 to AN 49	AN 173DD to AN 186DD
AN 73 to AN 81	AN 509DD
AN 173 to AN 186	MS 27039D
MS 20033 to MS 20046	MS 24694DD
MS 20073	
MS 20074	
AN 509 NK9	
MS 24694	
AN 525 NK525	
MS 27039	
MS 20004 to MS 20024	
NAS 144 to NAS 158	
NAS 333 to NAS 340	
NAS 583 to NAS 590	
NAS 624 to NAS 644	
NAS 1303 to NAS 1320	
NAS 172	
NAS 174	
NAS 517	

Steel shear bolt: NAS 464

NUTS

Steel Tension	Steel Shear	Steel Tension	Steel Shear	Aluminum Tension	Aluminum Shear
AN 310	AN 320	AN 310	AN 320	AN 365D	AN 320D
AN 315	AN 364	AN 315	AN 364	AN 310D	AN 364D
AN 363	NAS 1022	AN 363	NAS 1022	NAS 1021D	NAS 1022D
AN 365	MS 17826	AN 365	MS 17826		
NAS 1021	MS 20364	MS 17825	MS 20364		
MS 17825		MS 20365			
MS 21045		MS 21045			
MS 20365		NAS 1021			
MS 20500		NAS 679			
NAS 679		NAS 1291			

FINE THREAD SERIES

Nut-bolt size	Torque Limits in.-lb.		Torque Limits in.-lb.		Torque Limits in.-lb.		Torque Limits in.-lb.		Torque Limits in.-lb.		Torque Limits in.-lb.	
	Min.	Max.	Min.	Max.	Min.	Max.	Min.	Max.	Min.	Max.	Min.	Max.
8—36	12	15	7	9					5	10	3	6
10—32	20	25	12	15	25	30	15	20	10	15	5	10
¼—28	50	70	30	40	80	100	50	60	30	45	15	30
5/16—24	100	140	60	85	120	145	70	90	40	65	25	40
3/8—24	160	190	95	110	200	250	120	150	75	110	45	70
7/16—20	450	500	270	300	520	630	300	400	180	280	110	170
½—20	480	690	290	410	770	950	450	550	280	410	160	260
9/16—18	800	1,000	480	600	1,100	1,300	650	800	380	580	230	360
5/8—18	1,100	1,300	660	780	1,250	1,550	750	950	550	670	270	420
¾—16	2,300	2,500	1,300	1,500	2,650	3,200	1,600	1,900	950	1,250	560	880
7/8—14	2,500	3,000	1,500	1,800	3,550	4,350	2,100	2,600	1,250	1,900	750	1,200
1—14	3,700	4,500	2,200	3,300	4,500	5,500	2,700	3,300	1,600	2,400	950	1,500
1-1/8—12	5,000	7,000	3,000	4,200	6,000	7,300	3,600	4,400	2,100	3,200	1,250	2,000
1-1/4—12	9,000	11,000	5,400	6,600	11,000	13,400	6,600	8,000	3,900	5,600	2,300	3,650

COARSE THREAD SERIES

Nut-bolt size	Torque Limits in.-lb.		Torque Limits in.-lb.		Torque Limits in.-lb.		Torque Limits in.-lb.		Torque Limits in.-lb.		Torque Limits in.-lb.	
	Min.	Max.	Min.	Max.	Min.	Max.	Min.	Max.	Min.	Max.	Min.	Max.
8—32	12	15	7	9								
10—24	20	25	12	15								
¼—20	40	50	25	30								
5/16—18	80	90	48	55								
3/8—16	160	185	95	110								
7/16—14	235	255	140	155								
½—13	400	480	240	290								
9/16—12	500	700	300	420								
5/8—11	700	900	420	540								
¾—10	1,150	1,600	700	950								
7/8—9	2,200	3,000	1,300	1,800								
1—8	3,700	5,000	2,200	3,000								
1-1/8—8	5,500	6,500	3,300	4,000								
1-1/4—8	6,500	8,000	4,000	5,000								

*Torque values shown are for clean, dry, unlubricated threads.

unairworthy. If you know for sure (or suspect) that the threads of your nut or bolt are coated with any kind of solvent, be certain to wash the affected parts in methyl chloroform, methyl ethyl ketone, or acetone (which do not leave a film when they dry) before torquing everything.

Returning for a moment to the previous example, suppose that you followed the procedure for finding the proper torque range and torqued your wheel through bolts to 70 in.-lb. And suppose you later find out (by reading your airplane parts catalog) that the nuts you were working with are not AN365s but actually AN364s, which should be torqued to between 30 and 40 in.-lb. What do you do then?

The answer is, you trundle back out to the airport, remove the wheel, disassemble the improperly torqued nuts and bolts, throw those bits of hardware in the trash, and inspect your wheel halves for damage. (If possible, have an A&P inspect the parts, just to be sure.) Assuming there's been no damage, you can put *new* nuts and bolts of the proper type on the wheel and—this time—torque everything correctly. Mistakes of this type, as you can see, can be costly (in more ways than one), so watch what you're doing.

RULES FOR INSTALLING AIRCRAFT NUTS AND BOLTS

The proper installation of aircraft nuts and bolts calls for a good deal of common sense and a foreknowledge of what FAR 43.13 refers to as "accepted industry practices." On the assumption that you can provide the former, let us now review the latter.

First of all, whenever you torque a bolt, remember to tighten the *nut* down onto the bolt, rather than place your torque wrench on the head of the bolt. If you are screwing a bolt into a blind hole, or for some reason you cannot reach the nut and find that you must turn the bolt, good practice dictates (and the FAA mandates) that you torque the bolt to the higher torque limit. (When you rotate the bolt, the wrench is working not only against nut-bolt torque, but against the friction of rotation as well. This causes the desired torque to be reached prematurely. To correct for this, it is necessary either to measure the bolt drag torque and add it to the desired torque, or tighten the bolt to the higher torque limit.)

In the case of locknuts, the FAA requires that once the final torque has been reached, the end of the bolt shows through the nut. More specifically, flat-ended bolts must extend a minimum of $1/32$ in. through the locknut, while rounded or chamfered bolts must (according to the FAA) extend the full round or chamfer through the nut.

Regardless of the type of nut or bolt being used, it is always good practice to position the bolt in such a way that its head is on *top* of the structure, or facing *forward*, rather than down or back (unless, of course, the manufacturer's recommended service procedures advise otherwise). This tends to prevent the bolt from slipping out of place if the nut is accidentally lost.

Earlier, we mentioned the fact that the FAA requires the use of one washer beneath the head of every bolt and beneath every nut, except when the manufacturer specifies the omission of washers. It should also be pointed out that whenever a steel bolt is used to secure aluminum or magnesium alloy members, aluminum alloy washers should be used under the head and nut of the bolt. This way, any dissimilar-metals corrosion that occurs will attack the washers rather than the underlying structure. Naturally, steel washers should be used when steel members are being joined with steel bolts.

Occasionally, because of unusually tight working conditions, you may find it necessary to use a "crow's foot" or other extension-type adapter on the end of your torque wrench. In that case the final torque you reach will be different from the apparent torque indicated by the torque wrench. Accordingly, you'll have to adjust your indicated (or apparent) torque upward or downward somewhat, to obtain the correct final torque at the nut or bolt. This can be done with the aid of the following simple formula:

$$\frac{T \times L}{L + E} = T'$$

where T' = the proper *indicated* torque
T = the actual final torque at the nut
L = the handgrip-to-drive distance (minus adapter)
E = the adapter length

FIGURE 3-6 When a wrench adapter that changes the effective moment arm is used on a torque wrench, it is necessary to calculate the correct indicated torque by means of the formula shown here. Notice that when the adapter faces away from the handgrip, *E* is treated as a positive number; when the adapter faces toward the handgrip, *E* is treated as a negative number.

Naturally, if the adapter or extension points toward the handgrip of the wrench (thereby *reducing* your leverage), E in the above formula will be a negative number. (See Figure 3-6.)

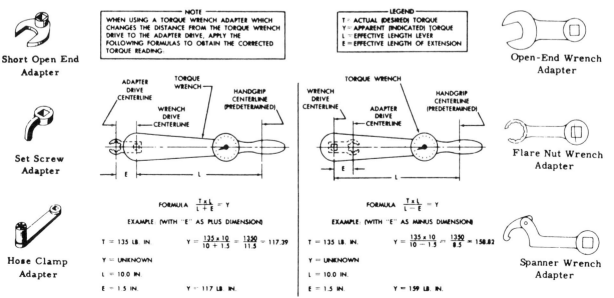

SAFETYING TECHNIQUES

According to the FAA, all non-self-locking fasteners used in aircraft primary structures *must be externally secured*, to ensure that said fasteners will not depart the aircraft—not without some difficulty, at least. When such fasteners are externally secured, usually with safety wire (MS20995) or cotter pins (MS24665), they are said to be "safetied."

Although oil filters, piano hinges, wing nuts, studs, and drain bolts (among others) can all be safetied, the most familiar type of safetied fastener is the AN310 or AN320 castle nut, which can be safetied with either cotter pins or wire. (Exactly which material you use will depend on the type of material present when you start the job.) Safetying one of these nuts is easy, providing you can get the nut's castellations (or slots) to line up exactly with the hole in the bolt tip after tightening the nut to its proper torque. As it turns out, this is quite often a problem; strict adherence to recommended torque values frequently prevents slots from lining up at all, since castle nuts are not "keyed" (i.e., the hex does not clock to the threads).

There are ways, naturally, of dealing with this situation. The first thing you can do is try torquing the nut to its minimum torque limit, then tighten the nut slowly in an attempt to get things to line up before reaching the maximum torque limit. If the moon and tides are with you, proper alignment will occur before the upper torque limit is reached, and that will be that.

The second thing you can do (if the foregoing procedure proves futile) is try a different washer under the nut. Quite often, the substitution of a shiny new washer for an old, flattened one will do the trick; if not, you can simply substitute a new washer of a different thickness. (Whether you knew it or not, AN960 flat washers come in two different thicknesses, to deal with just this situation. The thinner washers can be identified by the presence of a suffix L on their dash number: an AN960-5L is a thin-series 5/16-in. flat washer.) Of course, one thing you definitely will *not* want to do is use two washers where there was only one to begin with.

If all else fails, you have one final option—and that's to try an entirely new castle nut, an entirely new bolt, or both. Remember, a castle nut's threads are not keyed. The AN310 nut that didn't work on this particular bolt will work on another one somewhere else.

After you've achieved alignment between the bolt hole and the nut's slots, you can begin to secure the assembly with safety wire or a cotter pin (whichever was there originally). If you're using wire, select the largest diameter wire that will fit through the bolt hole. (You can buy safety wire in several sizes.) And be sure to use none other than aircraft-quality stainless steel safety wire with MS20995 printed somewhere on the package—not the barnyard-grade junk you see in hardware stores.

Incidentally, aircraft safety wire comes in brass, copper, soft iron, galvanized, and other special forms, in addition to stainless steel. If the assembly you're working on requires one of these special types of lock wire, use it. Consult a mechanic if you're not sure what to use.

The actual safety-wiring of a nut or bolt to another nut or bolt (or to an anchor

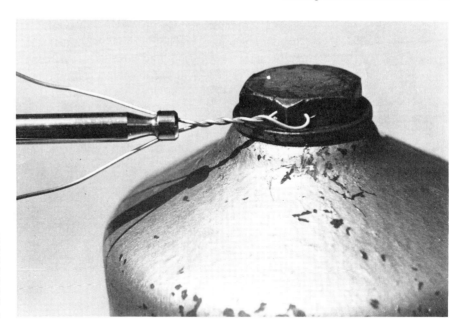

FIGURE 3-7 A wire-twisting tool in action. Here, a Gerdes wire twister (such as the one shown in Figure 2-5) is being used to safety the stud on a stud/cartridge type engine oil filter. Notice how the tool holds the wire automatically at the proper twisting angle.

lug, housing, etc.) is very simple, once you get the hang of it. Basically, it involves little more than looping a long piece of wire through the anchor point, twisting the wire together tightly (6 to 12 twists per inch) until the nut-bolt assembly is reached, passing one strand of wire through the bolt and the other around it, and making a ¼- to ½-in. pigtail past the last item to be wired. (Doing this in an artful manner with a pair of duckbill pliers takes a bit of practice. As pointed out in Chapter 2, it is much easier, the first few times you do this, to use a special wire-twisting tool rather than a set of pliers. See Figure 3-7.)

It should go without saying, but in case it doesn't: *Always* use new safety wire for each job. And route the wire in such a way that the only possible direction in which the wire can pull on the nut is in a *tightening* direction (Figure 3-8). Also, make certain that the wire is positioned so that the loop around the edge of the nut stays down and does not come up over the bolt.

Remember that your twists should be tight and even, but not excessively tight. Beginners have a tendency to overtwist the wire, creating a very taut run between anchor points; this is both unnecessary and imprudent. You don't want to work-harden the wire to the extent that normal airframe vibrations may cause it to fail, and yet that's exactly what can happen if the wire is overtwisted. So please, take it easy. Don't overtwist.

One more thing: Be sure to bend your pigtails back or under when you're finished so that there is no danger of them snagging other parts—or bare skin. Sharp-pointed pigtails can cut like razor blades.

Thankfully, the installation of cotter pins offers less opportunity for error than safety-wiring: even so, however, you'll want to watch what you're doing. Cotter pins, as you probably know, come in a variety of lengths, diameters, and alloy types. They also come in aircraft and nonaircraft grades. You want only brand new, never-been-used-before MS24665 (formerly AN380) aircraft-type cotter pins.

Here are some rules of thumb to bear in mind when working with cotter pins:

1. Check to be sure the pin fits neatly into the bolt hole with *little or no side play*.

2. Start the prongs apart (once the pin is in place) with a screwdriver; then tap them lightly with a mallet to get them to bend. Avoid making any sharp bends.

3. See that the top prong (i.e., the prong bent back over the end of the bolt) does not extend beyond the bolt diameter. If necessary, cut the prong back.

4. Make sure the lowermost prong does not rest against the surface of the washer, or the underlying structure. (Again, trim the prong back if need be.)

5. If you wish, you may bend the prongs around the sides of the nut, rather than bend one prong up and one down (Figure 3-9). In this case, be certain the ends of the prongs do not extend outward from the nut hex.

Appendix A of FAR Part 43 specifically lists the replacement of defective safety wire and cotter pins as one of the preventive maintenance procedures pilots may engage in. This means that any time you encounter *any* broken safety wire or rusted or missing cotter pins on your aircraft, even if it's in an area you normally wouldn't work on (the engine accessory case, say), you may legally replace the safety wire or cotter pins in question. The one exception to this is *turnbuckles*, the safety-wiring of which is somewhat complicated (and extremely critical to safety). If you happen across any poorly wired turnbuckles in your plane's control system,

FIGURE 3-8 Safety wire should always be routed in such a way that it can only pull on fasteners in a *tightening* direction. In the examples shown here, the wire is assumed to be installed in nuts, bolts, and studs with right-handed threads. In general, no more than three items should be safetied with a single piece of wire.

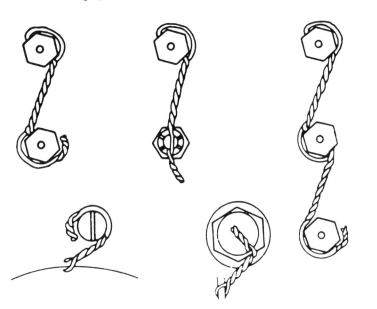

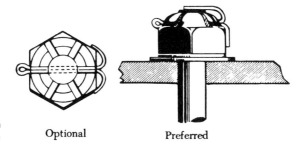

FIGURE 3-9 Accepted cotter-pin
configurations.

Optional   Preferred

call in a mechanic immediately; this is one area you'd be best off not touching, regardless of what the FARs say.

ADDITIONAL SOURCES OF INFORMATION ON AIRCRAFT HARDWARE

In this chapter, we have only been able to scratch the surface in terms of the classification and proper use of aircraft hardware; for space reasons, we've had to neglect completely such important hardware items as speed nuts, screws, and hose fittings and hoses. Likewise, our discussion of nuts, bolts, washers, and associated hardware has necessarily been brief. A great deal has been left unsaid.

Fortunately, most of what has been left unsaid in this chapter is said quite clearly in a handful of other publications, should you wish to pursue the matter. High on the list is the FAA's own *Acceptable Methods, Techniques, and Practices: Aircraft Inspection and Repair*, otherwise known as AC No. 43.13-1A, which contains a wealth of information on the design and use of aircraft hardware. As far as any discussion of FAA-approved procedures goes, that book is the ultimate authority. That manual, and its sister volume AC No. 43.13-2A: *Aircraft Alterations*, should be considered must reading by every maintenance-conscious pilot.

For a slightly more detailed, more easily digestible discussion of the hows and whys of working with aircraft hardware, you may wish to consult another FAA publication; AC No. 65-9A: *Airframe and Powerplant Mechanics—General Handbook*, which, unlike AC No. 43.13-1A & 2A, assumes absolutely no prior knowledge on the reader's part. Written for student mechanics, this book provides a very thorough discussion of aircraft hardware, along with many other topics.

Finally, if you wish to obtain more information on the kinds and sizes of AN, NAS, and MS hardware in common use, invest in a copy of Aero Publishers' *Aircraft Standards Handbook*, the Aviation Maintenance Foundation's *Aviation Maintenance Handbook and Standard Hardware Digest*, or the Pittsburgh Institute of Aeronautics' *Aircraft Mechanic's Specifications Handbook*. Each of these manuals will tell you more about aircraft hardware than any civilian has a right to know.

Have you looked at your plane's wheels and tires lately? *Really* looked at them? If you're like most pilots, you probably haven't checked the inflation of your tires for more than a week; there's probably no record in your aircraft logs of how long ago you gave your treads a thorough going over for bulges, skid burns, weather checking, foreign-object damage, etc.; and you've probably *never* given your rims a fine-tooth-comb inspection. Chances are, the last time your wheels and tires got a really thorough examination was at your last annual inspection, and the next time they'll receive such care will be at your next annual inspection.

This is no way to conduct wheel and tire maintenance. Your wheels and tires, after all, are no less important to the safe operation of your plane on the ground than your wings are to its safe operation in the air. In this sense, a plane's wheels and tires actually constitute a vital control surface, and they should be treated as such. You wouldn't think of flying a plane that had a loose rudder or improperly rigged flaps; nor should you consider entrusting your life to an aircraft whose wheels and tires have been less than carefully maintained.

What does routine wheel and tire maintenance consist of? Actual procedures vary somewhat from one airplane model to the next, so—regardless of what follows—you should check your service manual for the techniques applicable to your aircraft. However, the periodic servicing requirements for aircraft wheels and tires are pretty much the same for a Twin Beech as they are for a Cessna 150. As a rule, it is considered standard practice to inspect wheel halves for damage once a year (or at every tire change, whichever comes first), inspect and lubricate wheel bearings annually or every 100 hr, and check tires for condition daily (i.e., before every flight).

Pilots can be forgiven, perhaps, for not making thorough inspections of wheels and bearings periodically themselves, since these checks are always accomplished (by law) at each annual inspection, and since a once-yearly look-see is all that's needed. Pilots have no excuse, however, for neglecting their tires—although neglect is exactly what 90 percent of all pilots lavish on their treads right up until the time they wear out (which, under the circumstances, usually doesn't take long). Most pilots seem to think that routine tire maintenance consists of checking tires for inflation once a month (not daily, but once a month!) and glancing at them to see if they're still there before each flight. The fact that a tire may be unairworthy even though

FOUR
WHEELS
AND TIRES

it is holding air and has a good deal of tread left evidently has never occurred to some pilots.

Before we go any further, then, let us begin at the beginning and consider what constitutes an adequate "on the aircraft" inspection of an airplane tire—the kind of inspection that should be (but usually isn't) made before every flight.

HOW TO INSPECT A TIRE ON THE AIRCRAFT

There's more to judging a tire's airworthiness than merely checking its inflation; and there's more to checking inflation than meets the eye, as you'll shortly see. In determining whether a given tire is fit to fly, you should check it for *inflation*, *wear*, *damage*, and *slippage*. Let us consider each of these in turn.

Inflation

"Proper inflation," a B. F. Goodrich manual on tire care states, "is undoubtedly the most necessary maintenance function for safe, long service from aircraft tires." Too much air or too little air spells trouble. In particular, it means reduced service life—perhaps precipitously reduced.

Pilots have a tendency to believe that the most significant effect on tires of underinflation is rapid tread wear at the tire's shoulders, but this is the least important effect of underinflation. *Heat buildup* is the most worrisome consequence of low tire pressure. When properly inflated, an aircraft tire undergoes more than twice the deflection of a passenger-car tire, and that flexing liberates heat. When the tire is underinflated, it experiences extreme amounts of flexing and produces correspondingly increased amounts of heat—heat that can literally cause the tire to come apart internally.

Of course, in addition to causing overheating, underinflation also offers ample opportunity (through increased flexing) for the tire's sidewalls to be crushed by the wheel rims during a hard landing, or while taxiing across a pothole. Then too, the bead area (i.e., that portion of the lower sidewall which seals tightly against the wheel rim) may be damaged as the flaccid sidewalls flex over the wheel flange during sharp turns. Cord rupture and bruise breaks are then likely to occur.

To make matters even worse, underinflated tires are apt to creep or slip on the wheel during braking (or all the time, if the brakes drag). This eventually causes the inner-tube valve stem to shear off, leaving the tire without air and the pilot with a major problem.

Underinflation clearly is bad news for airplane tires. More so, perhaps, than most pilots realize.

Overinflation is arguably less hazardous to tires than underinflation, but its effects are no less undesirable. Overinflation lessens the shock-absorbing capacity of the landing gear, thereby allowing extra stress to be passed to the airframe during landing; it increases the susceptibility of the tire to impact breaks, bruising, cutting, and foreign-object damage; it puts excessive strain on tire cords (leading to reduced service life); and it subjects wheel components (tie bolts in particular) to unusually high stresses—to say nothing of rapid center-tread wear.

There's only one way to avoid the undesirable effects of underinflation and overinflation, and that's to check (and adjust, if necessary) tire inflation before every flight, using an accurate pressure gauge. The main thing to remember here is that tire pressure should always be checked when the tire is *cold*. If the aircraft has been flown, allow a minimum of 3 hr for the treads to cool before checking inflation. Also, remember to follow the *airframe manufacturer's* inflation recommendations (as given in the plane owner's manual or the service manual), rather than the more general inflation guidelines published by the tire manufacturer. The airframe manufacturer's data take into account the actual load conditions under which the tire is being used.

You should check tire pressures *daily* (or before each flight) because changes in air temperature can and do have a significant effect on tire inflation. This, plus the normal slow seepage of air from tires and tubes, will effectively cause your tires to have a different inflation pressure every time you fly. As a rule of thumb, you can count on a 1 percent pressure change for every 5°F change in outside air temperature. In other words, if your nosewheel tire pressure was 50 psi this afternoon, and the temperature drops 30°F overnight, your nosewheel tire pressure will be 6 percent lower—47 psi—tomorrow morning.

After you've gotten into the habit of carrying a tire gauge with you on every walkaround, you'll be surprised at how often you find yourself adding air to your tires. Surprised, and perhaps frustrated. (Taxiing back and forth to the nearest air hose tends to become tiresome after awhile.) The way to avoid the frustration, of course, is to carry your own air with you. Portable air tanks are handy for this purpose, although they do tend to be bulky and cumbersome. If you want to be able to carry your own air supply in the plane, you might consider investing $20 or $30 in one of the small air compressors that operate by being plugged into a cigar lighter. For even less money, you can buy a foot-operated air pump with a built-in dial-type pressure gauge (Figure 4-1). J. C. Whitney, the automotive-parts

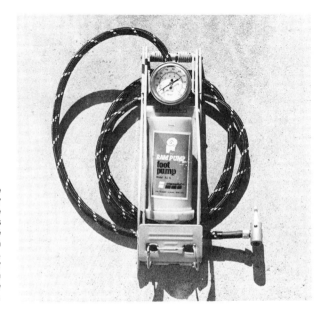

FIGURE 4-1 Foot-operated tire pumps similar to this one are fairly common now and may be obtained through auto-parts stores for about $15. Such pumps are easy to use (certainly easier than a hand-operated tire pump), they're compact enough to carry in the plane, and most come with a built-in dial-type pressure gauge.

supplier, offers a variety of low-cost tire pumps of this and other designs, if you find you can't obtain one locally through a hardware, auto-parts, or department store.

Checking for Wear
No preflight inspection is complete without a thorough examination of the tire surface for wear. Here, you'll want to examine not just the easily visible portion of each tire, but the *entire tread surface*. If necessary, roll the plane back or forward several complete tire revolutions to bring hidden portions of tread (i.e., any areas concealed by wheel pants) into easy view.

The first and most obvious thing to observe is the overall tread wear pattern. Ideally, the wear should be spread evenly across the entire tread surface of each tire. If the tires have been consistently overinflated or underinflated, the result will be clearly visible as accelerated center tread wear (if overinflated) or shoulder wear (if underinflated). Some degree of center-tread wear is considered normal (see Figure 4-2).

Aircraft with spring steel (Wittman-type) main landing gear tend to experience more rapid tread wear on the outboard half of each tire than on the inboard (fuselage-facing) half, as a result of the natural tendency of this kind of gear to bow together slightly when the aircraft is not under maximum static load. In flight, when there is no load on the main gear, the gear legs bow quite noticeably; as a result, the outboard edges of the tires always impact the runway first during touch-down, a situation that inevitably leads to rapid outer-shoulder tread wear. Owners of aircraft with this type of gear (for example, pre-1972 Cessna singles) will find that they can get 25 to 40 percent more useful tread life if they'll simply dismount each tire, turn it around, and remount it on the same wheel every 100 hr or so. This trick works for any tire (on any type of gear) that is wearing more on one side of the center-tread rib than the other.

In addition to checking for signs of chronic overinflation or underinflation, check your tires for uneven tread wear. Rapid inboard or outboard shoulder wear on main wheels could be a sign of wheel misalignment; on a nose wheel, differential shoulder wear could indicate a dragging brake. (In either case, the tire should be taken off, turned around, and remounted to even up the wear.) Spotty, uneven wear around the tire circumference could be due to brake problems, tire imbalance, or shimmy problems. On a nosewheel tire, such wear could also be due to improper towing techniques and/or high-speed swerving turns.

Skid burns, which show up as flat spots on an otherwise normal tire, should be watched carefully from the time they're first discovered; the flat spot generally grows with continued service, causing a steadily worsening tire imbalance. Also, the burned area is particularly vulnerable to foreign-object damage (FOD). A single skid mark can take months off the life of a tire, since the burned area is usually the first part to wear through (i.e., show cords or plies). When the skid area exposes cords, the tire must be replaced.

You may not have realized it before, but skid burns can be caused not only by locking a brake, but by hydroplaning. When a tire encounters water or slush

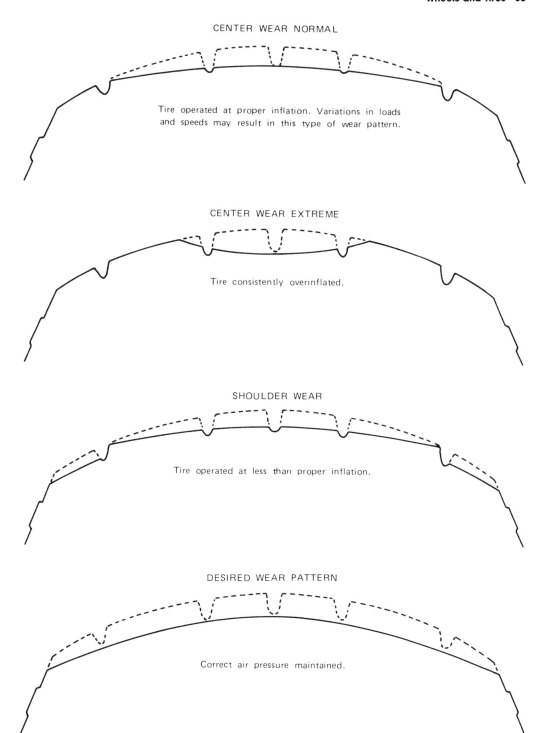

CENTER WEAR NORMAL

Tire operated at proper inflation. Variations in loads and speeds may result in this type of wear pattern.

CENTER WEAR EXTREME

Tire consistently overinflated.

SHOULDER WEAR

Tire operated at less than proper inflation.

DESIRED WEAR PATTERN

Correct air pressure maintained.

FIGURE 4-2 Effect of inflation pressure on tread wear patterns.

at high speed, traction is diminished and hydroplaning (a phenomenon well known to most automobile drivers) is said to occur; yet at the same time, sufficient friction may be present to cause a locked wheel's tire to suffer burning. The hydroplane burn that results shows up as an oval-shaped pattern of rubber reversion or deterioration on the tread surface. Usually, the tire may be kept in service, although it should be watched.

The National Aeronautics and Space Administration (NASA) has come up with a handy formula to predict the minimum ground speed at which hydroplaning (and thus tire burning) can occur. The formula is:

$$V_m = 9 \sqrt{P}$$

where V_m is the minimum hydroplane velocity in knots, and P is the tire pressure in pounds per square inch. It should be noted that this formula is valid only when the runway flooding depth is equal to or greater than the tire tread depth.

Skid and hydroplaning burns should not be confused with bald spots caused by out-of-balance wear. If you encounter a bald area on a tire, and the bald part shows no sign of burning, you've probably got an out-of-balance wheel or tire. The bald spot comes about as the result of the tire's heavy point being the first part to impact the runway on every landing. To correct this, it may be necessary to remove the wheel from the plane and have a mechanic add balance weights to it.

Checking for Damage

When you inspect your tires for damage, be on the alert not only for cuts, tears, and obvious signs of FOD, but also for cracks, blisters, chunking (missing chunks of tread), tread rib delamination, abrasion damage from contact with wheel wells or fairings, spillage of hydraulic fluid onto the tire, and severe weather checking. Some of these conditions are illustrated in Figures 4-3 through 4-6.

The most serious forms of damage are those that either (1) present evidence of internal delamination or (2) cause exposure of nylon cords or plies. Accordingly, any time you spot bulges or blisters anywhere on the tire or any time nylon cords become visible through a cut or crack, plan on replacing the affected tire immediately. It's possible the damage may be of a type that would allow the tire to remain in service, but this is a judgment only a qualified mechanic can make.

Cuts can be classified in terms of their direction as being either transverse (i.e., at right angles to the tread grooves) or circumferential (parallel to tread grooves). Regarding the former kind of cuts, the Firestone Tire and Rubber Company recommends that the following rules be observed in determining a tire's serviceability:

1. When a cut is deep enough to have penetrated body cords, the tire should be scrapped.

2. If the cut is deeper than existing tread grooves and extends the full length from one groove to the next, the tire should be replaced.

FIGURE 4-3 This tire, removed from a Cessna 182, shows the effect that wheel misalignment (toe-in), combined with the natural bowing tendency of spring-steel gear, can have on tread wear. In this case, the outboard portion of the tire (left) wore so rapidly that a hole was produced in the carcass before the inboard treads began to show significant wear.

FIGURE 4-4 The major tire manufacturers say that whenever wear has proceeded to the point where cords are visible, the tire should be taken out of service. On this basis, the tire shown here (a nosewheel tire taken from a Beech Baron) should have been retired long ago. This type of nosewheel tire wear (notice the dramatic difference between the two shoulders) is often due to a dragging brake on one or the other main wheel.

FIGURE 4-5 Classic signs of skid burning are evident on this tire, taken from a Baron main wheel. Notice the narrow area of rubber melting and advanced tread wear in adjacent areas.

3. Puncture cuts less than 1 in. in length that have not exposed body fabric are not cause for tire removal; however, the cuts should be monitored closely for growth.

As for circumferential cuts, Firestone recommends that when a cut extends deeper than a tread groove (but not into body cords) and its ends are displaced no more than ½ in apart measured transversely, the tire may remain in service. Also, so long as only one rib (the area between two grooves) is involved, a less-than-groove-depth cut of up to 12 in. in length may be left in service *if the ends of the*

FIGURE 4-6   Weather checking (the appearance of thousands of tiny surface cracks) inevitably afflicts all tires. Tire manufacturers consider weather checking perfectly harmless so long as cords cannot be seen through the cracks.

cut are displaced no more than ⅛ in transversely. If carcass cords are exposed, the tire must be replaced no matter what the size of the cut.

According to Firestone, there is no limit on how long a sidewall cut can be. A tire with any sidewall cut may remain in service so long as body cords are not exposed.

All tires eventually develop numerous minute, shallow cracks on their side-walls, a phenomenon known as "weather checking" (Figure 4-6). Although direct exposure of a tire to ozone (which is produced by electric motors and fluorescent lights), sunlight, or weather can speed the development of weather checking, normal aging will also produce it; in any case, it can be considered harmless as long as no body cords can be seen through the myriad tiny cracks. When cords can be seen, the tire should be replaced.

When you inspect tires for damage, be sure to look for oil, gasoline, tar, or hydraulic-fluid stains. Each of these substances is harmful to the rubber in aircraft tires. Hydraulic fluid in particular can produce a swelling and softening of tire rubber, leading to (at best) erratic wear and/or (at worst) internal damage. If you discover oil or hydraulic fluid on a tire, wipe the fluid off with a gasoline-moistened cloth; then wash the tire with soap and water. (Needless to say, if your plane has any leaking brakes, oleo struts, or gear-retraction hydraulics, you should have the leaks fixed at once.)

Finally, don't neglect the valve-stem area during your inspection for tire damage. Check to be sure the valve stem is not cocked due to tire slippage (see below). In addition, check to see that the stem is not coming in contact with wheel fairings or other obstructions. If threads are damaged, dress them up with a valve repair tool such as the kind shown in Figure 4-7. Also, if the stem is not capped, cap it to keep dirt from entering it and hanging up on the valve core (which is how many air leaks get started).

Tire Slippage   Many pilots are not aware that it is possible for an underinflated tire to creep or slip along the wheel on landing or during braking. The eventual result is heat damage and/or abrasion damage to the tire bead. In serious cases, the inner-tube valve stem can be sheared off completely, causing immediate and total loss of air.

The best way to keep tabs on tire slippage is to draw or paint a line across both tire and rim; then, at each walkaround inspection, you can simply look to see if the lines on the tire and wheel line up. If they don't, you'll know the tire is creeping.

HOW TO MOUNT AND DISMOUNT WHEELS AND TIRES   Knowing how to remove and reinstall wheels and tires should be a part of every pilot's preventive maintenance repertoire. The procedures involved are quite simple (much simpler, in fact, than for automobile wheels and tires); once learned, they'll enable you to save a sizable amount of money on routine maintenance over the years.

The hardest part of getting a plane's wheels on and off is lifting the landing gear up off the ground; therefore, let us address this problem first.

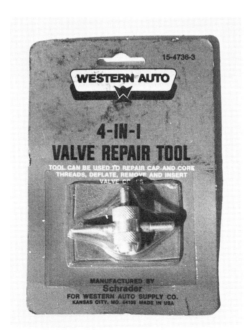

FIGURE 4-7 Small, inexpensive tools designed to remove, insert, and repair valve cores are made by Schrader and others. They pay for themselves quickly.

Jacking   Aircraft jacking is a subject not to be taken lightly. Grave injuries to people and equipment have resulted from carelessness in jacking. Even when performed correctly and with due caution, jacking entails a certain amount of risk; a sudden gust of air can cause thousands of dollars of damage in an instant. Thus it is imperative that adequate safety precautions be taken whenever any part of an airframe is raised off the ground. *Read and follow the directions given in your aircraft service manual regarding the jacking of your plane.* Only general guidelines can be given here.

When the entire aircraft is to be raised off the ground, three tripod jacks (or two jacks and a tail stand) must usually be used (Figure 4-8). Generally, jack pads are provided on each wing near the quarter-chord point, and at a point under the

MASONITE BLOCK 4'' SQUARE AND 1'' THICK
WITH DEPRESSION FOR JACK IN UNDER-
SIDE. PAD TOP SIDE WITH 1/4'' RUBBER.

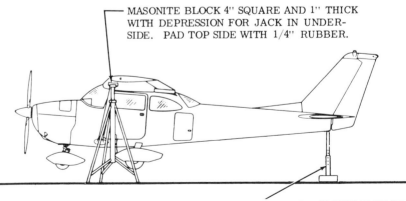

FIGURE 4-8 When the entire airplane is to be raised off the ground, large tripod jacks must be placed under the wings; also, the tail must be supported so as to keep the aircraft level. Some planes have built-in jack pads; others do not. (*Cessna Aircraft Company drawing.*)

WEIGHTED, ADJUSTABLE STAND
ATTACHED TO TIE-DOWN RING

nose or tail. The jacks must be positioned squarely beneath each jack pad (jack misalignment is a leading cause of jacking accidents). Then the surrounding area should be cleared, and the jacks raised simultaneously until the plane just clears the ground. During jacking, the aircraft must be kept as nearly level as possible to minimize the chance of its slipping off the jacks. When the work is finished, the plane is lowered, again in a level attitude.

As mentioned in Chapter 2, heavy-duty tripod jacks for aircraft can be quite expensive ($200 or more each), making their occasional use by plane owners somewhat less than practical. Fortunately, most preventive maintenance operations, including routine wheel and tire servicing, do not require jacking the entire aircraft off the ground. For most operations, it's only necessary to raise one wheel.

Nose wheels are best raised off the ground with the aid of a few sandbags placed on the horizontal stabilizer. (Remember to lay the bags on the *stabilizer spar only*, as close to the fuselage as possible, to avoid damaging the structure.) Alternatively, ballast can be attached to the plane's tail tie-down ring.

Getting a main wheel off the asphalt is usually a little more of a challenge. However, most planes do incorporate provisions for raising one wheel off the ground, usually by means of a small hydraulic jack placed under some portion of the main-gear fork or casting. Cessnas with spring steel gear can be raised via a special jacking adapter that clamps onto one gear leg; here, because of the springiness of the gear, it is usually necessary to raise the gear a few inches, then (as it bows together) let it back down, raise it again and (if it bows some more) let it back down, then finally reposition the jack and raise the gear off the ground. The later-model Cessna singles with tubular steel gear have a built-in jack point on the gear leg and require no adapter.

For some low-wing aircraft, a scissors jack placed beneath the main-landing-gear lower casting will suffice to raise one wheel (this is true, for instance, of the Beechcraft Sundowner). Some models require the use of a special adapter for this. In any case, *do not* place a jack under a brake casting. If you are unsure as to where to position the jack, consult your aircraft service manual and/or a qualified mechanic.

Regardless of the jacking method being used, certain safety rules should always be followed when an aircraft is to be jacked:

1. Jacks should be inspected before use to determine whether they are working properly and are of sufficient load capacity to support the weight of the plane.

2. Jacks should be placed on a dry surface only.

3. If only one wheel of an aircraft is to be raised, all other wheels should be securely chocked fore and aft.

4. The aircraft being raised must be *well protected from the wind*. A hangar should be used if possible.

5. No more than one wheel should be raised off the ground at a time with small,

individual main-gear jacks. When more than one wheel must be raised, tripod jacks should be used.

6. No one should be in, on, or under the aircraft while it is being raised. Also, the area immediately surrounding the plane should be cleared of bystanders and obstructions before any jacking is begun.

7. Never raise the airplane any higher than the minimum height necessary to accomplish the job.

8. *Always* follow the airframe manufacturer's jacking instructions to the letter. When possible, enlist the aid of an experienced mechanic.

Wheel Removal   The first step in removing the wheel from the aircraft (once the wheel is jacked up) is to liberate it from any brakes, wheel fairings, or other impedimenta that might be present. Main-gear wheel pants generally come off quite easily with the removal of a nut or bolt and numerous screws. In the case of a nosewheel, you'll probably need to slide the fairing straight up on the gear until the wheel can be removed; then, with the wheel gone, let the pant back down and turn it sideways to free it from the nose fork. (See Figure 4-9.)

If you're dealing with a main wheel, you'll have to free the wheel from the brake before you begin loosening the axle nut (after removing any fairings). With Goodyear brakes, this is a simple matter of loosening the brake-disc clips that hold the disc in the side of the wheel. (As the wheel comes off, the disc will stay.) With

FIGURE 4-9   To liberate the wheel from the axle, remove any wheel fairings and/or hubcaps that are present, then pull the cotter pin from the axle nut, and finally remove the nut itself.

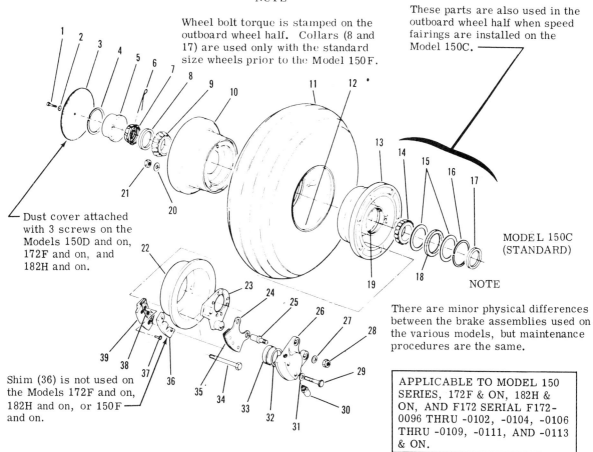

NOTE

Wheel bolt torque is stamped on the outboard wheel half. Collars (8 and 17) are used only with the standard size wheels prior to the Model 150F.

These parts are also used in the outboard wheel half when speed fairings are installed on the Model 150C.

Dust cover attached with 3 screws on the Models 150D and on, 172F and on, and 182H and on.

MODEL 150C (STANDARD)

NOTE

There are minor physical differences between the brake assemblies used on the various models, but maintenance procedures are the same.

Shim (36) is not used on the Models 172F and on, 182H and on, or 150F and on.

APPLICABLE TO MODEL 150 SERIES, 172F & ON, 182H & ON, AND F172 SERIAL F172-0096 THRU -0102, -0104, -0106 THRU -0109, -0111, AND -0113 & ON.

FIGURE 4-10 Exploded view of a typical Cleveland wheel and brake installation. This particular drawing shows Cessna 150, 172, and 182 wheel and brake components. (*Cessna Aircraft Company drawing.*)

Cleveland and McCauley brakes, the disc comes off with the wheel; therefore, the back plate (see Figure 6-3) must be removed from the wheel side of the brake disc before the wheel will come off the axle (see Figure 4-10). To remove the back plate, unscrew the two through bolts that hold it to the back side of the disc. (Leave the bolts in place in the brake cylinder.)

Before going any further, stop and *release all the air from the tire you're going to work on.* That way, should any or all of the wheel tie bolts have developed cracks (an unlikely situation, but possible nonetheless), air pressure will not cause the wheel to undergo "rapid disassembly" (i.e., blow apart) when you remove the axle nut from the axle. Depress the valve core plunger until air can no longer be heard escaping from the tire.

At this point, all that remains is to gain access to the axle nut and remove it. Unscrew or pry off any dust cover or hubcap that might be present; set it where it won't get lost. Then pull the cotter pin from the axle nut, unscrew the nut, and

FIGURE 4-11 When you remove the wheel from the axle, you'll also be removing the wheel bearings from the axle; the bearings will stay with the wheel (assuming they don't fall out onto the ground). If the axle itself looks or feels dirty, wipe it with a solvent-dampened rag and lightly grease it before returning the wheel to the gear. If the axle is scored, pitted, or bent, call a mechanic.

carefully slide the wheel off the axle (Figure 4-11). If you're working on a nose-wheel, you may find that you need to unscrew a small nut at one end of the axle, then pull (or tap) out the axle rod, then tap various spacers, end caps, or ferrules out to free the wheel. Consult your service manual for instructions pertaining specifically to your plane.

Dismounting the Tire You should have done this already (see above), but in case you haven't, deflate the tire completely before going any further. Ideally, you should remove the valve core from the tire's valve stem, using a *core key*. (You can pick up one of these tools at nearly any bike shop or auto-parts store, if you don't already have one.) Allow the tire to deflate before you unscrew the core all the way, or else it'll go shooting out of the valve stem like a bullet.

The reason you should remove the valve core completely, rather than deflate the tire simply by depressing the core plunger, is that it's possible (though not likely) for ice to form in the valve stem as you hold the core plunger down, causing some air to remain trapped in the tire. Subsequent removal of the wheel tie bolts would then be very hazardous, since any residual tire pressure might send bolts flying when the wheel is disassembled. So *remove the valve core completely* unless you are absolutely certain that all the air is gone from the tire.

The next step is known as "breaking the bead"; on small tires, it involves manually pressing the bead portion of the tire away from the wheel rim (i.e., toward the interior of the tire) all the way around the bead's circumference, on both sides of the tire. Goodyear recommends pressing with a 2-ft block of wood close to the bead, or else tapping the bead smartly with a rubber mallet. One thing you definitely must *not* do is attempt to break the bead free using a screwdriver, pry bar, or other metal tool; such tools can very easily nick or dent the soft aluminum (or magnesium) of which aircraft wheels are made, setting up stress concentrations that could later turn into fatigue cracks.

After the bead has been broken on both sides, you may proceed to disassemble the wheel tie bolts (see Figure 4-10). Remember that if any air pressure exists in the tire, these bolts can fly apart with explosive force. Exercise due caution.

Finally, pull the wheel halves away from the tire, beginning with the *inboard* wheel half (i.e., the brake-disc half). As you pull the tire apart from the outboard portion of the wheel, be careful not to snag the inner-tube valve stem.

Inspecting the Wheel   Any time you remove a tire from a wheel, you should make at least a cursory (and preferably a thorough) inspection of both wheel halves and associated hardware. The main things to look for are corrosion, cracks, and elongation of bolt holes. If minor corrosion is present, attempt to remove it with a moist sponge and a nonchlorinated household cleanser such as Bon Ami. Afterward, thoroughly rinse the affected region and blow it dry; then follow up with a coating of zinc chromate primer and aluminum lacquer (or whatever your mechanic recommends). Any damage more advanced than minor surface corrosion should be brought to the attention of a mechanic immediately.

Cracks are most likely to be found in the rim area of each wheel; go over these parts with a magnifying glass, if you can. While you're at it, examine the tie bolts too, paying particular attention to the thread areas and the shank-head junction region. If any doubt exists as to whether a crack is present, consult a mechanic.

Elongated bolt holes are not all that uncommon in aircraft wheel halves, so be sure to check for this condition. Elongation results from undertightening of the wheel tie bolts and subsequent movement of the rims with respect to each other; thus, to check for bolt hole "stretch" all you have to do is bolt the wheel halves back together—sans tire—and try to move the two halves in opposite directions. Noticeable movement is cause to suspect elongation. Fortunately, this condition can sometimes be cured by the use of inserts; check with your mechanic for details.

Replacing the Tire   Remounting an aircraft tire is only slightly more difficult than removing it—which is to say, not very difficult at all.

If you intend to remount your old tire (if, for example, you are simply turning the old tire around to equalize uneven tread wear), it would be a good idea to give the doughnut a quick inspection before putting it back in service. In particular, examine the *bead area* (a part of the tire you don't often get to see) for signs of chafing, burning, and/or damage in the form of kinks or protruding bead wires. (The bead contains steel reinforcing fibers.) If any of these conditions is evident, if there are any unusual bulges anywhere, or if the tire has any cuts or skid marks that expose cord fabric, plan on buying a new tire rather than reinstalling the old one.

While you're at it, be sure to inspect your inner tube, if your tire is of the tube type (it probably will be). The valve-stem base warrants especially close scrutiny; this area is highly susceptible to damage. (If damage is found, the tube can usually be saved, so don't throw it out.) Examine the entire tube for wrinkling, chafing, and thinning. Wrinkling and chafing often go together; they indicate improper seating of the tube to the tire. (See Figures 4-12 to 4-14.) Thinning is the direct result of overheating and frequently occurs at the tire bead, where heat due to braking and tire slippage is the greatest. Learning to recognize thinning by feel takes practice. If you have any doubts, call in a mechanic.

By the way, if you suspect a leaky inner tube, check it the way you would a bicycle tire tube: Inflate it and put it under water. Should repairs be necessary, you can make them in the same way, using the same materials, as you would for a bicycle tube (Figure 4-15). The FAA recommends that you use vulcanized patches, however, whenever possible.

With new inner tubes costing fully half as much as new tires, the question often arises of whether an old tube can be used with a new tire. The answer, of course, is yes—providing the old tube is still airworthy. Next time you go shopping for a new tire, don't automatically assume that you must also buy a new inner

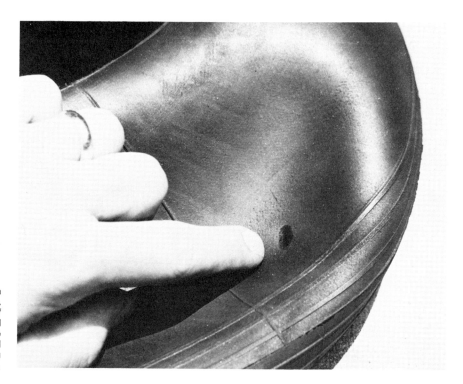

FIGURE 4-12 Before reusing an old inner tube with a new tire, inspect the tube for signs of damage. Chafing has produced a small, thin weak spot in the tube shown here. Such a spot could easily be overlooked during a hasty inspection.

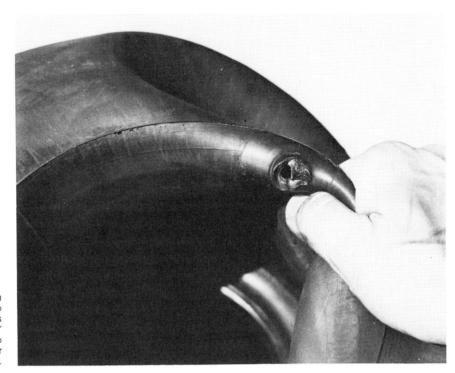

FIGURE 4-13   The valve area of a tube is especially prone to damage. This is what happens when a tire and tube "creep" relative to the wheel, owing to chronic tire underinflation and/or overbraking.

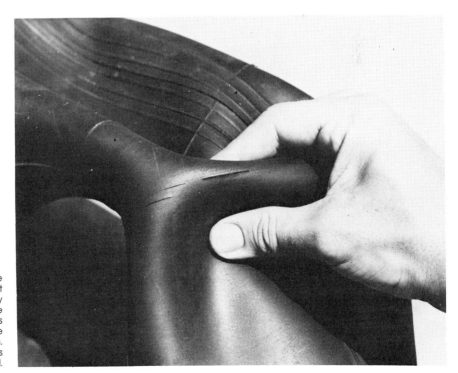

FIGURE 4-14   Radial surface cracks can be very hard to detect without "feeling" for them carefully around the entire circumference of the inner tube. These cracks were, in fact, invisible until the tube was squeezed as shown. Replacement of the tube is indicated.

FIGURE 4-15 Small punctures in aircraft inner tubes can be repaired using the same materials and techniques that would be used to patch any other inner tube. When the area of puncture damage is large, however, the tube should be scrapped. The puncture shown here is large enough (3 cm across) and close enough to several rib-like protrusions at the tube's perimeter to make patching inadvisable.

tube (particularly if your "old" tire was relatively new when it died). Your old tube may well be reusable, in which case you can save yourself $15 or $20 over what a shop might have charged you for a new (and unnecessary) one.

With regard to buying new tires, remember that you don't have to buy from an FBO. All the well-known pilot supply houses stock the major brands of tires, and in fact there is a good deal of price competition among the mail-order firms in this area (something that's not true of FBOs). Some mail-order companies sell tires separate from tubes; others don't. None of them wants your old tire in trade.

Another shopping tip: If you are intent on buying new tires, be sure you get what you are paying for. Some FBOs will sell you retreads unless you specifically ask for new, fresh-from-the-factory tires. If a tire has been retreaded, it will be marked with a letter R followed by a number (1, 2, 5, etc.) signifying the number of times the carcass has been retreaded. (The FAA sets no limit on the number of times a tire may be retreaded.)

The main thing you should know about retreads is that many airframe manufacturers specifically recommend against their use on retractable-gear models, the reason being that retreads (more than new tires) tend to swell after being put into service, thereby creating gear-well clearance problems. (The recaps may pass a gear-retraction-cycle test performed immediately after installation, but they may *fail* the same test a week—or a month—later.) Check your airframe manufacturer's tire recommendations carefully before deciding to buy retreads.

The procedure for mounting a new tire-tube combination is exactly the same as for remounting an old tire and tube (or a new tire and an old tube):

1. Wipe all debris from the inside of the tire and the surface of each wheel half.

2. Locate the balance mark (a yellow or white stripe) on the tube, if there is one. (This indicates the tube's *heavy* point.)

3. Dust the tube with tire talc or soapstone.

4. Tuck the tube into the tire, aligning the balance mark on the tube with the red dot on the tire sidewall. (This dot marks the tire's *light* side.) If there is no balance mark on the inner tube, align the valve stem with the red dot.

5. With the valve core in place, introduce just enough air into the inner tube to give it shape.

6. Install the tube and tire on the outboard wheel half. Use care when inserting the valve stem through the opening in the wheel. Do not use any kind of lubricant on the tire bead.

7. Mate the inboard wheel half to the assembly, being careful not to pinch the tube between the wheel halves. If there is a letter L on each wheel half (to indicate the part's *light* side), arrange the rims so that the Ls will be 180° apart. Most small wheels do not have the Ls.

8. Align all bolt holes, and insert the tie bolts so that their heads rest against the *inboard* wheel half.

9. Tighten the tie-bolt nuts alternately in crisscross fashion until the manufacturer's recommended torque is reached. (This torque is usually stated on the wheel.) Measure the friction drag torque of the locknuts, and *add this amount of torque to the manufacturer's recommended torque.* Don't forget to use washers.

10. Inflate the tire to normal operating pressure, and then *deflate it completely.* Afterward, reinflate the tire to its proper pressure and screw the valve cap on finger tight. (The inflation, deflation, reinflation procedure helps ensure proper mating of the tube to the inside of the tire.)

Relatively few light aircraft employ tubeless tires these days; many of those that used to have since been converted to inner-tube use. If your plane uses tubeless tires, you'll follow much the same procedure for mounting new tires as that given above. The principal difference is that you will be installing a large O ring in a groove where the two wheel halves meet. Manufacturers' recommendations regarding the lubrication of this O ring (and the tubeless tire bead area) vary; be sure to follow the instructions given in your aircraft service manual.

Remounting the Wheel   Reinstalling the wheel-tire assembly on the aircraft is usually a simple matter of going through the disassembly steps in reverse order (see above). The only problem you may encounter is deciding how tight to tighten the axle nut.

Some manufacturers actually call out a specific torque value for the axle nut; obviously, you'll want to check your service manual to see if this is the case for your plane. Most manufacturers, however, merely say that the axle nut should be tightened enough to prevent any side play of the wheel yet allow free rotation. The standard practice is to tighten the nut just enough to produce a noticeable drag (with no side play), and then back off half a turn. (When in doubt, call for a mechanic.)

Of course, when you've finished adjusting the axle nut, you'll want to install a *new* cotter pin of the correct size to keep the nut in place. (Axle nuts are never on very tight, which means they will come off if not safetied properly.) Consult your aircraft parts catalog for the actual cotter pin number, if you're not sure.

TIRE AIR LEAKAGE   After mounting a new tire on your aircraft, you may well find that the tire loses quite noticeable amounts of air in its first week of service. In most cases, this is normal. At the time of mounting, air usually gets trapped between the tire and tube; a day or two later, as this trapped air seeps out of the tire, the tire may become severely underinflated. Subsequent reinflation and observation will generally show the tire to be sound.

It is also important to realize that whenever a new tire is put in service, the nylon cords will tend to stretch somewhat over the first 12 to 24 hr. This results in a significant increase in tire volume, and hence a pressure drop.

For the above reasons, it is important to monitor the pressure of a new tire closely during the first few days (the first week, really) that it is in service. No particular significance should be attributed to moderate pressure losses during this initial break-in period.

For old tires, or tires that have been in service more than a week, a pressure loss of 5 percent (plus or minus 1 percent for every 5°F temperature change) in any 24-hr period can be considered normal. A temperature-corrected pressure loss of more than 5 percent in 24 hours suggests the need for further investigation to determine the cause of the leak.

With tubeless tires, pinpointing the source of a leak can be an exhausting (and sometimes fruitless) task; the best one can do is apply a soapy water solution to the valve, bead, and sidewall portions of the tire in hopes of detecting the source of the leakage. Tube-type tires, on the other hand, leak less frequently than tubeless tires and are easier to fix when they do leak. For the most part, tube-type tire leakage comes about either as the result of damage to the inner-tube carcass, or contamination of the valve stem with dirt. To check for leakage through the valve stem, simply apply a small amount of soapy water to the end of the stem and watch for bubbles. If bubbles appear, buy a new 98¢ valve core and install it yourself. (*Note:* When letting air out of the tire to replace the valve core, do not allow the weight of the plane to rest on the flat tire; jack the wheel up instead.) Inner-tube damage, as mentioned earlier, may be diagnosed by the familiar submerge-it-in-water method and repaired with a patch kit obtained from any bicycle shop.

If it should become necessary to repair tears around the base of a conventional all-rubber-type valve stem, take it to a gas station. According to the FAA's AC No. 65.15A: *Airframe and Powerplant Mechanics Airframe Handbook*, page 396, "Replacement of this valve can be made by most any gasoline service station or garage, providing they have the proper valve for replacement."

SERVICING WHEEL BEARINGS

Not everyone agrees on how often wheel bearings should be serviced. Some manufacturers (Beech, Piper) say that wheel bearings should be inspected and greased every 100 hr; others (Cessna, Mooney) recommend longer intervals. Cleveland Wheels and Brakes, one of the largest wheel manufacturers, recommends a maximum servicing interval of 500 *wheel miles*. In addition to (or despite) all this, the FAA requires that wheel bearings be inspected once a year by an Inspection Authorization-rated A&P mechanic, regardless of whether they need inspecting or not. (See FAR Part 43, Appendix D.)

Whether you should service your wheel bearings oftener than they are already being serviced is, of course, up to you. Most mechanics feel that it is a good idea to inspect and relubricate wheel bearings any time a wheel is removed from the airplane (such as during tire replacement). In any case, more frequent inspections certainly can't hurt—and they might turn up hidden problems.

As you can see from Figure 4-10, aircraft wheel bearings are of the tapered roller bearing type and consist of a cone (made up of a cage and rollers) inserted into a cup, or outer race. The cup is pressed into place and does not come out for servicing. Holding the bearing cone in place are various rings, seals, and retainers, all of which do come out.

To get at the bearing cones (there is one on each side of every wheel), it is necessary first to remove a snap ring or (in some cases) a retainer plate. Then you can lift out rings, felt seals, and the bearing cone itself.

Once removed, all the bearing components should be rinsed in a dirt-free (unused) petroleum-based solvent (Figure 4-16). Before you rinse the bearing cone, take a look at the grease on it; if you can see or feel bits of metal or other large impurities, you may be in need of new bearings. Consider yourself forewarned.

As you rinse the bearing cones in solvent, examine them closely for signs of damage. Look for evidence of pitting, uneven wear, discoloration, and brinelling, in addition to obvious, serious damage (e.g., missing rollers). Brinelling, if present, will be more clearly seen in the outer races, where numerous tiny indentations (caused by hammering of the rollers against the cup) will be evident. Brinelling occurs when bearings are exposed to severe impact loads or vibration under static conditions—that is, when the plane is not moving. The condition is most often seen in airplanes that are not flown often and that, as a result, sit on the ramp for weeks at a time, rocking back and forth on their wheels in the wind.

Discoloration can be of two types. One type is brought about by the action of

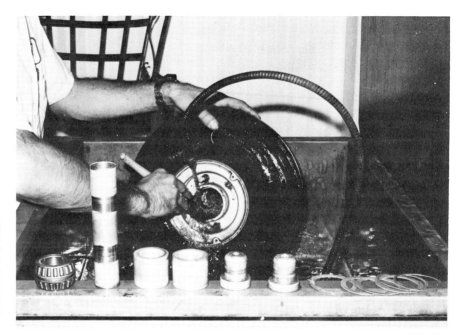

FIGURE 4-16 Wheel bearings, grease seals, etc., should be washed in Varsol (or the equivalent) prior to lubrication and reassembly. It doesn't hurt to wash the wheel halves, too, if a wash bin is available. The bearing cones, axle tube, spacer blocks, and retainer rings shown here are from the nosewheel of a 1968 Cessna 182.

moisture and involves simple staining; generally, the color is light brown to black. As a rule, stain-discolored bearings may be continued in service, providing there has been no corrosion.

The other main type of discoloration affecting bearings is *heat discoloration*. Overloading and/or the use of an inferior grade of grease will cause this kind of discoloration, which takes the form of a bluish tinge that will not go away with light polishing. Its presence generally means that the steel of which the bearing is made has lost its temper and thus cannot be reused—not on an airplane, anyway.

New cones and cups cost about $15 apiece and can be ordered through any of the large pilot supply firms. Don't hesitate to buy new ones if your present bearings look questionable.

If your bearings are in good shape, blow-dry them after removing them from the solvent bath. To do this, hold an air nozzle about 10 in. away from the cage, and apply air in a direction *parallel* to the rollers. *Never blow air across the rollers*, spinning them at high speed, as you could easily damage them (or set up the kind of stresses that could culminate in a fatigue failure).

Greasing a clean-and-ready-to-go bearing prior to reinstalling it is a simple job—messy, but simple. The first thing to do is round up some high-temperature bearing grease (MIL-G-81322 or equivalent); some familiar names to look for are Mobilgrease 77, Texaco Marfak All Purpose Grease, and Shell Alvania EP Grease 2. Place a glob of grease the size of a small peach in the heel of one hand. Then, holding the bearing cone small-end-up in the other hand, press the grease up into the bearing's rollers. Continue greasing around the circumference of the cage until every roller is packed with grease. (See Figure 4-17.)

Now go over to the wheel, and wipe the bearing cups clean. Then apply a thin film of grease to the races. Do not, under any circumstances, fill the bearing cups with copious quantities of grease, as the grease will be pushed (by centrifugal force) between the wheel halves to the inner tube, where it will wreak havoc. (Grease is a natural enemy of rubber.)

Next, clean any large globs of excess grease from the cones, and insert them carefully into the outer races. (Maintain sanitary conditions at all times.) If the felt seals are hard or gritty, they should be replaced. If not, they may be reused. Apply a light coating of SAE 10 oil to the felt seals, and then reinstall them in the wheel. Finally, reinstall all retainers, snap rings, etc., in the proper order, and return the wheel to the axle.

PREVENTIVE MEDICINE FOR WHEELS AND TIRES

The best way to reduce wheel and tire maintenance costs and associated downtime is to operate the equipment in such a way that maintenance (except for routine inspections) is never needed. There are several things pilots can do in this regard.

Crack formation and bolt-hole elongation are the leading causes of early wheel death; both conditions are fairly easily avoided. As mentioned earlier, bolt-hole elongation occurs when the wheel tie bolts are not torqued properly and the wheel halves begin to move with respect to each other. This can be prevented by periodic rechecking of the bolts.

Cracks come about as the result of minor damage during handling of the

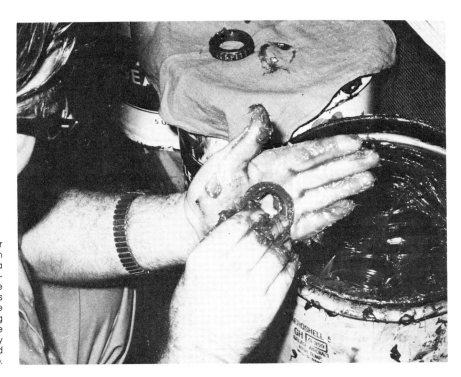

Figure 4-17 The proper technique for lubricating a clean wheel bearing is to place a generous amount of high-temperature aircraft grease in the palm of one hand and then press the bearing's rollers lengthwise down into the grease, working around the entire circumference of the cone. In the end, every roller should be solidly packed with grease.

wheels (e.g., scratching a rim with a metal instrument while dismounting a tire) and/or repeated hard landing impacts. The message here is clear: Smooth out your landings. Keep tires inflated properly. And be careful never to nick or dent rims during servicing operations. Because rim cracks usually cannot be fixed in any permanently safe fashion, cracked wheels are almost always scrapped. Don't count on having a cracked rim repaired.

Getting maximum service life out of a set of tires is usually a matter of keeping them inflated properly, protecting them from corrosive agents (oil, hydraulic fluid, etc.), and operating them so as to keep internal temperatures down. Contrary to what many people think, the toughest demand on aircraft tires is not posed by the impact of landing, but by the rapid heat buildup that occurs during protracted ground operations—a fact borne out by Goodyear's finding that more blowouts occur on takeoff than on landing. To reduce heat buildup, it is necessary to minimize sidewall flexing (by keeping tires inflated properly and avoiding swerving turns), keep taxi speeds slow, and cut down on the needless use of brakes. Remember that dragging brakes, and excessive use of brakes in general, cause the liberation of enormous amounts of heat into tires, wheels, and wheel components (nuts, bolts, bearings, grease, etc.), thereby shortening the lives of all these parts.

Maximizing tread life is mostly a matter of operating the plane on the ground in a manner consistent with common sense: Slow down before making turns, keep sudden braking to a minimum, avoid pivoting on one wheel while turning, and so on.

Needless to say, tread life can also be increased by keeping touchdown speeds low; so if you're in the habit of carrying an extra 5 knots on final approach for no reason, slow down. Also, if your engine idle speed is set too high, have it adjusted downward. This will make your landing rollout shorter and help keep tire wear to a minimum. It'll pay dividends in terms of longer brake life, too.

If you aren't already doing so, keep all valve stems capped tightly when not in use to prevent dirt, ice, etc., from hanging up inside the core (which will cause chronic air leakage). This applies equally to tube-type and tubeless tires. Valve stem contamination accounts for a significant portion of all air-loss problems.

And, finally, remember to give your tires a thorough preflight inspection each and every time you fly. Often, problems detected in the course of a walkaround inspection are still minor enough to be corrected. If you wait for a mechanic to spot the defect, the damage may be expensive to repair—or irreparable.

Air-oil, or oleopneumatic, shock struts ("oleo struts" for short) are now a very common sight at airports across the country. Except for a relative handful of Grummans, Beeches, and Mooneys, virtually all modern tricycle-gear aircraft have at least one oleo strut.

Unfortunately, flat oleo struts—and struts leaking fluid—are also a common sight at airports across the country. For whatever reasons, pilots (as a group) are not very good at keeping their shock struts in A-1 condition.

There's no reason why this should be so. Oleo strut maintenance is neither difficult nor time-consuming; nor is it particularly messy (unless, of course, you're planning on rebuilding a strut completely). In fact, once you've tried servicing your own struts and seen for yourself how easy it is, you'll wonder why you ever waited so long to get involved. You may also wonder why the people who fly and sell non-oleo-equipped aircraft make such a big deal of oleo maintenance requirements, when those requirements are so few and so easily met.

HOW OLEO STRUTS WORK

Despite what you might think, all oleos operate pretty much the same way, whether you're dealing with a Cessna 152's nose strut or the mains on a jumbo jet—so if you understand how *one* oleo works, you pretty much understand them all.

As you can see from Figure 5-1, an oleo strut consists of a strut *housing* or *cylinder* capped off at the top by a combination filler plug and valve stem, a *piston tube* that slides in and out of the housing, and various retainer rings and seals. And that's about all.

The strut housing is effectively divided into two compartments by an *orifice assembly*. In normal operation, the lowermost compartment is filled with MIL-H-5606 hydraulic fluid, while the upper compartment is filled with high-pressure air. Thus, whenever the piston is subjected to forces that tend to push it up into the housing (as during landing), the piston's movement is slowed by (1) the slow passage of hydraulic fluid through the small opening in the orifice assembly, and (2) the further compression of the air trapped in the top compartment. As a result, the strut acts as a shock absorber.

Obviously, for an oleo (any oleo) to function properly, it must contain sufficient amounts of both air and oil. If there is a lack of either, the strut may no longer be able to absorb landing shocks—or even the shock caused by a small bump in

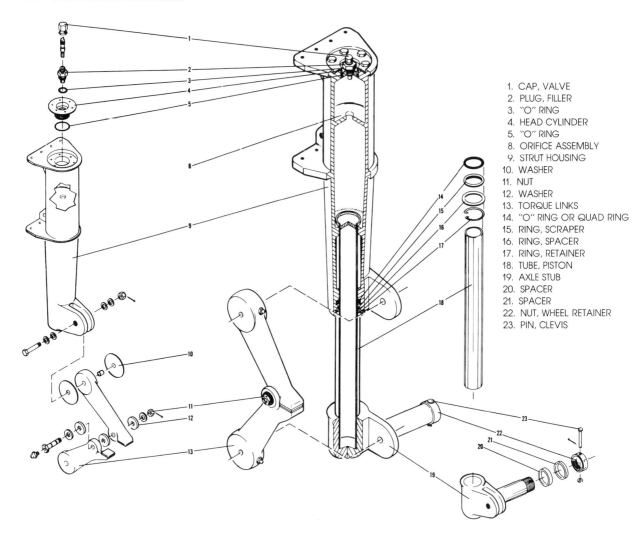

1. CAP, VALVE
2. PLUG, FILLER
3. "O" RING
4. HEAD CYLINDER
5. "O" RING
8. ORIFICE ASSEMBLY
9. STRUT HOUSING
10. WASHER
11. NUT
12. WASHER
13. TORQUE LINKS
14. "O" RING OR QUAD RING
15. RING, SCRAPER
16. RING, SPACER
17. RING, RETAINER
18. TUBE, PISTON
19. AXLE STUB
20. SPACER
21. SPACER
22. NUT, WHEEL RETAINER
23. PIN, CLEVIS

FIGURE 5-1 A typical main-gear oleo-strut assembly (minus brake and wheel). (*Piper Aircraft Corporation drawing.*)

the taxiway—and harmful stresses may be passed directly to parts of the airframe (e.g., the wing spar or engine mount). Needless to say, a low-on-air or low-on-oil strut demands immediate attention if potentially serious damage is to be avoided.

SOURCES OF TROUBLE

Lack of air in an oleo strut can come about in a number of ways. Often, it is the result of slow (but sure) leakage past the air valve or filler plug due to (1) improper tightening of the filler plug, (2) a worn plug seal, and/or (3) a contaminated valve core. The latter condition can be prevented by keeping the strut valve capped between servicings. (If there is not a little yellow MS20813-1B high-pressure valve cap on each one of your plane's oleo struts, plan on buying valve caps soon. Your local FBO should be able to sell you as many caps as you need; otherwise try any of the mail-order aircraft parts suppliers.)

It should be noted that a small amount of air leakage is unavoidable with oleos, particularly in winter, when rubber seals contract and harden to such an extent that a "perfect" seal is impossible to achieve. (Ever notice how many oleo struts go flat in the fall, with the arrival of the first truly cold temperatures?) And, of course, the air pressure inside a strut will diminish slightly with the arrival of cold weather, in much the same way (and for the same reasons) that tire pressures fluctuate with changes in ambient temperature. If anything, the effect is more noticeable with oleo struts than with tires, since a relatively small change in strut pressure can produce a fairly large drop in strut height.

Loss of fluid from a strut comes about as a result of damage to the strut's rubber seals. Seal damage, in turn, is caused primarily by dirt, which either enters the strut via the filler plug at the top, or collects on the shiny portion of the piston and gets forced into the strut as the piston travels back and forth. There are two very simple and effective ways to keep dirt from wearing away a strut's seals: One is to periodically clean the filler-plug area at the top of the strut with a Varsol-soaked rag. (This area tends to get grimy in a hurry, since fluid is often slopped around it during servicing. All it takes is for a little bit of accumulated dirt to fall into the filler hole during routine maintenance, and you've bought yourself a strut overhaul.) The other thing you can do is wipe away the layer of pumicelike grit particles that collects on oleo pistons between flights. Allowing this grit to build up on a strut is the surest way I know to convert a perfectly sound oleo into a leaker (Figure 5-2). Carry a rag with you on every preflight inspection, and wipe off your

FIGURE 5-2 When the piston portion of an oleo strut is allowed to accumulate dirt—and that dirt is not wiped away prior to flight—rapid wear of the strut's lower seal results, leading eventually to fluid leakage, loss of damping action, and (at the very least) a complete strut overhaul.

oleos whether they look like they need it or not. You'll be surprised how much dirt an oleo can collect in a day or two—and how much longer seals last when this dirt is regularly removed.

Nose-strut oleos, as it turns out, are somewhat more prone to fluid-leakage problems than main-gear oleos (on single-engine airplanes, at least), owing to their close proximity to the spinning propeller. Prop blast sends sand, dirt, small rocks, etc., smashing against the exposed portion of the nose-gear piston, giving it a craterlike surface which rapidly wears away the soft rubber of the lower strut O ring. To get around this problem, some mechanics recommend keeping nose-gear oleos inflated to no more than the *minimum height allowed by the manufacturer.* The idea is that if you have a 15-in.-long nose-strut piston that travels, say, 10 in. on landing, and if only the bottom 3 or 4 in. are scarred or pitted, much less damage will be done to the strut's lower O ring than would be done if the piston were uniformly scarred over half its length (as a result of the strut being kept overinflated).

Of course, in no case will you want to keep your nose strut (or any other oleo) inflated to less than the minimum height recommended by the manufacturer. Check your airplane owner's manual and/or the service manual before adjusting strut heights up or down.

DIAGNOSING STRUT PROBLEMS

So much for preventive measures. The question now is, what do you do when, during a preflight inspection, you find that one of your plane's oleos is lower than the manual says it should be?

Obviously, one thing you definitely don't do in this situation is go ahead and fly anyway. If you do, you stand a good chance of turning a relatively minor strut problem into a potentially major rearrangement of the firewall or wing.

What you should do, first of all, is determine whether the strut is low on oil or air: Just rock the plane up and down on the gear a few times, and observe the strut's reaction. If the oleo travels in short strokes and stops moving after just one or two cycles, the strut needs *air.* If, on the other hand, the piston travels in long strokes and the plane continues to bob up and down after the rocking force is discontinued, the strut needs *oil.*

Of course, if fluid leakage is clearly evident to begin with, you'll already know that the strut needs fluid. Chances are, it needs a new O ring too.

But let's say you're not sure what the strut needs, even after performing the rocking test. In this situation, the standard practice is to add air to the strut (enough air to bring it back up to its normal height), then rock the plane as above and note the strut's reaction. If the strut acts "spongy" (that is, if it travels in long strokes and exhibits poor damping), you'll know that what it needed was fluid, not air. Which means you'll have to start from scratch and service the oleo with both oil and air (in that order) in accordance with the manufacturer's servicing instructions.

FIGURE 5-3 All oleo struts leave the factory with a decal or placard giving abbreviated servicing instructions. Find and follow the instructions on this decal and you won't go far wrong. (If the decal is gone from your struts, consult your service manual for information on how to fill the struts with air and oil.)

HOW TO SERVICE A STRUT

Most airframe manufacturers recommend that oleos be serviced (with oil and air) once every 100 hr, or any time strut extension falls below minimum acceptable limits. Happily, this is one preventive maintenance procedure that you won't (strictly speaking) need a service manual to carry out; virtually every oleo strut carries a decal or placard on it somewhere giving complete servicing instructions (Figure 5-3).

Of course, before you can proceed with servicing, you'll need to gain access to the top of the strut, which in itself can be quite a project. If you're dealing with a nose strut, you'll generally have to remove the cowling (on a fixed-gear single) or grope around in the wheel well (on a retractable). In the case of a main-gear leg, access to the oleo filler plug is usually available either via an inspection plate atop the wing (this is true of fixed-gear Pipers, for example) or through the wheel well (if one exists).

Once the problem of access has been solved, the next order of business is to remove the load from the strut you intend to work on, either by weighing down the plane's tail or (if you're working on a main gear) putting the plane on tripod jacks. (Refer to Chapter 4, page 68, for more information on the subject of jacking.) Whatever you do, don't try to service the strut with the weight of the plane still on the gear. If you begin to let air out of the strut while it is compressed under the weight of the plane, a geyser of red fluid will very likely spew forth from the top of the strut, possibly causing injury to person or plane (and certainly creating a mess).

Now then. With the strut fully extended and the wheel off the ground, unscrew the little yellow cap on the valve stem at the top of the strut. (All you're doing here is exposing the valve core; no air will come out yet.) Then, using a penknife, a valve repair tool, or some other appropriate device, depress the valve core and begin letting the air out of the strut. *Be extremely careful not to let the escaping high-pressure air come near your face or arm. Serious injury could result.*

Once all the air is gone from the strut, you may proceed to add oil (actually, MIL-H-5606 hydraulic fluid) to it. One way of doing this is to (1) remove the valve core from the filler-plug assembly, using a core key, (2) attach one end of a clean piece of Tygon tubing (¼ in. inside diameter) to the valve stem, (3) submerge the other end of the tube in a clean container of fresh MIL-H-5606 fluid, and (4) begin exercising the strut. As you compress and extend the piston, fluid will be drawn from the container, and excess air purged from the top of the strut. At first, of course, some air will be drawn into the strut—but much less air than fluid. After a couple of cycles, the small amount of air trapped in the strut will be purged completely, and bubbles will cease to appear in the fluid container. (If the strut fails to draw fluid by this method, it needs new seals.)

When you're done, remove the filler plug from the top of the strut, and look to see if the strut contains the proper amount of fluid. (With the oleo fully compressed, the fluid level should come right up to the filler opening.) If necessary, add more fluid. Finally, reinstall the filler plug and valve core, torquing the plug according to the instructions given on the strut or in the aircraft service manual.

You'll probably notice that the valve core in your oleo filler plug looks very much like the valve core from a tire. The two types of valve cores are not the same, however, and should not be intermixed. The AN809-1 high-pressure valve core used in oleo struts is of a special "closed cup" design that can withstand extremely high pressures and temperatures—not to mention exposure to hydraulic fluid. Unlike the natural rubber in tire valve cores, the neoprene used in AN809-1 high-pressure valve cores is resistant to attack by MIL-H-5606 hydraulic fluid.

The foregoing method is only one of two widely practiced methods for servicing oleo struts with fluid. The other major method involves releasing all air from the strut, removing the entire filler-plug assembly (containing the valve core) from the strut, compressing the strut completely, and pouring fluid into the filler opening until the fluid level reaches the hole. (Chances are, you won't have room enough to stick a funnel in the filler hole and pour hydraulic fluid into it from a bottle or can. No problem: Just hook a piece of clear plastic tubing over the end of a $1.98 oil squirt can filled with MIL-H-5606, and finger-pump the strut full of fluid.) When you've serviced a strut by this method, it's generally a good idea to reinstall the filler plug finger tight and exercise the strut several times to purge trapped air from the top of the housing. Then compress the oleo, remove the plug, and (if necessary) add more fluid. Afterward, screw the filler plug back in, and torque it down to aircraft-manual specs.

Regardless of which of these two methods you use to service your oleos with fluid, be exceedingly careful not to introduce any dirt or other contaminants into the uncapped strut, since dirt is a strut's worst enemy. Use only *new* MIL-H-5606 hydraulic fluid, and maintain sanitary working conditions at all times.

After you've added fluid to the strut, you will need to add compressed air (via the valve stem atop the strut). Just how much air you'll add depends, of course, on the recommendations given in your plane's service manual or on the strut decal. It will vary from plane to plane.

Generally, main-gear struts must be inflated to give so many inches of piston extension with a normal static load (the empty weight of the plane, plus full fuel and oil) applied to all the struts. The catch here is that while the plane must be sitting on the ground when you check strut extension, you can't usually inflate the strut while the weight of the plane is on it. (The 100 to 200 psi of air pressure you'll get from a shop air line or from your portable air tank simply won't be enough to inflate a loaded-down strut.)

With a main-gear oleo, then, you have two choices. Either you can jack the plane up, apply low-pressure (120-psi) air to the strut, let the plane down, check strut extension, jack the plane back up, add more air, let her back down, etc. Or, you can hook a device known as a *strut pump* to your FBO's air hose, couple the strut pump to your oleo, and (with the plane *not* on jacks) watch the strut extend. (The strut pump is nothing more than a very compact pneumatic force pump that boosts ordinary shop air from 100 or 200 psi all the way to 1500 psi, which is about what you'll need to inflate a fully loaded main-gear oleo. You can buy one through sources listed in *Trade-A-Plane* for around $80.)

Nose struts, fortunately, are somewhat easier to inflate than main-gear oleos. All you need to do is sandbag the plane's tail or have someone hold it down, apply low-pressure air to the strut (100 psi will usually do), and stop when the desired pressure is reached. Some aircraft manuals specify nose-strut inflation limits in terms of pounds of air pressure (which you can measure with a tire pressure gauge, the same as you would a tire); others specify a certain number of inches of piston exposure.

If you find, when you're done, that the strut is extending a bit too much, let some air out. But *go slow* (and again, protect your skin from the blast). You won't have to release much air to produce a fairly large reduction in strut height.

A word of caution: No matter how tempted you might be, do not attempt to inflate your strut with air from a high-pressure gas bottle. The pressure in such a bottle is usually so extreme (4000 psi), and the flow of gas so difficult to control, that you could well blow your strut apart. I have actually heard of a Cessna 210 sustaining serious tail damage as a result of too-rapid inflation of its nose strut with air from a high-pressure air bottle. Whatever you do, *don't use bottled gas to inflate a strut.*

One more thing: Before you put that little yellow cap back on the valve stem, dab some soap suds on the tip of the stem to check for air leakage. If bubbling occurs, you'll know the valve is leaking and needs a new valve core. Replacement AN809-1 high-pressure cores cost about a dollar apiece and can be bought wherever aircraft parts are sold.

Also check for leakage around the filler-plug hex. To do this, apply soap suds around the base of the plug, and watch for bubbling. Leakage past the filler plug is a common source of oleo troubles that occurs either because of improper torquing of the plug hex or damage to the little O ring that (in most cases) the plug rests on. You can correct either one of these problems yourself, if need be.

SEAL REPLACEMENT

Replacement of oleo strut seals is not generally considered preventive maintenance for the purposes of FAR Part 43; as a result, if you wish to replace a defective oleo lower seal on your plane, you will have to do so under the direct supervision of a licensed mechanic or repairman (who will later have to sign off your work in the plane's logs). As long as you can get a mechanic to oversee and sign off your work, however, there is no reason why you should feel hesitant about replacing a strut O ring yourself. It's not a difficult job, by any means. Messy, yes—but not difficult.

The actual procedures involved differ somewhat from one plane model to another, and often from main gear to nose gear on any given plane model, so only general guidelines can be given here. (For more specific instructions, obviously, you'll need to consult your own plane's service manual.) Basically, here's what you'll do:

First, jack the plane up if you're working on a main-gear leg, or raise the nose high off the ground. Slide a drip pan under the strut you intend to work on. Next, deflate the strut (see above), remove the filler plug (see above), insert a clean piece of tubing into the filler opening, and siphon as much fluid out of the strut as you can. (Do not reuse this fluid; plan on throwing it away.)

If you're working on a main-gear strut, disconnect the flexible brake line from the brake casting, and allow fluid to drain into the drip pan. Cover the end of the brake line and the connection point on the brake housing, to prevent dirt from contaminating the system.

At this point, getting to the strut's main O ring is a simple matter of taking apart one of the gear's torque link bolts and then sliding the piston tube out of its housing. (Be sure to note the arrangement of the various spacers, washers, etc., so you can put everything back together properly later.) On some types of aircraft, the piston tube will slide right out, creating a big mess if you haven't previously drained all the fluid out of the strut. On others, it will be necessary to remove a snap ring in the lower part of the strut housing before the piston will pull all the way out. Also, you should know that on some airplanes (Piper PA-28 aircraft, for instance), the O ring is located in an annular groove inside the strut cylinder, while on others (Cessna nose struts), the O ring is installed on the piston itself. In either case, you may need to remove spacers, scraper rings, etc., to gain access to the seal. (Wire the rings together, if you need to, to keep them properly oriented with respect to each other.) You may need a narrow, blunt-ended lifting tool to get the old O ring out.

Putting the new O ring in place will be easy, once you've seen how the old one comes out. Just be sure to follow your airframe manufacturer's recommendations to the letter when it comes to lubricating and handling the new O ring. (Some manufacturers recommend lubricating the new seal sparingly with Dow Corning DC-4 compound.) Also, remember not to drag the new O ring over any rough edges, or damage it in any way whatsoever, when reinstalling it. Replacement O rings cost only a dollar or two, but they should be handled as if they cost a hundred dollars.

To reassemble the strut, go through the disassembly steps in reverse order. Remember to *lubricate the piston thoroughly with MIL-H-5606 hydraulic fluid* before inserting it—slowly and carefully—into the strut housing.

When you're done, service the strut with fluid and air. Also, service and bleed the brake (if one was present when you started) using fresh hydraulic fluid. (See Chapter 6 for details.)

Finally, congratulate yourself; you now know everything that a pilot working under the preventive maintenance provisions of FAR Part 43 needs to know about oleo strut maintenance (and then some).

Few things are as frustrating as performing a 20-min preflight inspection, climbing into a plane's cockpit, fastening your seat belt, and finding—just as you begin to turn the ignition key—that one of the brake pedals goes flat to the floor when you press on it. Kaput. No brake.

Oddly enough, almost everybody who's logged more than 100 hr of flight time has had this happen at one time or another. Brake problems, it seems, are not at all uncommon. Exactly why the brakes on today's light planes are so temperamental is anyone's guess; suffice it to say, if automobile brakes failed as often as airplane brakes seem to, there would be nonstop Congressional hearings on the subject. (And the problem might even be solved.)

For now, though, in the absence of Congressional inquiries, a pilot's best bet in coping with brake problems is simply to become well informed—informed not only in the area of *preventive* measures, designed to reduce the likelihood of brake malfunction, but in brake *troubleshooting* and *repair* as well. We'll touch on all three areas in this chapter.

HOW TO KNOW WHAT KIND OF BRAKES YOU HAVE

The majority of all light aircraft now flying in the United States (including most single-engine Pipers, Mooneys, and Cessnas) carry Cleveland brakes; a good many of these are single-disc, single-cylinder brakes of the type shown in Figures 6-1 and 6-3. Some aircraft (including many pre-1966 Cessnas and Beeches and quite a few light twins) carry Goodyear disc brakes (Figure 6-2). Others carry brakes made by Firestone, Gerdes, or Bodell, not to mention the "house brands" of Beech and Cessna.

If you're not sure what kind of brakes your plane has, consult your aircraft equipment list or service manual, or simply examine the brakes yourself. If your brakes are of the type that has a very prominent brake disc which stands well away from the wheel, chances are good you've got Clevelands or McCauleys. (McCauley brakes are functionally identical to Cleveland brakes and are found mainly on late-model Cessna singles. McCauley is Cessna's house brand.) If, on the other hand, your brake disc is nestled tightly in the side of the wheel and has a scalloped or serrated outer edge, you've probably got Goodyears.

It could be that your brakes don't fit either of the above descriptions. In that case, you probably have one of the minority-brand types of brakes mentioned earlier. You may even have drum brakes.

FIGURE 6-1 Typical Cleveland brake installation. In this picture, the main brake housing (containing the piston) sits at 9 o'clock on the brake disc, which in turn is rigidly bolted to the wheel. The two bolts on the left side of the housing extend just beyond the brake disc, terminating at the back plate (not visible). The first step in disassembling any Cleveland (or McCauley) brake is to remove these two through bolts from the housing. (Some installations have more than two through bolts.) Note the presence of a bleeder attachment at the *top* of the brake housing.

FIGURE 6-2 Typical Goodyear brake installation (dual cylinder). In contrast to the Cleveland-type brake (which has a floating caliper riding on a rigidly mounted disc), the Goodyear brake features a cylinder assembly that's bolted firmly to the gear, and a *floating disc* that's free to move back and forth inside the outboard wheel half. (Notice the interlocking tooth-and-slot design of the disc and wheel.) To reline a Goodyear brake, it is necessary to remove the wheel from the gear leg. As the wheel is removed, the disc stays with the plane.

One of the reasons Cleveland brakes are so popular is that they're relatively easy to work on. (Ask any mechanic what kind of brakes he'd prefer to work on if he could only be around one kind of brake the rest of his life, and he'll probably answer "Clevelands.") To replace a set of Cleveland brake linings, for instance, you don't have to jack up the plane and remove the wheel, as you do for a Goodyear installation. In fact, in many cases you can replace Cleveland linings without even removing the plane's wheel pants. This would not be possible with Goodyear brakes.

There's no getting around the fact that, for beginners, at least, Goodyear brakes are not as easily worked on as Cleveland brakes. Parts costs are generally higher, too, with Goodyear installations than with Cleveland systems, which means that mistakes tend to be costlier with the former than with the latter. For this reason, and because Cleveland installations outnumber Goodyear installations by a considerable margin, we'll limit our discussion of brake maintenance here mainly (though not totally) to just those techniques and procedures applicable to Cleveland brakes and the very similar McCauley brakes.

HOW YOUR BRAKES WORK

If you already understand how and why aircraft disc brakes work, you may skip this section and go on to the next. If not, take a minute now to study Figure 6-3, which shows an exploded view of a typical lightplane brake installation (Cleveland brakes). It's not important that you understand Figure 6-3 in minute detail. You should, however, take note of the following facts:

1. The entire brake assembly slides in and out of a *torque plate* on a pair of smooth *anchor bolts*. The torque plate is rigidly attached to the main gear and remains stationary at all times.
2. The *brake disc* (not shown in Figure 6-3, but see instead Figure 4-10) is bolted rigidly to the inboard wheel half and rides between a set of *brake linings*. (Goodyear discs, by contrast, fit somewhat loosely in the side of the wheel; they're not bolted down.)
3. The brake linings—small, curved, ¼-in.-thick slabs of organic or metallic material—are attached to steel "holders" known as the *pressure plate* and *back plate*. (The phenolic, or organic, type of linings used in most Cleveland installations are riveted to these plates. The metallic linings used in many light-twin applications simply snap on and off their holders.)
4. The back plate rides against the wheel side of the brake disc and is held in

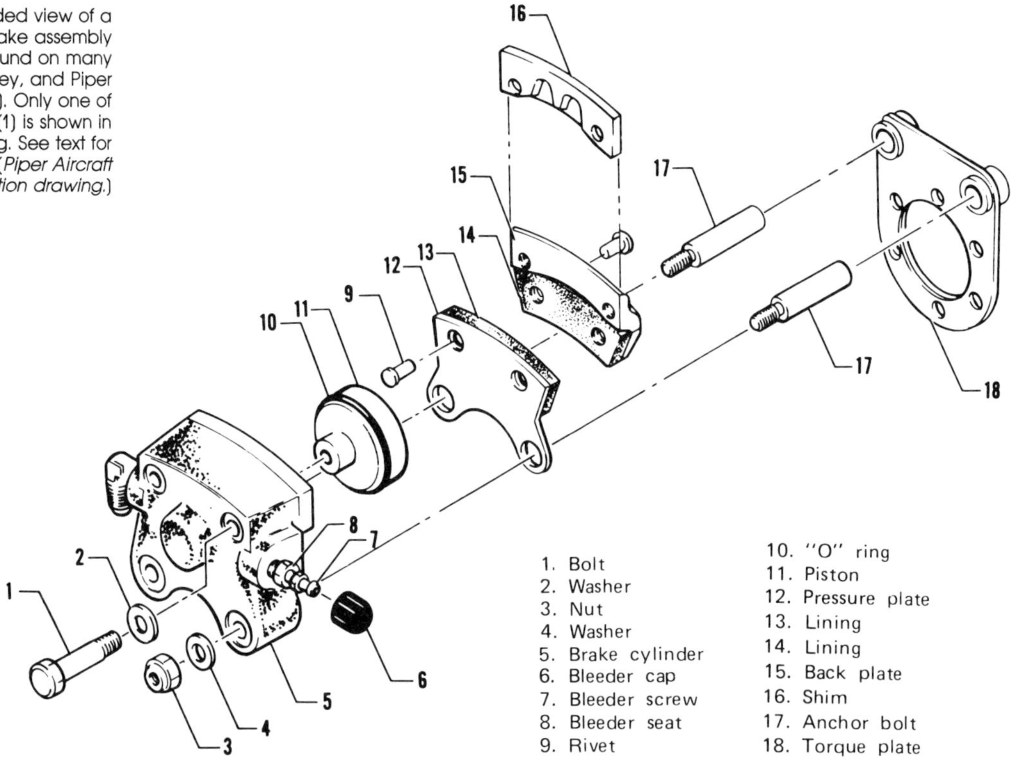
1
2
3
4
5
6
7
8
9
10
11
12
13
14
15
16
17
17
18
1. Bolt
2. Washer
3. Nut
4. Washer
5. Brake cylinder
6. Bleeder cap
7. Bleeder screw
8. Bleeder seat
9. Rivet
10. "O" ring
11. Piston
12. Pressure plate
13. Lining
14. Lining
15. Back plate
16. Shim
17. Anchor bolt
18. Torque plate

FIGURE 6-3 Exploded view of a typical Cleveland brake assembly (such as is found on many Cessna, Mooney, and Piper aircraft, for example). Only one of two through bolts (1) is shown in this drawing. See text for explanation. (*Piper Aircraft Corporation drawing.*)

position by a pair of *through bolts* that pass through the brake cylinder. These bolts terminate at the back plate; they do not connect with the torque plate.

5. The pressure plate rides against the airplane side of the brake disc and slides in and out on the anchor bolts. The pressure plate is, in effect, sandwiched between the brake disc and the brake *piston*; hence, the amount of pressure exerted by the pressure plate on the spinning brake disc is determined by the degree to which the piston moves.

6. A hydraulic line originating at the cockpit-located *master cylinder* (Figure 6-4) attaches to the brake housing and feeds brake fluid to the "back" side of the piston. It is by means of this line that pedal pressure in the cockpit is converted to piston movement at the brake and, subsequently, to braking action.

As you can see, the pressure plate and back plate act in caliperlike fashion to grab the spinning brake disc whenever pedal pressure is exerted by the pilot, in much the same way that the front brakes on a 10-speed bicycle grab the front wheel to slow the bike down. Notice that whenever the pressure plate is forced against the disc, the entire brake housing (including the back plate, which is connected to it by two through bolts) moves in the *opposite* direction (in accordance with Newton's third law), causing the back-plate lining to rub against the disc also. This "free-floating" feature of the Cleveland brake is what allows both sets of linings to wear at the same rate. Obviously, if the housing is prevented from moving freely in and out (as will happen, for instance, when the anchor bolts become caked with dirt), the free-floating feature is lost, the pressure-plate lining will wear faster than the back-plate lining, and problems will begin.

COMMON BRAKE DIFFICULTIES

The Cleveland-type aircraft disc brake, you'll have to admit, is remarkably simple. There are very few moving parts; thus, there is very little to break down. Understanding that "very little," however, can mean the difference between spending $200 a year on brake work and going 500 maintenance-free hours on one set of linings (which is actually possible to do). Let us therefore take a moment now to discuss some of the more common problems affecting lightplane brakes, and what—if anything—pilots can do to remedy them.

FIGURE 6-4   (*Opposite*) A Cessna-type brake master cylinder. On this type of master cylinder, the fluid reservoir is integral with the cylinder body; other types of master cylinders are fed by a reservoir located at the engine firewall (or elsewhere). The rudder pedal connects to the clevis (1) at the top of the cylinder. Each pedal has its own master cylinder. Notice the position of the Lock-O-Seal (15) relative to the piston (14); the purpose of the 0.040-in. clearance between the seal and the piston is to allow the return of excess fluid to the reservoir during periods of no braking, to compensate for heat expansion. Otherwise, heat expansion of the fluid downstream of the piston would cause the brake to drag. In some master cylinders, this seal is sometimes called the compensating-port seal. (*Cessna Aircraft Company drawing.*)

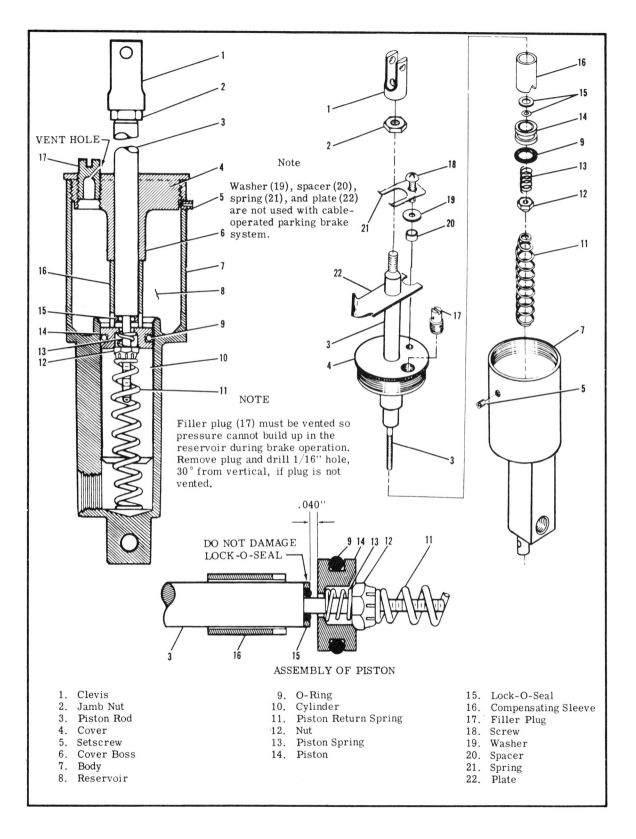

VENT HOLE

Note

Washer (19), spacer (20), spring (21), and plate (22) are not used with cable-operated parking brake system.

NOTE

Filler plug (17) must be vented so pressure cannot build up in the reservoir during brake operation. Remove plug and drill 1/16" hole, 30° from vertical, if plug is not vented.

.040"

DO NOT DAMAGE LOCK-O-SEAL

ASSEMBLY OF PISTON

1. Clevis	9. O-Ring	15. Lock-O-Seal
2. Jamb Nut	10. Cylinder	16. Compensating Sleeve
3. Piston Rod	11. Piston Return Spring	17. Filler Plug
4. Cover	12. Nut	18. Screw
5. Setscrew	13. Piston Spring	19. Washer
6. Cover Boss	14. Piston	20. Spacer
7. Body		21. Spring
8. Reservoir		22. Plate

Brake problems are usually identified and diagnosed on the basis of the amount of pedal travel and/or pedal pressure available (or not available) to the pilot in the cockpit. The problems tend to fall into four categories:

1. Pedal pressure is normal, but braking action is poor.

2. There is no pedal resistance whatsoever. The pedal goes completely flat to the floor when pressed.

3. Some pedal pressure exists, but the pressure (such as it is) gradually bleeds off under sustained pedal effort.

4. The pedal feels "spongy"; that is, it travels in long strokes and builds inadequate pressure, but the pressure does not bleed off.

Let us consider the first possibility: poor braking action with normal pedal pressure. The problem here obviously cannot be lack of brake fluid; the fact that you have normal pedal pressure and some degree of braking action means that you do have fluid. More than likely, one or more brake linings have completely worn out (a lining may even have departed the aircraft). With Cleveland or McCauley brakes, you can check this quite easily on a walkaround inspection, simply by examining the back plate and pressure plate where they meet the brake disc.

Alternatively, the brake housing may not be free floating; that is, the brake's anchor bolts may have frozen in the torque-plate bushings. To check this possibility, kneel down and grab the brake housing firmly with one hand, and try to twist it back and forth or up and down. The casting should move just a little—not much, but enough to let you know that the anchor pins aren't frozen in their bushings. If the housing seems to be frozen solidly in place, you'll need to clean the anchor bolts thoroughly with an alcohol-soaked rag. To get at the anchor pins, simply unscrew the two through bolts that hold the back plate to the disc (catch the back plate as it falls free). Then pull the brake housing straight out of the torque plate, being careful not to kink the brake line. After cleaning up the two anchor bolts, lubricate them with dry graphite or silicone spray (Figure 6-5) to prevent future sticking problems. (Whatever you do, *don't* use oil or grease to lubricate the pins. Oil will attract dirt and grit, thereby ensuring future sticking problems.)

If you have a hard pedal and poor braking action, but your linings look good and the caliper appears to be free floating, one or more brake linings may have been contaminated with oil (i.e., brake fluid) or grease. Check to see if the disc is wet or oily. Also look to see if the piston is oozing brake fluid (in which case you can be fairly sure the piston O ring is shot). If you find brake fluid on the disc, plan on relining your brakes immediately, and degrease the disc. And, of course, plan to have any fluid leaks corrected.

Once in a while, the hard-pedal, weak-brake syndrome can be explained by a bad twist in the flexible brake line that connects to the brake at the wheel. Occasionally (but not often), a twist in this line can introduce a side load to the

FIGURE 6-5 It helps to apply silicone spray to the brake's anchor pins periodically, to keep them moving smoothly in and out of the torque-plate bushings. If the anchor pins are not kept lubricated (or if dirt is allowed to accumulate on them), the free-floating feature of the caliper will be lost, and uneven lining wear will result (among other things).

caliper, causing the anchor bolts to bind in the torque plate and the brake to work inefficiently. (This is not a problem with Goodyear brakes, in which the brake disc floats while the housing is bolted rigidly to the gear.)

So much for problems falling into the hard-pedal, brake-doesn't-work category. What if you climb into your plane, press on each brake pedal, and find that one of the pedals goes *completely flat*, without offering so much as token resistance? Most pilots, in this situation, automatically assume (in knee-jerk fashion) that the brake in question must be out of fluid. This is an entirely unnecessary assumption in many cases. Depending on how your brakes' master cylinders are designed, it may be possible for you to have a flat brake pedal even with the system completely full of fluid.

Before you disrupt your mechanic's digestion by telling him that your lifeless left brake "needs a shot of fluid," stop and determine whether there's fluid in the system already. Start by checking the hydraulic reservoir. (On Beech, Mooney, and Piper products, the hydraulic reservoir is generally at or near eye level on the firewall. On Cessnas, the brake reservoirs are integral with the master cylinders for each brake, as shown in Figure 6-4.) Also, look for a puddle on the ground directly below the brake housing, indicating a popped or worn-out piston O ring. Check for the presence of red fluid on the plane's belly (possibly indicating a ruptured brake line between the cockpit and the landing gear). And look for fluid in the cockpit (indicating a defective master cylinder).

If you can't find any fluid leaks anywhere (it's quite possible you won't) and the hydraulic reservoir looks full, it may be that a piece of foreign matter has lodged under the tiny seal in the master cylinder. This seal normally prevents fluid from flowing the wrong way during braking (i.e., from the brake side of the piston to the reservoir side). When dirt hangs up the seal (the Lock-O-Seal in Figure 6-4), brake fluid can slosh from the master cylinder back into the brake reservoir or reservoir return line when pedal pressure is applied, which is exactly what this seal is designed to prevent. As a result, the piston cannot build any pressure downstream of the master cylinder.

The only way to fix this problem is to have the master cylinder disassembled and carefully gone over by a mechanic. If you're lucky, you won't need any new parts; more than likely, though, you'll be socked with a master-cylinder overhaul. The thing to do is find a mechanic who'll let you watch as the master cylinder is opened up and inspected. That way, you'll be able to see for yourself whether a master-cylinder overhaul is necessary. If you can't attend the postmortem personally, ask your mechanic to present you with the worn-out parts that are replaced during the overhaul, so you'll know whether the overhaul was indeed needed.

Sometimes it is not the Lock-O-Seal (or *compensating port seal*, as it is sometimes called) that causes a lack of pedal pressure, but the main master-cylinder O ring instead. If this O ring wears out, the brake pedal offers a fair amount of resistance when pumped vigorously, but slowly goes to the floor when constant pedal pressure is applied. Figure on spending $20 to $40 to have this condition corrected. Replacement O rings are cheap (usually only a buck or so), but unfortunately you're going to have to pay an A&P for the labor involved in disassembling the master cylinder, putting in the new O ring, reassembling the cylinder, reinstalling it in the airplane, adding new brake fluid, and bleeding the system.

There's one more type of pedal-pressure-related problem you can have, and that's where a pedal builds pressure, but only after an alarming amount of travel (i.e., you have soft or spongy brakes). Here, the culprit is almost certainly air in the system, and the only cure is to bleed the brakes.

HOW TO BLEED YOUR BRAKES

There are two methods of brake bleeding in common use: the *gravity* method (Figure 6-6) and the *pressure* method (Figure 6-7). In terms of the number of tools necessary to do the job, the gravity method is simpler; however, it is generally considered to be less reliable than pressure bleeding (or "back bleeding"), since air bubbles do not flow in the same direction as gravity. In either case, you'll need at least a quart (possibly more) of fresh MIL-H-5606 hydraulic fluid, an adjustable-

FIGURE 6-6 (*Near right*) Bleeding a brake by the gravity method. (*Piper Aircraft Corporation drawing.*)

FIGURE 6-7 (*Far right*) Bleeding a brake by the pressure method. (*Piper Aircraft Corporation drawing.*)

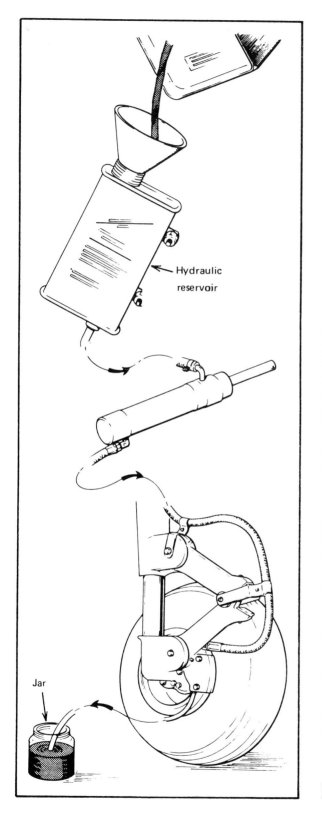

Hydraulic
reservoir

Jar

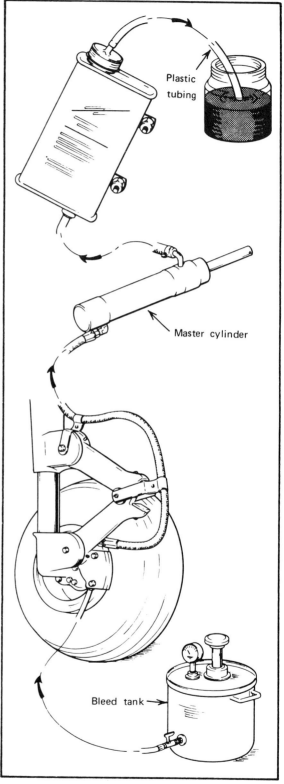

Plastic
tubing

Master cylinder

Bleed tank

end wrench with which to crack the bleeder fitting, some clear plastic tubing, and (very important) a volunteer to pump the brake pedal as you open and close the bleeder valve at the wheel. (You'll also need an A&P to sign off your work when you're done; brake bleeding, unfortunately, is not considered preventive mainte- nance by the FAA.)

To bleed a brake by the gravity method, first ensure that the hydraulic reservoir is completely full and that the parking brake is off. Then attach a clean, short piece of clear plastic tubing to the bleeder attachment on the brake at the wheel. (If there is a rubber cap on the bleeder fitting, remove it.) Submerge the free end of the tube in a clean container partially filled with MIL-H-5606 hydraulic fluid.

Next, have someone in the cockpit begin pumping the brake pedal as you open the bleeder fitting one-half turn or until fluid passes freely. Have the person in the cockpit continue pumping, approximately 30 times or until bubbles no longer appear in the clear plastic bleeder line. Meanwhile, keep a close watch on the hydraulic reservoir, and *replenish it as necessary with fresh hydraulic fluid* to keep air from entering the system.

When air bubbles are no longer appearing in the clear tubing at the wheel, retighten the bleeder fitting one-half turn or as much as necessary to stop the flow of brake fluid. Do not overtighten it. Tell your assistant to discontinue pumping the brake. Recheck the hydraulic reservoir and, if need be, adjust the fluid level.

That's all there is to the gravity bleeding method.

In the pressure method, the brake is bled in the opposite direction, and air bubbles are expelled through the high point in the system (i.e., the hydraulic reservoir). To get the brake fluid to flow in the opposite direction, it is necessary to introduce new fluid under pressure to the bleeder fitting at the wheel. The standard means of accomplishing this is to attach a special $50 device known as a *bleed tank* or *pressure pot* to the bleeder fitting, usually by means of a special $12.50 adapter. (You've probably seen your mechanic use one of these devices to service your brakes in the past.)

Happily, there's no need for you to rush out and spend $62.50 just so you can bleed your brakes. As it turns out, a $2.98 oil squirt can equipped with a short piece of clear plastic tubing will do just as well for all but the mightiest of bleeding jobs. (See Figure 6-8.)

Rinse out the can, if necessary, to remove traces of old oil. Fill the oil can with fresh MIL-H-5606 hydraulic fluid, and slip one end of the clear plastic tubing over the spout. Then, after finger-pumping the tubing full of fluid to eliminate air bubbles, slip the free end of the hose over the bleed fitting on the brake housing. Crack the bleeder fitting one-half turn.

Next, attach a second piece of plastic tubing to the vent fitting atop the brake- fluid reservoir.(*Note:* On Cessnas and planes having Cessna-like master cylinders it will be necessary to remove the small filler plug at the top of the appropriate master cylinder, screw a threaded AN fitting into the hole, and slip the plastic tubing over the AN fitting.) Submerge the free end of the reservoir tube in a container of hydraulic fluid.

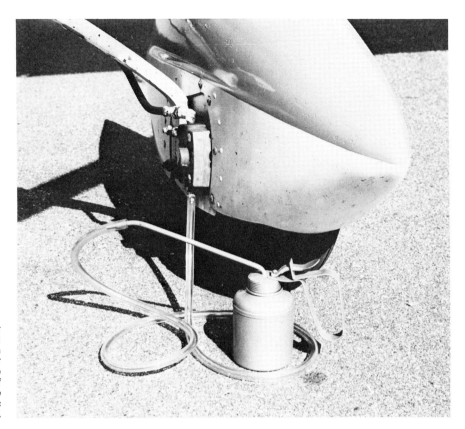

FIGURE 6-8 A brake bleeder can be fashioned from an oil squirt can and a piece of Tygon tubing, should you not have (or not want to buy) a $50 "pressure pot." Be sure to rinse all traces of old oil from the squirt can before filling it with MIL-H-5606 hydraulic fluid.

Now, while somebody in the cockpit *slowly* pumps the appropriate brake pedal, finger-pump fresh fluid into the system at the bleed fitting, using the oil squirt can. Hold the squirt can high so that you won't be fighting gravity. Watch for the emergence of bubbles in the fluid-filled container next to the hydraulic reservoir. When bubbles cease to appear, retighten the bleeder valve and determine whether the brake pedal is now hard. If it is not, reopen the bleeder valve and bleed some more. If the pedal is hard, you're finished—after you siphon off any excess fluid from your brake reservoir.

Thus far, we have only talked about bleeding the pilot's brakes, and then only one or the other of the two brakes (right and left). Obviously, if both brake pedals are soft, you'll need to bleed each brake separately, since the left and right brakes are independent. Also, if there is a soft brake pedal on the copilot's side, you will need to (1) bleed the pilot's side as described above; (2) tighten the bleeder valve at the wheel; (3) pump the copilot's brake pedal (which will have the effect of changing the position of the shuttle valve that connects the pilot's and copilot's brake system); and (4) reopen the bleeder valve and bleed the copilot's brake, following the same procedure that was used for the pilot's brake.

Regardless of which of the plane's brakes you're bleeding, and regardless of which bleeding method you use, remember to be careful at all times not to introduce any air into the system. Any time you open the bleeder valve at the main brake housing, you want to have a fluid-filled hose attached to it so that no air can be sucked into the brake. Likewise, do not at any time allow the hydraulic reservoir to go dry.

Even more important, be extremely careful not to let even the smallest trace of dirt enter the system at any point, since dirt will quickly cause all your rubber seals to self-destruct. (It has rightly been said that dirt causes more brake problems than any other single thing.) *Maintain sanitary working conditions whenever you bleed your brakes.*

One more thing: When you're done bleeding your brakes, throw away the fluid that you bled out of the system, along with any other contaminated fluid that may be left over. Brake fluid—like mouthwash, bath water, and antifreeze—is best used only once.

REPLACING WORN LININGS

Probably the most common brake problem encountered by pilots is worn linings, a condition that arises only once every 200 hr for some aircraft, but as often as every 20 hr for others. Why do linings wear out so much faster on some planes than on others? Usually, the rapid wear is due to a rusted, scored, or pitted brake disc. A badly rusted disc can leave a set of linings noticeably worn after a single hard brake application.

There are three ways of getting around the problem of rapid pad wear due to a rusty disc. One way is to switch over to Cleveland heavy-duty linings. (Cleveland offers a separate line of heavy-duty organic linings that, by virtue of their much higher brass content, last about twice as long as ordinary organic linings under rusty-disc service conditions.)

Another way of dealing with the problem is to dismount the offending disc (which, in effect, you do every time you disassemble your wheels to mount new tires) and sand the rust off, first using 200-grit and then 400-grit sandpaper. If you do this, though, you'll have to measure the disc's thickness with a micrometer before remounting it, to determine whether the disc is still within factory specs. Check your service manual for the appropriate dimensions and service limits.

A third possibility is simply to replace the rusted discs (at a cost of $40 to $70 each) and be done with it. Ideally, you should invest the extra few dollars and buy a set of chromed brake discs, which will greatly retard corrosion formation. Chromed discs are available for a number of Goodyear and Cleveland brake models; check with your nearest Goodyear or Cleveland dealer for details.

Now, then: how can you tell when your brake linings are worn to the point where they need replacing? The only sure way to tell is to visually examine your linings where they meet the brake disc. (You cannot judge lining wear from the cockpit. The brake pedals will "feel" normal right up until the time the rivets shear and your linings depart the aircraft.) With Clevelands, this is a simple matter of kneeling down next to the wheel and comparing the thickness of each lining to items (drill bits, Allen wrenches, etc.) of known thickness. According to the Cleveland factory, linings are ready to be replaced when they're worn to a thickness of 0.10 in. or less. In other words, if you can fit a ³⁄₃₂-in. drill bit between the disc and the pressure plate or the back plate, the linings need to be replaced—both linings. (Linings are always replaced in sets. It is never permissible to mix old and new linings on one brake.)

Lining replacement is a very simple task—so simple, in fact, that the entire operation takes about 20 min, once you get the hang of things. Essentially, all you need to do is remove the back plate and pressure plate from the brake in question, punch the rivets out of the plates, rivet new linings to the same plates, and reinstall the parts on the plane.

Start by unbolting the brake cylinder from the back plate. (*Caution:* Be sure the parking brake is off before you begin.) To do this, clip and remove any safety wire that may be present in the heads of the two brake-cylinder through bolts (some Cleveland installations do not have safety-wired bolts, but rely instead on special fiber-insert self-locking through bolts). Then take a ⁷⁄₁₆- or ⁹⁄₁₆-in. wrench to the bolts. *Do not unscrew the nuts securing the anchor pins to the housing.*

As you unscrew the last through bolt, be ready to catch the back plate as it falls free. A shim may also fall free, depending on the particular model of brake you have. Leave the through bolts in the brake housing for the moment.

Next, pull the brake housing straight out of the torque plate. It will slide right out, unless your anchor bolts are caked with dirt. Be careful not to kink or twist the hydraulic line that connects to the cylinder.

Lift the pressure plate off the two anchor bolts now, and set it aside; then stop and examine the brake cylinder. Are the anchor bolts clean and smooth? Is the piston relatively sanitary, with no evidence of fluid leakage? (If leakage is present, you may have a worn piston O ring, in which case you should call in a mechanic.) Clean the entire cylinder assembly with alcohol, if need be, paying particular attention to the sides of the piston. Dirt in this area, unless carefully cleaned away, is apt to be forced into the cylinder when the brake is reassembled. Do not use gasoline or dry-cleaning solvent to wash the cylinder, since these agents attack the rubber in brake O rings.

Now place the brake cylinder back on the wheel by slipping the anchor bolts back into their torque-plate bushings. Or, wire the brake assembly to a convenient point on the landing gear. The important thing is not to leave the cylinder dangling by the flexible brake line.

With the back plate and pressure plate thus removed from the brake, you can move on to the actual relining part of the operation. Begin by placing the pressure plate face down (i.e., lining side down flat, rivet heads facing the table) on a suitable work surface. Next, center a ⁹⁄₆₄-in. punch, or the punch that comes with the riveting kit shown in Figure 2-7, in one of the rivets, and deal the punch a firm blow with a hammer. Punch out any remaining rivets in the same manner, being careful not to hit the punch so hard that you enlarge the holes in the pressure plate (Figure 6-9). The old lining should fall loose.

Now place a new lining on the pressure plate in exactly the position previously

FIGURE 6-9 To remove the old lining from the pressure plate (notice how thin the old lining is in this picture), all you need to do is center a ⁵⁄₆₄-in. punch in the "tail" end of one of the rivets holding the lining in place; then deal the punch a firm blow with a hammer. Do this for each attaching rivet, and the lining will fall free.

FIGURE 6-10 After the old lining has been detached from the pressure plate, a new lining is laid against the plate, new rivets are placed in the properly aligned rivet holes, and the rivets are clinched using a special rivet-setting punch. In the bottom of the jig, supporting the head of the rivet being clinched, is a small plug of metal (the anvil, not visible in this photo); this rivet-supporting plug was not present earlier, when the old rivets were being knocked out of the old lining. The punch being used here has a special dimpled end, designed to curl the ends of (and thus clinch) new rivets. One rivet has already been installed in the assembly shown here.

occupied by the old lining. Be sure the countersunk side of each rivet hole faces *away* from the plate; the countersunk area accepts the head of the ne ᵛ rivet. Place fresh rivets in the holes, and check to see that they fit easily. If the holes in the pressure plate do not appear to line up properly with the rivet holes in the new lining, you've got the wrong kind of lining. (McCauley linings have slightly different rivet spacing than their Cleveland counterparts; it's quite possible that somebody sold you the wrong kind of lining, since the two kinds often look the same but are not.) Take any unsatisfactory parts back where you got them and ask for replacements.

Now secure your rivet-setting tool (i.e., the brake-relining tool discussed in Chapter 2, on page 27) in a vise or clamp it to your work table. Set the pressure-plate-lining-rivet assembly in the jig, with the lining facing *down* and the rivet head resting on the circular anvil, as shown in Figure 6-10. Insert the rivet-clinching punch vertically in the jig, and bring the tip of the punch down to the lips of the rivet. Then, while holding the pressure plate firmly against the lining, strike the punch with a hammer. Give the punch several good blows, turning the pressure plate and lining from side to side between blows so that the rivet will be evenly clinched around its edges. Repeat this procedure for all remaining rivet holes in the assembly, thereby securely fastening the new lining to the plate.

When you're done, check to see that the lining is tightly fastened to the plate. (There should be no looseness.) Examine the lining carefully to be sure that you haven't cracked, chipped, or otherwise damaged it in hammering the rivets. If the new lining isn't perfect, replace it. Linings cost only a couple dollars each.

If everything checks out okay, you are done relining the pressure plate and can now go through the entire procedure again with the back plate. Knock the old rivets out as you did with the pressure plate; remove the old lining; and, exactly as before, install a new lining in place of the old one.

That, basically, is all there is to relining a Cleveland or McCauley brake.

Putting everything back together is essentially a matter of going through the disassembly steps in reverse order. Before you begin, though, you'll want to take a moment to push the brake piston back into the cylinder (as shown in Figure 6-11). The purpose of this operation is twofold: One, it helps ensure that during normal brake use following reassembly of the relined parts, the piston won't exceed

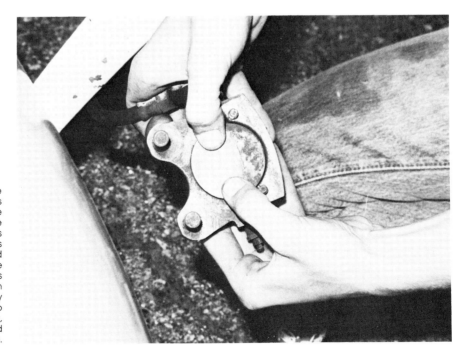

FIGURE 6-11 Before reassembling the brake, it is always a good idea to press the brake piston back into the cylinder with your thumbs as shown here (unless the piston is dirty, in which case you should clean it with alcohol first, before pressing it back in). If the piston is not repositioned in this fashion after each brake relining, it may exceed its travel limits (i.e., pop out) during subsequent service, causing loss of brake fluid and braking action.

FIGURE 6-12 If your brake's anchor pins are rusted up, remove the rust and dirt with 400-grit sandpaper (and treat the pins with silicone spray to prevent further rusting) before placing them back in their bushings. Good preventive maintenance calls for sanitizing the entire brake area each time the brake is apart for relining. The ends of the brake's two through bolts can be seen protruding through the right-hand side of the brake casting in this picture.

its proper travel limits (a situation that could cause a sudden loss of brake fluid). Two, it brings the brake casting closer to the disc during reassembly, making it that much easier for you to thread the through bolts into the back plate. The bolts may not reach to the back plate if the piston is fully extended when you remount the brake.

To reassemble the brake, slide the relined pressure plate back onto the anchor bolts so that the plate meets the piston and the lining faces the disc. Next, slide the brake assembly onto the wheel. That is, insert the anchor bolts into their torque-plate bushings. Then insert the two original through bolts into the brake casting (don't forget to use washers); place the back plate and shim (if you have one) in their proper position behind the brake disc; and thread the through bolts into the back plate. (See Figure 6-12 for another assembly hint.)

The last step, incidentally, is easier said than done if there's a wheel fairing in the way. Cessna wheel fairings, in particular, tend to envelop the brake disc and thus hide the back plate from view. Even so, you should have no trouble installing the back plate by feel, with a few minutes of practice.

When both bolts have engaged the back plate, cinch them up alternately, little by little, until you reach the manufacturer's recommended torque (which may be stated somewhere on the brake itself). If the through bolts have drilled heads, safety-wire them with stainless steel MS20995 lock wire, using the largest diameter wire that will fit through the holes. (As mentioned before, some Cleveland installations do not have head-drilled bolts but instead utilize a self-locking type of bolt having a nylon insert in the threaded tip. These bolts are of a special type that *must not* be replaced with nondrilled, non-self-locking AN4 or AN5 equivalents.)

When you're done, congratulate yourself: You've just relined your brakes at a total cost of less than $10. You can forget about ever again paying anyone $40 or $50 or more to have this done.

HOW TO BREAK IN NEW LININGS

After you've relined and reassembled your brakes, you'll want to climb into the cockpit and feel your brake pedals to make sure everything is working all right. If everything checks out okay, you'll then want to break in or "condition" your new linings according to factory recommendations.

Amazingly, many A&Ps are unaware of the existence of a recommended break-in procedure for new brake linings—despite the fact that if phenolic (asbestos-resin) linings are not conditioned properly before being put into service, a single hard brake application can carburize the lining material and prevent the design braking coefficient from being reached throughout the life of the linings. And that won't be long, since carburized linings wear out rapidly.

To break in a set of organic linings, you'll need to begin a 25- to 40-mph straight-line taxi, and then brake to a stop or a near stop *using light pedal effort*. Then allow the brakes to cool for a minute. Again start a 25- to 40-mph taxi run, and once more brake to a stop using light pedal pressure. Let the brakes cool briefly.

Repeat this taxi-stop-cool cycle a minimum of four more times (or six times in all). This procedure will generate sufficient heat in the linings to completely cure the resins in them, but will not allow sufficient heat buildup for carburization to occur. Thus conditioned, your new linings should (according to the Cleveland factory) be able to deliver 50 to 100 stops from 72 mph at a 10-ft/sec/sec deceleration rate before lining replacement is again needed (with standard steel discs in like-new condition). This means, for instance, that if you average one landing for every flight hour, you should be able to go 100 hr or more without needing new linings.

So far, we have been discussing the break-in procedure only for organic or phenolic linings. The conditioning procedure is quite a bit different for metallic brake linings, such as are used in many light-twin applications. To break in a set of metallic linings, it is necessary to perform three consecutive hard brakings from a taxi speed of 45 to 50 mph, *without allowing the brakes to cool substantially between stops*. This procedure, which can be used on Goodyear or Cleveland metal linings, will have the effect of glazing the surface of each lining. The glaze significantly increases the linings' service life while ensuring smooth braking performance and, at the same time, minimizing the chance of brake-disc scoring.

STRATEGIES FOR GETTING EXTRA LIFE OUT OF YOUR BRAKES

At the beginning of this chapter, reference was made to the fact that lightplane brakes are seemingly temperamental—compared to automobile brakes, at least. Probably the reason aircraft brakes seem to give out so often is that pilots, as a group, tend to abuse their brakes to an inexcusable degree. If small-plane brakes were operated properly, with a view toward maximizing reliability and minimizing downtime, present brake system maintenance requirements could probably be cut in half.

With this in mind, the following tips for getting extra "mileage" out of your brakes are offered:

1. Quit using your brakes on landing, unless you operate from a very short field. Use the second (or third, or fourth) turnoff. Employ aerodynamic braking.

2. Keep touchdown speeds low. Don't carry more speed on final approach than you need to. Close your throttle all the way before flaring. If need be, have your engine's idling speed adjusted: a too-high idle setting will increase the length of your rollout needlessly, forcing you to use brakes to slow the plane down.

3. Break in new brake linings in accordance with factory recommendations (see above).

4. Ensure that the brake anchor bolts (Cleveland-type brakes) are kept clean at all times. Periodically lubricate the bolts with silicone spray.

5. If your brake discs are rusted, scored, or pitted, recondition them or buy new ones. If your discs are not rusted, coat them with silicone spray between flights and any time the aircraft is washed.

6. Maintain sanitary conditions when replenishing the brake reservoir. Do not allow dirt to accumulate near the reservoir filler opening.

7. Do not leave your parking brake on in hot weather. Brake lines, connections, and seals can rupture as brake fluid undergoes heat expansion.

8. Periodically check to be sure the brake piston (at the pressure plate) is positioned so that it will not exceed its proper travel range. Push the piston back into the cylinder at every relining interval; otherwise, the piston may pop out, causing loss of brake fluid.

9. Use your brakes as they were meant to be used—to stop, not to turn. Use brakes for tight turning only when absolutely necessary.

10. Always abide by manufacturers' service recommendations. If you don't have a service manual for your brakes, order one. (See Appendix B for brake manufacturers' addresses.)

Whatever kind of plane you fly, and whatever kind of brakes it has, go easy on your brakes. With a little luck, you may never have to perform the procedures discussed in this chapter.

It has been said (and rightly so) that the best way to ensure long life for an airplane is to fly it often—the more often, the better. Novice pilots are frequently quite startled to hear this, since in the nonaviation world it is axiomatic that the more often one uses a mechanical device, the more quickly the device wears out. Such is not the case for an airplane, however. When brake discs, control hinges, and engine parts sit idle, they corrode; and corrosion in an airplane is much less tolerable than it would be in any type of earthbound machinery. Keep a plane's moving parts moving, however, and corrosion scarcely has a chance to begin.

If frequent usage offers the best hope of ensuring an airframe's longevity, then the second most important factor in stretching a plane's lifespan must surely be keeping the airframe clean. Cleanliness is vitally important to an airframe's long-term well-being, for the simple reason that grit and grime hasten the development (and obscure the presence) of corrosion—corrosion being the ultimate killer of all airplanes. The grime layer that builds up on the surface of an airframe over time contains both *corrosives* (salts, acids, solvent residues, and—where bugs have impacted—enzymes) and abrasives (principally silica, from sand). The corrosives attack the airframe directly (chemically), while the abrasive constituents of the grime physically remove the paint layers that protect the airframe from corrosion. (Contrary to what you might think, the primary purpose of the paint on an aircraft is to protect the underlying structure from corrosion. Any cosmetic benefits are secondary in importance.)

Thus, washing an airplane becomes, in effect, a maintenance function, and an important one at that. In fact, the FAA considers it so important that in Appendix D of FAR Part 43, a "thorough cleaning" of the airframe and engine is specifically listed as one of the procedures that mechanics must perform at every annual inspection. Let us, then, begin our discussion of airframe maintenance with a careful consideration of the "how to" and "how not to" of cleaning an airframe.

HOW TO WASH AN AIRPLANE

Washing an airplane is only slightly more difficult than washing a car, owing to the larger surface areas involved; but, as in all other preventive maintenance operations, there is a right way and there is a wrong way to do the job.

Doing the job the right way means, first and foremost, following the instructions given in the aircraft service manual.

(Look under "Cleaning, Exterior" in the section on routine servicing.) Some manufacturers make specific brand-name recommendations regarding cleansers to be used on various parts of the airframe. Also, special instructions are sometimes given concerning particular airframe subassemblies. Needless to say, you'll want to heed the manufacturer's recommendations in these areas, since the specific instructions given in the airplane manual always take precedence over any general recommendations given here.

Unlike an automobile, an airplane needs to be subjected to certain preparatory procedures before the water is turned on; your service manual will no doubt have some specific suggestions in this regard. One thing you'll want to do is cover the main wheel brake discs (using Saran Wrap, or whatever's available); otherwise, the discs may rust. Likewise, you'll want to mask off the pitot tube and static ports. There's no need to block off the engine air filter or cowl openings; for now, though, avoid blasting these areas with water. (The procedure for washing an engine is slightly different from that for cleaning the airframe exterior. We'll get to engine cleaning in the next chapter.)

When sensitive parts of the airframe have been covered, you may begin to hose the plane down. Work around the plane in a circle, as you would in a preflight inspection. Try to avoid spraying water in cabin vent openings. (Did you remember to close that little window on the pilot's side? Are all the doors shut tightly?)

After the plane has been wet, you can begin the job of actually washing it. Here, you'll need at least a bucket, a soft-bristle brush of the type made for washing boats and cars, some nylon scouring pads, and a box of soap flakes. Beech Aircraft specifically recommends Ivory or Lux soap. (There are more expensive "aircraft soaps" on the market, but you needn't buy them.) Airframe manufacturers are unanimous in recommending that detergents, no matter how "mild," and household cleansers *not* be used on airframe exteriors, since such cleansers can attack the airframe chemically and/or by abrasive action. Chlorinated cleansers, in particular, are to be avoided at all costs.

Mix your soap solution in a bucket, using (if possible) lukewarm tap water. Then apply copious amounts of the solution to a portion of the airframe, and use your brush or a large sponge to spread it around. A gentle circular motion is best.

You should never need to apply more than light pressure to the brush or sponge to dislodge most dirt and grime. If you come across a bug-stained (or bird-stained) area that appears to require more than light effort with the brush, lay down the brush and go at it with a plastic scouring pad; use liberal amounts of soap and water. Doing an entire wing this way requires a good deal of muscle—not to mention the patience of a Zen master—but it's the only thing to do. The alternative is repainting the wing.

Wash only small sections of the airframe as you go, rinsing each section before any part of it begins to dry. The idea is not to let any soap dry on the plane's surface. All soaps are alkaline and thus capable of damaging paint. As long as you keep the soap dilute, no damage can occur. Proceed in this manner (i.e., scrub

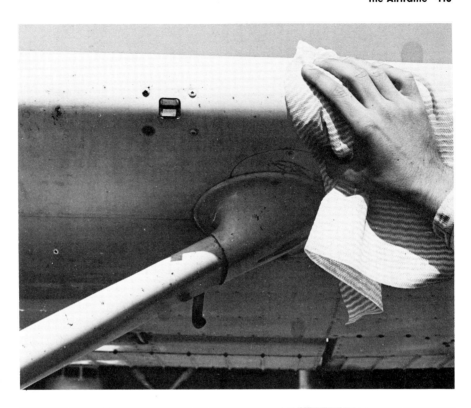

FIGURE 7-1 The leading edges of wings, struts, fins, and stabilizers tend to accumulate dirt, bug remains, and other debris in a hurry. For this reason, leading edges should be given special attention during washing operations. A one-to-one solution of commercial degreaser in water, applied by hand with a nylon scouring pad or tough cloth, may be required to budge persistent bug stains. Shown here is a wing before (a) and after (b) degreasing.

for 5 min, then rinse, scrub the next section, rinse again, etc.) until you've worked your way around the entire plane. (*Note:* Leave the windows for later.) Then hose the plane down once more, to remove any last traces of soap.

At this point, there will still be areas of the airframe needing attention. Concentrated grease, oil, and soot, such as you'll find around exhaust openings, on landing-gear torque links, etc., won't yield to mild soap solution (Figure 7-1). There are two ways of dealing with these exceptionally dirty trouble spots. One way is to get hold of a trigger-action plastic spray bottle of Fantastik (or the equivalent) and go around zapping any particularly ugly or persistent grime buildups. Carry a supply of throwaway cloth wipes in your free hand, with which to rub out the offensive spots. Some plane owners like to substitute a commercial-grade degreaser for the stuff that comes in the supermarket-style plastic spray bottles. It doesn't matter. The strong surfactants used in most commercial degreasers will not harm the finish on an aircraft or on Plexiglas windows, as long as they are eventually flushed away with water.

Another way of dealing with extremely grimy areas is to come at those areas with a rag soaked in solvent. Naphtha, Varsol, kerosene, and Stoddard solvent are among the most widely used solvents for this purpose, since none of these substances will harm the finish of the average enamel-coated metal aircraft. (Prolonged contact with these solvents can, however, produce dermatitis on the average skin-coated human being. Take appropriate precautions.) Under no circumstances should you use acetone, benzene, carbon tetrachloride, gasoline, isopropyl alcohol, lacquer thinner, methyl ethyl ketone, or window cleaning sprays in place of the above-mentioned solvents, since some of these agents will dissolve paint and Plexiglas before your very eyes. (Used carelessly, they'll dissolve your very eyes!) When in doubt, perform a spot test on the underside of, say, the horizontal stabilizer, to see whether the solvent you're using will, in fact, ruin paint.

If the underside of your fuselage looks like the hull of the Amoco Cadiz, solvent is really the only answer. A thick layer of "belly oil" simply will not be budged by spray-bottle degreaser, unless you have dozens of bottles of the stuff and endless patience. To get an oily airplane belly clean, you'll need a bucket of Stoddard or some other solvent, some rags, and a dolly to lie on while you work under the plane. After rubbing each area with a solvent-soaked rag, reach up with your other arm and wipe off the solvent with a dry rag (to keep the liquid from evaporating and redepositing the grime back on the plane's surface). When you're done, flush the entire belly of the plane with water, and wipe it dry with a towel or chamois to eliminate any solvent residue.

Done washing? Before you forget, take time now to untape the pitot tube and static ports; also, uncover the brake discs. Wipe the plane dry, or—better yet—*fly* it dry, but not before relubricating anything that needs lubrication (see the section on lubrication that follows).

Most airframe manufacturers recommend that a plane's finish be restored with wax after every washing; check your manual on this. Waxing not only makes the plane look better, but, more important, it forms a clear barrier that protects the paint from chemical attack (by bug juice, bird juice, salts, and acids) as well as abrasive attack. A good wax job also makes the plane easier to wash next time around.

Most airframe manufacturers recommend the use of good-quality automotive waxes on airplane finishes. (Again, though, check your service manual for specific suggestions in this regard.) Bare aluminum may be polished with any good aluminum polish. Regardless of what you end up using, be sure to follow the wax or polish manufacturer's instructions exactly. Also, use only light rubbing effort and very soft cloths. High-abrasive polishes and waxes should be avoided.

If you lack the time or inclination to wax the entire airframe, by all means at least wax—and wax *liberally*—the leading edges of the wings, the front of the cowl, the prop spinner, and all empennage leading edges. Heavy waxing will significantly reduce abrasion problems in these areas.

A word of caution: If your aircraft is brand new or has recently been repainted, *do not apply polish or wax until after the finish has cured completely*. This is usually 60 to 90 days for enamel, and 2 to 3 weeks for lacquer. Application of wax during this period interferes with normal outgassing and curing of the paint.

AIRFRAME LUBRICATION Knowing how to locate and service the lubrication points on your plane is an important aspect of airframe preventive maintenance. It is all the more important if your plane is among the many that receives a thorough lube job just once a year, at annual inspection time. If you fly a great deal (or even if you merely wash your plane a lot), your aircraft may well be in need of more frequent lubrication than it is now getting at the hands of mechanics.

If you've never taken the opportunity to study the lubrication charts in your aircraft service manual, plan on doing so soon. Your owner's manual will give you some idea of what the periodic lubricating requirements are for your plane, but the lubricating instructions set forth in the aircraft service manual will be much more complete and useful. The lubrication section of your service manual will be several pages long; in fact, the main lubrication diagram is likely to be printed on an extra-large foldout page. In it, you'll find words, pictures, charts, and diagrams showing, for each subassembly that needs periodic lubrication, the type of lubricant to apply, the method by which to apply the lubricant, and the recommended frequency of lubrication. (See Figure 7-2.)

Since most planes (even small trainer aircraft) have a minimum of about 50 lubrication points, and since details of design, lubrication frequency, application procedures, etc., vary significantly from one plane type to the next, no complete, point-by-point rundown of how to lubricate the "average" plane can be given here. Some general guidelines, however, are probably in order:

First of all, remember that the frequency requirements stated in your owner's manual or service manual are based on average usage and average environmental conditions. As one manufacturer states, "Airplanes operated for air taxi or other than normal operation and airplanes operated in humid tropics or cold and damp

LUBRICATION POINTS

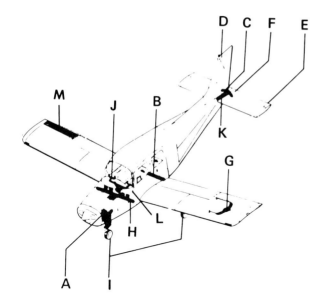

DETAIL A

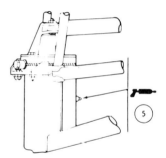

NOSE GEAR STEERING

SPRAY   GREASE GUN   HAND OR PACK

OIL CAN   BRUSH   HYDRAULIC FLUID

NOTE

Numbers refer to items in the consumable materials chart. Lubricate all plain bearing bushings as required or every 500 hours with SAE No. 30 oil. Apply SAE No. 20 oil to push-pull control housings as required. Lubricate flight control pulleybushings with SAE No. 30 oil every 1000 hours.

SAE 10w/30 oil is an acceptable replacement for SAE 20 or SAE 30 oil.

DETAIL B

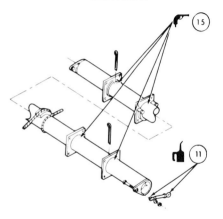

FLAP MECHANISM

DETAIL C

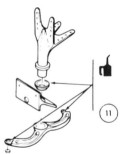

RUDDER BELLCRANK

FIGURE 7-2 Lubrication chart for the Beech C23 Sundowner.

DETAIL D

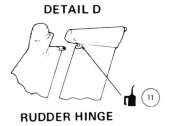

RUDDER HINGE

(11)

DETAIL E

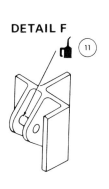

(4)

OR

(10)

ELEVATOR HINGE

DETAIL F

(11)

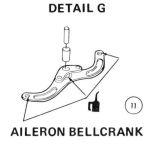

STABILATOR HINGE BRACKET

DETAIL G

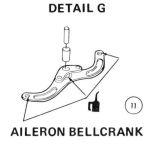

AILERON BELLCRANK

(11)

DETAIL H

(11)

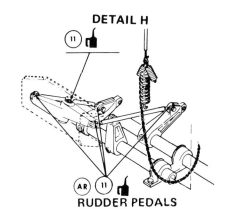

(AR) (11)

RUDDER PEDALS

DETAIL I

(8)

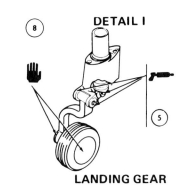

(5)

LANDING GEAR

DETAIL J

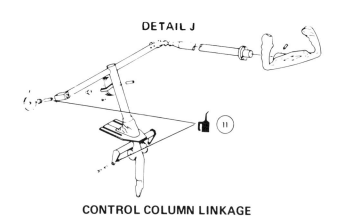

(11)

CONTROL COLUMN LINKAGE

DETAIL K

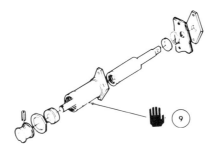

TRIM TAB ACTUATOR

DETAIL L

(For Airplanes Prior to M-1486)

This screw must be completely tight to prevent binding.

(16) LOOSEN NUT, REMOVE VALVE CONE, AND LUBRICATE CONE WITH VERY THIN COATING OF LUBRICANT.

NOTE: DO NOT OVER LUBRICATE VALVE CONE. APPLY MINIMUM AMOUNT OF LUBRICANT FOR COATING

FUEL SELECTOR VALVE

NOTE: FUEL SELECTOR VALVES ON M-1486 AND AFTER NEED NO LUBRICATION.

DETAIL M

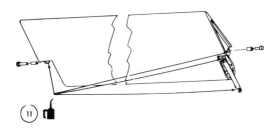

AILERONS

FIGURE 7-2   Lubrication chart for the Beech C23 Sundowner. (*Cont.*)

CONSUMABLE MATERIALS

ITEM	MATERIAL	SPECIFICATION	ITEM	MATERIAL	SPECIFICATION
*1	Engine Oil	SAE No. 20 (Below 10°F) SAE No. 30 (0° to 70°F) SAE No. 50 (Above 60°F)	††9	Grease (High & Low)	MIL-G-23827
2	Solvent	PD680	10	Lubricating Oil (Low Temperature)	MIL-L-7870
**3	Fuel, Engine	91/96 Grade (blue)	11	Lubricating Oil	SAE No. 20
***4	Lubricant, Powdered Graphite	SS-G-659	12	Lubricating Oil	SAE No. 30
			†††13	Grease (General Purpose)	MIL-G-7711
†5	Grease (High & Low Temperature)	Aero Lubriplate	††††14	Lubricant, Rubber Seal	Oakite 6 Compound
6	Corrosion Preventive, Engine	MIL-C-6529	†††††15	Lubricant, Silicone Spray	Krylon #1329 (or equivalent)
7	Hydraulic Fluid	MIL-H-5606	16	Lubricant, Fluorosilicone	Corning FS-1292
8	Grease (High Temperature)	MIL-G-81322		Synthetic Solvent Resistant Grease	Anderol L-237

*It is recommended that a straight mineral based (non-detergent) oil be used until the oil consumption has stabilized, and then change to an ashless dispersant oil for prolonged engine life.

**If 91/96 (blue) grade fuel is not available, use 100/130 (green), or 115/145 (purple) grade.

***Mix with quick evaporating liquid naphtha and apply with a brush.

†Product of BRC Bearing Company, Wichita, Kansas.

††In extremely cold climates, MIL-G-23827 grease should be used in place of MIL-G-7711 grease. Care should be exercised when using either MIL-G-7711 or MIL-G-23827 grease, as they contain a rust-preventing additive which is harmful to paint.

†††Product of Oakite Products, Inc., New York 6, New York.

††††Product of Krylon Inc., Norristown, Pa.

climates, etc., may need more frequent inspections for wear, corrosion, and/or lack of lubrication." The object of periodic relubrication of airframe components is not to adhere unwaveringly to a set schedule, but to keep the components operating properly. In other words, if a hinge looks dry, lubricate it—whether or not the manual says it's time to lubricate the hinge.

Second, don't let all the military specifications (MIL-G-6711 and so on) in the lubrication section of your service manual put you off. FAR 43.13 requires that you perform your preventive maintenance in accordance with "accepted industry practices." And it so happens that, in aircraft maintenance shops, the accepted practice is to substitute high-quality "civilian" lubricants for the mil-spec materials called out in the shop manuals. (I have yet to see an A&P mechanic check a can of grease for its mil-spec number.) The airframe manufacturers are aware of this. Cessna, in fact, states in its 100 Series shop manual: "The military specifications listed are not mandatory, but are intended as guides in choosing satisfactory materials. Products of most reputable manufacturers meet or exceed these specifications."

Something else you should keep in mind is that the recommended lubrication intervals for exposed control hinges are valid only if you do not wash all the lubrication off these hinges between scheduled lube jobs. In other words, any time you give your plane a soap-and-water wash, you should plan on relubricating aileron, elevator, rudder, and trim-tab hinges.

Control hinges come in different styles. Some are Teflon coated; others are not. Teflon-coated hinge points generally need no lubrication. Non-Teflon hinges (regardless of design) should be cleaned with Stoddard solvent prior to relubrication if they appear dirty. Piano hinges, bell cranks, and hinge bolts are generally lubricated with MIL-L-7870 general-purpose oil or the equivalent (i.e., lightweight engine oil); however, some mechanics like to touch up control hinges with a shot or two of WD40, LPS #1, or some other spray-type penetrating oil. (One advantage of using penetrant oils such as WD40 is that they are good at driving out moisture, so that if you've just finished washing the plane, you can be sure, after coating your hinge points with penetrating oil, that the hinges will emerge dry and lubricated. In addition, most penetrating oils have excellent anticorrosion properties. If penetrating oils have a drawback, it's that they tend to be too thin to stick around for very long.) Some manufacturers (Cessna, for instance) recommend that piano hinges be lubricated with powdered graphite rather than lightweight oil.

Rod-end bearings deserve special attention; if they are not lubricated properly, they can crack in the threaded area, resulting in loss of controls in flight. When you inspect the rod-end bearings on your aileron and flap pushrods, always grab the neck of the rod and twist it back and forth to see that the ball is free in its race. If the rod end sticks or looks dry, lubricate it with silicone spray (if the race is Teflon lined) or general-purpose oil, as appropriate. A "frozen" rod end should be brought to the attention of an A&P mechanic immediately.

Not counting the engine itself, the single portion of the airframe requiring more lubrication than any other system or assembly is the landing gear. The landing gear depends, for proper operation, on (1) frequent lubrication of the wheel bearings and (2) in the case of oleo-equipped aircraft, periodic servicing of the struts with air and oil and periodic greasing of the struts' torque-link bushings. On retractable-gear aircraft, lubrication of the entire retraction system must be considered. However, since the lubrication of actuator rods, motor gearboxes, uplock roller bearings, and other retraction-system components often involves disassembly of critical items, and since lubrication chores involving such disassembly fall outside the purview of preventive maintenance as defined in FAR Part 43, Appendix A, we shall not discuss the relevant procedures here.

Many pilots are surprised to learn that the average oleo-equipped lightplane has a minimum of three (and often as many as six) grease fittings on and around each gear leg. Many aviators are surprised, too, to learn that these grease points generally need servicing once every 50 hr or so. According to Cessna, for example, "The nose gear torque links should be lubricated at least every 50 hours, or oftener when operating in dusty areas. Under extremely dusty conditions, *daily lubrication is recommended.*" (Emphasis added.) With new torque links often costing several hundred dollars a set, it only makes sense to heed the manufacturer's lubricating recommendations in this area.

Servicing landing-gear grease fittings is easy: in most cases, an ordinary automotive grease gun will do the job. (Care must be taken, however, to ensure that the gun is filled with new, clean grease of the appropriate grade, usually MIL-G-23827 or MIL-G-81322. Note that both these commonly used greases contain a rust preventive that will, if carelessly used, discolor painted surfaces.) Simply clean the area around the grease fitting with a rag moistened with Varsol, couple the end of the grease gun to the fitting, and apply grease (preferably while someone turns the head of the torque-link bolt slowly with a wrench). Wipe away any excess grease when you're done.

If you feel particularly ambitious, you may wish to open up a few inspection panels and lubricate some bellcranks and pulleys, or possibly the entire control system. Let your service manual be your guide here. Most pulleys used in aircraft have sealed bearings and require no periodic lubrication; however, it is worth looking at the pulleys closely to determine whether any unusual wear patterns exist (Figure 7-3). The manufacturers don't like to admit it, but a certain number of new airplanes leave the factory each year with control cables misrouted or misaligned—conditions that sometimes go undetected until the planes' third or fourth annuals. You never know what you'll find until you pull the inspection plates off. Even if you find nothing unusual, it won't hurt to rotate the pulleys 180° by hand before putting the inspection plates back on. Most control-system pulleys turn a good deal less than 360° during normal operation. They thus tend to wear out faster on one side than the other unless someone—a mechanic, usually—rotates the worn side of each pulley away from the cable every 100 hr or so. Unfortunately, many mechanics seem to have forgotten this trick.

Exactly how many inspection points you decide to hit on your between-inspections lube job is up to you. The FARs say that you can lubricate anything

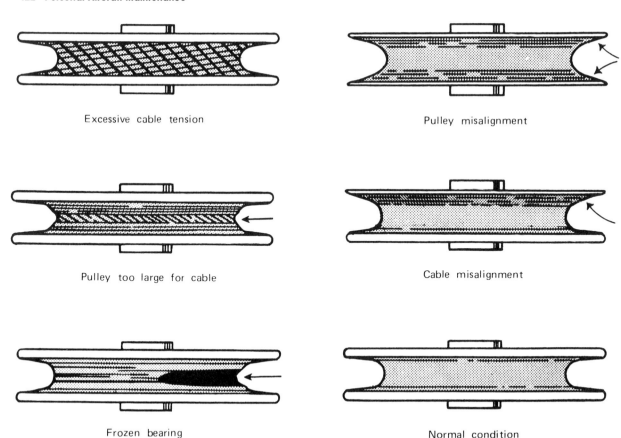

Excessive cable tension

Pulley misalignment

Pulley too large for cable

Cable misalignment

Frozen bearing

Normal condition

FIGURE 7-3 Normal (lower right) and abnormal pulley wear patterns. (*FAA.*)

you want, so long as you stay with items "not requiring disassembly other than removal of nonstructural items such as cover plates, cowlings, and fairings." Regardless of what you decide to lubricate, however, you should make it a point to observe the following "good lubrication practices":

1. Make sure that whatever it is you are going to lubricate is clean before you lubricate it. Clean bearings, bushings, and hinge points with a dry-type solvent before proceeding.

2. Do not apply lubricant where it is not needed. Overlubrication of bearings, hinges, etc., will only hasten the collection of dust and grit, leading to rapid component wear. This rule applies especially to cables, roller chains, and cockpit controls.

3. Except as allowed by the aircraft manual, do not apply lubricant to rubber parts. Rubber is deteriorated by many types of lubricants.

4. Always check the component to be lubricated for evidence of excessive wear. Report discrepancies to a mechanic at once.

5. Apply lubricant sparingly. Upon completion of the job, wipe away any excess lubricant to prevent the collection of dirt and sand in abrasive quantities.

One more thing: When you're done for the day, be sure to make an entry in the airframe log. State the date, the tach time or total airframe time, as appropriate, and (in some detail) the nature of the work done. That way, you'll have a record, 50 or 70 or 90 hr from now, of exactly which components you did or did not lubricate, and when. Without such a record, you may end up duplicating your earlier efforts prematurely.

A WORD ABOUT RUBBER FUEL CELLS

Many aircraft (Cessna and Beech products in particular) employ rubber fuel cells in the wings, rather than storing fuel in sealed-off compartments integral to the wing. This arrangement has advantages, but of course with time all rubber products, including rubber fuel cells, tend to wear out. And, unfortunately, when these cells start to go, the repair bills that inevitably ensue tend to resemble the gross national product of a developing country. Fuel-cell repairs are not cheap.

Pilots can't do much in the way of do-it-yourself repairs when fuel cells have deteriorated to the extent that repairs are needed. However, there is something that pilots can do to extend the life of healthy rubber tanks. It involves keeping the tanks wet.

According to the U. S. Rubber Company, whenever a new synthetic rubber fuel cell is placed in service, the gasoline has a tendency to extract the plasticizer from the inner liner of the cell. This extraction of plasticizer is not detrimental to the cell as long as the cell is kept full of fuel, inasmuch as aviation gasoline will itself act as a suitable plasticizer. However, when gasoline is removed from the cell, the plasticizing effect of the gasoline is lost; the inner liner can begin to dry out, and cracking or checking of the rubber will occur (causing chronic fuel leakage from that point on) unless preventive action is taken.

Preventive action, in this case, consists of smearing a thin coating of SAE 30 (or lighter) engine oil along the inside surface of any cell that is expected to remain without fuel (or remain only partly full of fuel) for 10 days or more. The oil acts as a temporary plasticizer and prevents the cell's inner liner from drying out and cracking, thereby staving off some potentially devastating repair bills.

The moral of the story is this: Don't let your rubber fuel cells remain dry or even partially dry for any length of time. Keep the tanks topped off between flights, and if you have any auxiliary tanks you're not using, smear a little oil inside them. Thus cared for, your rubber tanks should last a minimum of 10 (and maybe 20) years in service before "cracking up," if, in fact, they ever do crack up.

CORROSION CONTROL

Many pilots have come to assume that corrosion is a problem only with seaplanes, wooden aircraft, and antiques. Not so. All planes from jets on down, even new ones, are subject to corrosion, because virtually all the metals from which aircraft are fabricated are subject to some form of chemical and/or galvanic attack.

While it is true that corrosion is much more of a problem in regions where the air is humid or salty, corrosion can occur on any aircraft, in any climate. Battery fumes, bug and bird juices, detergent residues, certain types of greases and hydraulic fluid, dissimilar-metals contact, and even perspiration salts can cause corrosion to form under any climatic conditions. (In smoggy areas, precipitation can interact with sulfur dioxides in the air to form highly corrosive sulfuric acid, giving rise to the well-known phenomenon of acid rain.) Thus, no matter where you live, and no matter where you fly, corrosion detection and removal should be an important part of your airframe inspection and lubrication routine.

Corrosion normally appears in one or more of four forms: chemical, local cell, concentration cell, and galvanic. Each can be controlled by careful preventive maintenance.

Chemical corrosion occurs where exhaust gases, battery acid, bird dung, etc., come in contact with metal surfaces. You've probably seen this kind of corrosion on the posts of your car's battery. Prevention consists in making sure your battery box and vent tube are in good, clean working order, regularly removing exhaust deposits from cowl flaps and other surfaces, and repainting scratched and worn spots on the airframe. (*Note:* If you should discover battery acid spilled on any metal surface, including the bottom of your battery box, flush the entire area with baking soda and water. Rinse the solution away with fresh water; then blow all crevices dry with compressed air.)

Local-cell corrosion, unlike chemical corrosion, often goes deeper than the surface of the metal. In its early stages, local-cell corrosion will show up as a light, whitish powder on bare metal surfaces; in the more advanced stages, deep pitting will be evident. On painted surfaces, the first indication of local-cell corrosion is paint blistering.

Corrosion forming under rivet heads, along faying surfaces, at skin-to-longeron contact areas, and similar places is called concentration-cell corrosion. Owing to the nature of this type of corrosion, detection requires careful inspection. Removal of the corrosion usually requires the complete separation of corroded skins, panels, etc., and a thorough scouring of the affected areas with aluminum wool soaked in methyl ethyl ketone. Before reassembly, both joined surfaces must be treated with zinc chromate.

Galvanic corrosion results when certain dissimilar metals come in contact with each other (Figure 7-4). Because some metals are more electronegative than others, a galvanic action, not unlike electroplating, occurs at the point of contact of two dissimilar metals. Electrons flow between (and chemical changes take place on) the two metals in the same way, and for the same reasons, that electrons flow between the cathode and anode of a battery. The result is a type of corrosion that can take the form of either a mild surface corrosion or (in advanced cases) deep pitting.

Some good places to look for galvanic corrosion are piano hinges, including

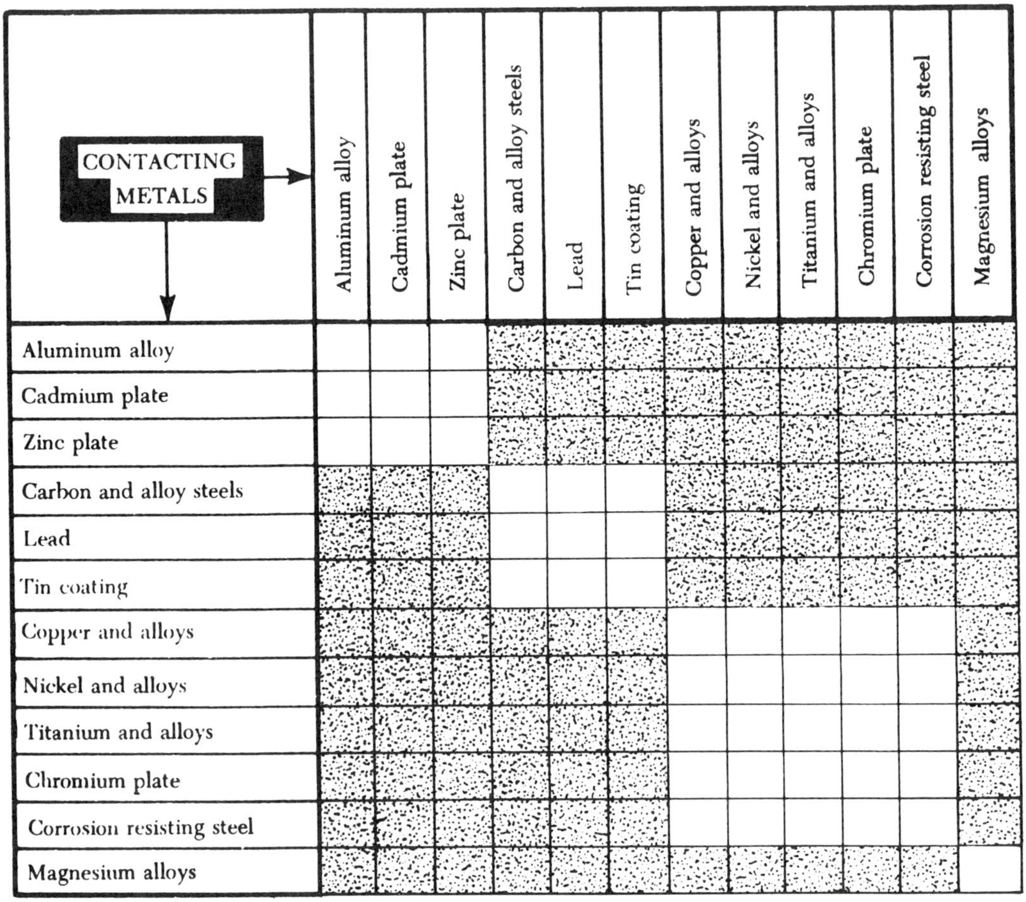

CONTACTING METALS →	Aluminum alloy	Cadmium plate	Zinc plate	Carbon and alloy steels	Lead	Tin coating	Copper and alloys	Nickel and alloys	Titanium and alloys	Chromium plate	Corrosion resisting steel	Magnesium alloys
Aluminum alloy				X	X	X	X	X	X	X	X	X
Cadmium plate				X	X	X	X	X	X	X	X	X
Zinc plate				X	X	X	X	X	X	X	X	X
Carbon and alloy steels	X	X	X				X	X	X	X	X	X
Lead	X	X	X				X	X	X	X	X	X
Tin coating	X	X	X				X	X	X	X	X	X
Copper and alloys	X	X	X	X	X	X						X
Nickel and alloys	X	X	X	X	X	X						X
Titanium and alloys	X	X	X	X	X	X						X
Chromium plate	X	X	X	X	X	X						X
Corrosion resisting steel	X	X	X	X	X	X						X
Magnesium alloys	X	X	X	X	X	X	X	X	X	X	X	

FIGURE 7-4 Incompatible dissimilar metals. Shaded areas indicate dissimilar-metals combinations that will result in galvanic corrosion (*FAA.*)

door hinges, and under the heads of wheel bolts. (The wheel halves are magnesium or aluminum; the bolts, steel.) Piano hinges are likely candidates for corrosion not only because they employ a steel pin inside an aluminum hinge, but because they are natural traps for dirt, salt, and moisture. All the more reason to keep your hinges clean and well lubricated.

When any of the above forms of corrosion is detected, the corrosion should be removed down to sound metal immediately, either by mechanical or (if need be) chemical means. In no case should corrosion be left untreated, even briefly. Once begun, corrosion tends to spread; it is rarely, if ever, self-limiting.

Some specific suggestions:

1. If the base metal is aluminum, the corrosion product will usually be a white or gray-white powder. Clean the affected area by scrubbing with aluminum wool or a nonmetallic scouring pad (such as the nylon pads made by the Carborundum Company, P.O. Box 477, Niagara Falls, NY 14302). *Do not use steel wool on aluminum.* Steel wool will leave tiny slivers of steel embedded in the aluminum, giving rise to much worse corrosion problems in the future.

2. If the base metal is steel, remove the corrosion product (ordinary rust, usually) with steel wool or 320-grit emery cloth. *Do not* attempt to clean highly stressed steel parts such as those in landing-gear structures; tiny scratches in the metal surface could produce abnormal stress concentrations of the kind that may lead to a later fatigue failure. When in doubt, call in a mechanic.

3. If the base metal is magnesium (chemically the most active of all structural metals), use only nonmetallic scouring pads to remove surface corrosion. After mechanical cleaning has been tried, further cleaning with a chromic acid pickling solution (Dow No. 1 or the equivalent) may be tried. Anything more serious than light surface corrosion should be brought to the attention of a mechanic.

Once the corroded surface has been cleaned down to the bare metal, the affected area should be prepared for zinc chromating. This can be done by wiping the exposed metal down with a clean cloth moistened in cleaning solvent. Some solvents that are widely used for this purpose are methyl ethyl ketone, Turco T-657, and Enmar No. 3094 wash thinner. Once it is applied, the solvent should be wiped dry with a second piece of clean cloth, to prevent it from drying and thus redepositing dissolved soil and other impurities on the exposed surface. (*Caution:* Most wipe solvents are highly toxic and flammable. Follow the manufacturer's instructions when using these potentially dangerous substances.)

After the affected area has been wiped clean as described above, zinc chromate primer may be applied (spray cans are widely available), and the area repainted. Enamel may be applied immediately, but acrylic lacquers should not be applied until the zinc chromate has had a chance to age for several days.

Obviously, the most effective form of corrosion control is *prevention*. In this regard, you can do a number of things, starting right now:

1. Keep your airplane clean. Mud, oil, exhaust stains, and grime tend to hide corrosion where it exists, and promote its formation where it doesn't.

2. Keep all systems well lubricated. Most lubricants form an airtight and watertight film on moving parts, thereby shutting out chemical corrosion. Except for graphite, most lubricants insulate parts from one another, preventing galvanic corrosion as well.

3. If possible, hangar the aircraft when it is not in use.

4. Eliminate standing water wherever it is found to exist (by drilling drainage holes, if necessary). Standing water not only invites corrosion, it *ensures* it. Inspect drain holes frequently to see that they are free of obstructions. If you decide to make your own drain hole in the fuselage, drill from the inside out. Unless you're extremely careful, you're apt to hit a control cable, a wire, or a structural member when drilling from the outside in.)

Corrosion control is a very complex subject, much more so than is perhaps indicated by the preceding paragraphs. The purpose of this discussion is simply to give you some idea of the scope and nature of the problem as it relates to private aircraft. If you wish to learn more about the subject, you'll find a comprehensive yet concise treatment in the FAA's Advisory Circular AC No. 43-4: *Corrosion Control for Aircraft*, available free of charge from the Department of Transportation, Publications Section, TAD 443.1, Washington, DC 20590.

HANGAR RASH It is an unfortunate fact of life that as airplanes become older, they don't perform quite like they used to. Cruise speed and rate of climb, in particular, begin to suffer noticeably as an airframe racks up hours. Partly, this is due to simple engine wear. There's no getting around the fact that an engine with several hundred—or several thousand—hours on it lacks the zip of a newer powerplant. Much of the time, however, the degradation in performance shown by an older plane can be attributed to propeller nicks, cracked fairings, peeling paint, minor door damage, scratches, dents, etc.—the sorts of miscellaneous wear and tear that collectively come under the heading of "hangar rash."

Sad to say, not all forms of hangar rash can be easily corrected. It would be impractical, for instance, to rebuild a wing in order to fix a 1-in. dent in the leading edge. And of the forms of hangar rash that can be fairly easily corrected, not all are correctable by the pilot working under FAR 43.3(h). For example, propeller nicks cannot be filed out by the pilot, since this constitutes a "minor propeller repair" which must, technically speaking, be done by a licensed mechanic.

There are, however, some forms of minor airframe damage that can be repaired by the pilot working alone. These forms of damage include most small cracks, damage to fairings, damage to paint, and rips or holes in fabric.

Crack formation is a recurrent problem for older aircraft, particularly in and around the cowling area. (There are only two types of aircraft cowls: those that have cracked, and those that are going to.) The many sharp bends incorporated into cowling designs, the light-gauge material used in cowling construction, and the high degree of vibration to which cowlings are exposed all tend to ensure the crackability of this vital airframe component. Consequently, examination of the entire area forward of the firewall for cracks should be part of every pilot's preflight inspection routine.

Whenever a crack is found in a cowling or any other airframe component, its location should be noted for future reference, and its ends stop-drilled as shown in Figure 7-5. This applies not only to cracks in metal cowls, but cracks in fiber glass, Plexiglas, and plastic components as well. If there is more than one crack, stop-drill each crack at its propagation point. Use a drill bit no larger than ⅛ in. in diameter, and no smaller than 3/32 in.

If the crack is a small one, its growth may (depending on the nature of the factors contributing to its original appearance) be entirely stopped by stop-drilling. Then again, it may continue to grow. Obviously, you'll want to keep an eye on it for awhile. If the original crack is more than an inch or two long—or if it is short but continues to grow after stop-drilling—a patch (Figure 7-6) should be made and applied. However, the crack should be stop-drilled *whether or not* a

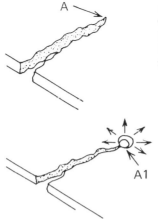

A

All the strains which originally caused crack are concentrated at point A, tending to extend crack. Therefore, drill a small hole at end of crack point A1 to distribute strain over wider area.

A1

FIGURE 7-5 How to stop-drill a crack. *(FAA.)*

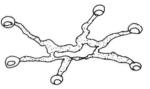

Each crack occurring at any hole or tear is drilled in same manner.

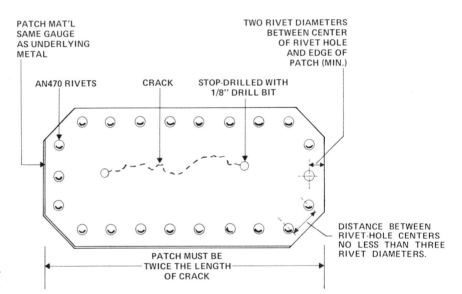

PATCH MAT'L SAME GAUGE AS UNDERLYING METAL

TWO RIVET DIAMETERS BETWEEN CENTER OF RIVET HOLE AND EDGE OF PATCH (MIN.)

AN470 RIVETS   CRACK   STOP-DRILLED WITH 1/8″ DRILL BIT

DISTANCE BETWEEN RIVET-HOLE CENTERS NO LESS THAN THREE RIVET DIAMETERS.

PATCH MUST BE TWICE THE LENGTH OF CRACK

FIGURE 7-6 Guidelines for patching a crack.

patch is to be applied. The FAA has a number of firm requirements regarding patches of this sort:

1. The patch plate must be of the same material (2024-T3 aluminum, or whatever) as the item to be patched: also, the patch material must be of the same or next heavier gauge as the original. The relevant material specifications can usually be found in the front of the aircraft service manual.

2. The patch plate must have a total length not less than twice that of the stop-drilled crack.

3. The patch must accommodate a minimum of four rivets on each side.

4. All rivet holes must be at least two rivet diameters from the edge of the patch and from the crack itself.

5. The rivet spacing must be at least three times the rivet-hole diameter.

Cowl patches are frequently made with ⅛-in. AN470-A rivets, which can be driven without using a rivet set (because they are made of soft aluminum). Cut your rivets just long enough so that they protrude about ³⁄₁₆ in. through patch and cowl. Drive the rivets one by one, holding the head of each rivet against a hard, flat surface while you flatten the ³⁄₁₆-in. end to about ¹⁄₁₆ in. with a ball peen hammer. (*Hint:* Arrange for each row of rivets to line up with a factory-installed row. That way, with a little luck, you'll end up with a patch that looks like standard equipment.)

Metal-to-metal patches of this type, under FAR Part 43, Appendix A, be made by pilots to any portion of the airframe—not just cowlings—so long as the patch does not change the contour of the underlying structure in such a way as to interfere with proper airflow. Bear that in mind, and you won't go far wrong. Just remember to be careful where you drill.

Repairs to fiber glass airframe components are, if anything, easier to make than repairs to metal. This is fortunate, considering the ease with which fiber glass wing tips, cowlings, tail cones, and wheel pants go to pieces. Start by removing the cracked part and cleaning the interior surface with methyl ethyl ketone. Next, buy yourself an inexpensive fiber glass repair kit, such as are sold through boat dealers; this is what most mechanics use to make fiber glass repairs. Mix the resin and catalyst, following the instructions that come with the kit. Also, cut several large pieces of fiber glass cloth to cover the damaged area. Coat the damaged portion with resin, and lay in the first piece of cloth; then apply more resin. Follow with additional layers of resin and cloth, with each new piece of cloth extending about ½ in. beyond the edges of the preceding piece. Be sure to work all air bubbles out of each layer. When a total of four layers of cloth have been laid, allow the resin to cure.

After the repair has been made to the inside surface of the cracked component, you can sand the outside surface smooth, fill in the damaged area with resin, and (after allowing the resin to cure) sand and refinish the exterior.

Working in this fashion, it is often possible to repair (to better-than-new condition) a cracked cowling or wheel fairing that might otherwise have cost $100 or more to replace. A set of new wheel fairings for some of today's aircraft can cost upward of $500. Obviously, it's worth it to try to fix the old ones, if possible.

Most forms of hangar rash require touch-up painting or repainting to be made aesthetically acceptable. This, again, is something pilots may legally do unaided, so long as the removal of any primary structure is not required. For fiber glass components, this means sanding the surface with 320-grit wet-or-dry sandpaper, applying a coat of epoxy primer, and finishing with three coats of spray enamel.

Allow the enamel to dry for two days before taping or masking, if a second color is to be applied. For best results, the entire component should be sanded and refinished, rather than just the damaged portion.

The repainting of an aluminum surface is not quite so easy, particularly if (as is often the case) you are not interested in stripping and repainting an entire panel to touch up a small area. A mistake in the choice of paint, paint color, or primer system can be costly and embarrassing, since the wrong combination of materials and methods can result in the curdling or lifting (now, or several weeks from now) of the paint surrounding the touched-up area. Not a very pleasant thing to think about.

Rule number one, therefore, regarding the application of touch-up paint to an aluminum surface is: Know what kind of finish your plane has. Often, your airplane service manual or the parts catalog will state what kind of finish (acrylic lacquer, acrylic enamel, polyurethane enamel) your plane has, and—equally important—the exact colors used. (You wouldn't want to substitute shamrock green for mint green or jade mist green, any more than you'd want to substitute lacquer for enamel.) Frequently, the only way to get this information is to call the factory. Alternatively, if your plane has been through several paint jobs since leaving the factory, it may be necessary to take the plane to a paint shop. An experienced painter can tell you what kind of paint you've got.

In any event, the important thing is not simply to go ahead and paint without due regard for what you are painting over. Acrylic lacquers, particularly, should not be wantonly applied. When in doubt, get an expert's opinion. After that, make a patch test on a not easily visible portion of the airframe to determine the compatibility of the existing finish with whatever it is you're applying.

If you need to remove paint from the area being touched up, use methyl ethyl ketone (MEK) or a commercial paint stripper, applied with a rag. Afterward, scrub the area to be painted with aluminum (not steel) wool, and wipe away any impurities with a clean, MEK-moistened rag. (Commercially recycled shop towels are not recommended here, as they frequently contain silicones picked up from previous polishing operations.) Next, apply a thin but wet coat of epoxy primer, and allow it to dry. Zinc chromate primer may be substituted for epoxy primer, but *only* if the bare aluminum is pretreated with an Alodine-type conversion coating before the primer is applied, and *only* if the paint to be used is an enamel. Acrylic lacquers tend to lift zinc chromate.

Now you can apply the top coat, whatever it happens to be. Acrylic lacquer should be applied in numerous thin coats rather than a few thick coats, with at least 30 min drying time between coats. If you're applying conventional enamel, first break the glaze on the primer by scuffing it with crumpled kraft paper; then apply a light mist coat of paint. Allow the solvents in the mist coat to "flash off" (which takes about 15 min) before applying a second thicker coat.

Polyurethane enamel may be applied in the same manner as conventional enamels, except that a great deal of restraint must be exercised to keep from applying too much enamel. (Coverage will seem poor at first, tempting you to apply thicker coats than are necessary. Since polyurethane tends to flow long after it has been applied, the end result will be sagging or running.) The proper procedure is to apply thin coats until you feel that "just one more pass" will do the job; then stop. Within a day or two, the paint will flow out and cover all thin spots, much to your amazement.

Take appropriate safety precautions when working with paint. Wear eye and hand protection, and breathe through a filter mask. Work in a well-ventilated area, and do not smoke or create fire hazards. Bear in mind that most paints and wipe solvents are not only flammable, but highly toxic (and probably carcinogenic). Polyurethane spray mist is particularly noxious; it has sent many an inexperienced user to the hospital. Exposure to polyurethane mist for as little as 30 min causes some people to experience flu symptoms the following day.

One more thing: Regardless of the type of paint you use, be sure to follow the manufacturer's application instructions to the letter. No one knows the properties of a particular pigment/solvent/resin formulation better than the original manufacturer—not even the FAA.

WINDOW MAINTENANCE

The acrylic windows used in today's aircraft are strong, lightweight, and shatterproof. Even if a window is holed by flying objects, there is no danger of injury from flying glass. The one major disadvantage of acrylic windows is that they scratch easily. Thus, window maintenance consists in large part of preventing and repairing scratches.

Improper cleaning, without a doubt, results in more surface damage than all other causes combined. (Very few pilots—let alone gas-pump attendants—know how to clean a Plexiglas windshield properly.) There is only one way to clean a Plexiglas window without creating scratches, and that's to use plenty of water in combination with plenty of soft, clean cloths. *Flannel* cloths are preferable, although any soft cotton cloth will do. (*Note:* Cotton blends containing polyester or nylon are not acceptable.)

Always start by flushing the entire surface of the window several times with clean water before touching it with anything. Then, using a thoroughly wet cloth, wipe the surface gently, in short, straight strokes, while adding more water to flush away loosened dirt. If you wish, you may omit the cloth altogether, and simply use your fingertips to dislodge dirt and grime. But again, use copious amounts of water. Be sure to pay special attention to the edges of the window; dirt left in crevices around the edges will be picked up during waxing and polishing, thereby creating scratches.

Oil and grease spots may be removed using a cloth moistened with kerosene or Stoddard solvent. Neither of these solvents will damage Plexiglas. Under no circumstances, however, should you attempt to remove grease or grime with gasoline, alcohol, benzene, acetone, carbon tetrachloride, lacquer thinner, or ammonia-containing window sprays, since these materials will soften and craze acrylic windows (maybe not right away, but in several weeks' time).

After cleaning, wipe away excess water with a wet cloth; then allow the surface to air dry. *Do not rub the surface dry with a dry cloth.* This will (in addition to increasing the chance of scratching) build up an electrostatic charge that will attract dust particles to the surface like a magnet.

When the window is dry, you can and should apply a light coating of wax. Waxing imparts a high gloss, inhibits electrostatic buildup, and, more important, provides a protective coating that lessens the chance of scratching and makes future cleaning operations easier. (Bugs don't stick as well to wax as they do to bare plastic.) Any of the widely available aircraft window polishes will do a fine job here; however, ordinary supermarket-variety Pledge spray wax will do a perfectly satisfactory job too, at a much lower cost. (I use the regular, rather than the lemon-scented Pledge.) Never use a rubbing compound or automotive wax on an aircraft window, as these products usually contain large amounts of abrasives.

Properly washed and cared for, Plexiglas windows will give many years of scratch-free, crack-free service. Eventually, however, all airplane windows become nicked, pitted, and scratched in the course of normal ground operations as sand, carried by prop blast, impacts on the plastic. When this happens, the question becomes: What is the best way to *restore* Plexiglas to its original scratch-free condition?

The answers to this question vary quite a bit, depending on whom you ask. Cessna, in one of its manuals, recommends a polishing routine based on the use of successively finer grades of sandpaper followed by rotary-wheel buffing with fresh tallow. The FAA (in AC No. 43.13-1A, Chapter 9) suggests that scratches be rubbed out by hand, using a cloth dampened with a mixture of turpentine and chalk. Then, too, many mechanics have worked out successful routines based on the successive use of wet sandpaper, jeweler's rouge, and toothpaste. (It would not surprise me to learn that somebody has worked out a system based on ox bile and bone dust.)

Perhaps the most dependably successful system for restoring scratched Plexiglas is the "cushioned-abrasive" system used by commercial airlines and the military. In this system, an assortment of cloth-backed, ultrafine abrasive pads is used with or without a dilute soap solution, in conjunction with a soft-rubber block to rub out surface imperfections. Because the pads and block are very soft, they conform exactly to the shape of the surface being restored; thus, the ultrafine abrasive crystals in the pads, rather than simply abrading the surface, effect a smooth shaving action on the Plexiglas. The result is a very smooth finish indeed.

Cushioned-abrasive kits containing materials identical to those used by the airlines are marketed by Micro-Surface Finishing Products, Inc., Box 456, Wilton, IA 52778, under the name Micro-mesh. In the Micro-mesh system (Figure 7-7), anywhere from seven to nine color-coded and numbered grades of abrasive pads (the coarsest of which is much finer than any grade of sandpaper) are used to restore scratched surfaces. Each mesh creates its own distinctive "scratch pattern" on the plastic surface—a pattern that is gradually worn down by finer and finer meshes until, in the end, no pattern remains. After all scratches have been re-

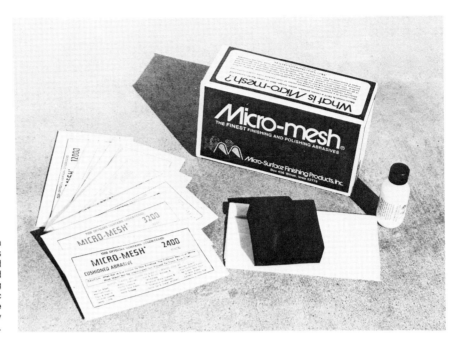

FIGURE 7-7 A Micro-mesh "cushioned abrasive" Plexiglas restoration kit containing assorted abrasive pads (in color-coded envelopes), foam-rubber rubbing block, a bottle of antistatic cream, and paper wipes. These materials are used by many airlines to restore plastic windows.

moved, a thin film of antistatic cream (supplied with each kit) is applied to remove any abraded particles held to the plastic surface by static.

The Micro-mesh system works well, not only on Plexiglas windows, but on landing-light lenses, watch crystals, and silverware. The method's principal drawback is that it is time-consuming: a half hour is needed to do one square foot of window area. (An orbital vibrator or buffing wheel can be used, but it will cause "fish hooks" in the plastic. The manufacturer recommends straight-line-motion hand rubbing to avoid this effect.) Nonetheless, when the choice is between spending several hours rubbing a window down by hand and spending several hundred dollars buying a new window, it's hard to complain about the technique—especially when the end result is so gratifying.

Of course, one thing that abrasive restoration won't do is repair deep stress cracks in Plexiglas. (When such cracks form under the surface of the plastic, it's known as *crazing*.) Cracks in Plexiglas windows can and should be stop-drilled in the same way as cracks in metal; however, such drilling should be considered a temporary measure only. The proper way to deal with a cracked window is to replace it.

Under present regulations, you may legally replace cockpit windows yourself, without the aid of a mechanic, so long as the windows are side windows and not part of the windshield. (See FAR Part 43, Appendix A.) In most cases, this is a fairly simple operation. Getting the old window out is usually just a matter of removing the surrounding upholstery panels, detaching the window retainer strips, and working the window from the frame. (A typical side window installation is

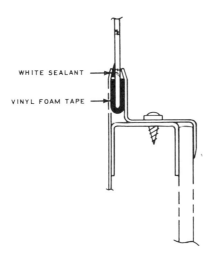

WHITE SEALANT

VINYL FOAM TAPE

FIGURE 7-8 Typical side-window
installation. (*Piper diagram.*)

shown in Figure 7-8). In some planes, the retainer strips are riveted in place,
which means that you'll have to drill out the rivets to remove them. Have a
mechanic walk you through this step if you feel nervous about drilling holes in
the fuselage.

Before installing the new window, check the pane's fit and, if necessary, grind
or file away any excess plastic around the edges. Most new Plexiglas windows come
from the factory with a paper or plastic film bound to the surface, to protect the
surface from scratching. You can remove some of this film around the edges if
need be, to facilitate mounting, but leave most of the film in place until the
installation is complete.

Be sure that any holes you make in the flange area of the new window are
significantly larger than the diameter of the screws or rivets you intend to use, to
allow for expansion and contraction of the plastic. Otherwise, dimensional changes
in the window will set up the kind of stresses that can later lead to crazing and
cracking. If you wish, you can melt rather than drill holes in the Plexiglas, using
a flame-heated punch of the appropriate size. (First make some practice holes in
the *old* window.)

Your aircraft service manual will tell you what kinds of gasket material or
sealants to use around the edges of the replacement window. Some commonly
used sealants are 3M EC-1202 tape, Behr-Manning 560 vinyl foam tape, and
Presstite 576. Any traces of old sealant remaining on the window frame should,
of course, be removed before you install the new window. A putty knife and an
MEK-dampened cloth will do the trick here, but be careful not to let the cloth
contact upholstery or paint.

After applying the proper new sealant to the edges of the new window, carefully
work the pane into place, beginning with an upper corner. Use clecos to hold the
window and retainer strips in place temporarily, if riveting is required. If riveting
is not required, simply screw the retainer strips down and you're finished (after
making the appropriate logbook entry, that is).

The periodic replacement of air and oil filters and the draining and replacing of old crankcase oil have become familiar routines to most automobile owners—so routine and so familiar, in fact, that a significant number of motorists could probably perform these procedures blindfolded and wearing a tuxedo, and emerge unsoiled.

Aircraft owners, alas, have not yet reached this level of maintenance consciousness. Even today, with shop rates at many airports climbing through $30 per hour, it is somewhat unusual to come across a pilot who does oil and filter changes; it's even more unusual to find a pilot who also regularly checks the sump screen and oil-filter elements for signs of metal. The pilot who routinely does all this and washes down the engine once a month is a rare bird indeed.

Of course, there is nothing wrong with paying a shop $50 (twice that for a twin) to change your oil and filters for you. But if someone else does the work, how do you *know* whether there were chunks of metal in the old oil filter? (Most shops lack the time or equipment to slice spin-on filters open to look for metal; old oil filters usually go straight into the garbage can.) How do you *know* whether the correct part number replacement filter was installed? (In some shops, it is common practice to replace the old oil filter with a new one just like it, perhaps perpetuating the use of an incorrect part number for months or years.) How do you *know* the new filter was torqued correctly, or that old gaskets were not reused? How do you *know* the correct grade of oil was put in the engine? (Do you really believe what invoices tell you?)

The only way to be really sure about any of these things, of course, is to do it yourself. And that's exactly what this chapter is designed to help you do.

EIGHT
OIL AND FILTERS

WASHING THE ENGINE

Because checking for oil leaks is (or should be) an essential test procedure following any oil or oil-filter change, and because oil leaks are almost impossible to detect on an engine that's generally grimy to begin with, the first bit of engine preventive maintenance you should undertake is a complete engine washdown. In addition to being a fire hazard, dirty engines make maintenance of any kind difficult. That's why the FAA requires a complete engine washing be performed in conjunction with every annual inspection. (See FAR Part 43, Appendix D.)

Step one in washing the engine is, of course, to get the cowling off—all the way off—and for some aircraft that is a whole chapter in itself. Most aircraft cowls are held on by quick-release fasteners (Dzus nuts, Camloc fasteners, wing nuts, etc.) and a handful or two of Phillips-head screws; be sure to put the screws in a safe place, and plan on replacing any rusty ones. With high-performance aircraft, it's usually also necessary to disconnect cowl flaps to remove the lower cowling. (Just take apart the clevis bolts, and, after the cowl flaps are free, put them back in place in the clevises, the nuts finger tight.) On some planes there are also a diabolically well hidden screw or two in the induction air box; these must be taken out with the aid of a contortionist before the lower cowl can be taken off. (Have someone walk you through all this the first time, if you're not that familiar with your plane.)

It should be mentioned that with some aircraft (Bonanzas, Cessna 310s), the lower cowl half is riveted in place and does not come off. Try not to let this bother you.

Step two in washing an engine is to cover up (with stout plastic bags, or plastic wrap and masking tape) all the engine's electrical accessories: the generator or alternator, the starter motor, and both magnetos. Generator brushes are treated with special lubricants that could well be washed away by engine cleaning solvents; likewise, a magneto's internal parts are usually waxed to prevent flashover, and unless the mag's vent holes are covered up, this protective wax layer could be dissolved during engine washing.

Once these two steps have been carried out, you may begin washing the engine down with solvent. Varsol and Stoddard solvent are the most frequently used solvents for this purpose. The easiest way to apply the solvent is to use a 2- or 3-gal pressurized garden sprayer, of the type used to spray weeds and insects. Put about a gallon and a half of solvent in the tank, pump up the tank pressure, and begin spraying the engine, working from top to bottom. (*Note:* Some people like to add a pint of Gunk, an emulsifying degreaser, to the cleaning solvent.) Try not to get too much solvent on windows or painted areas. While not immediately harmful, Varsol and Stoddard solvent should not be allowed to stand on Plexiglas or paint for long periods of time. Keep a rag handy to wipe up any overspray.

You'll notice that the solvent tends to evaporate rather rapidly. (Used on a hot engine, it could well *flash* rather than merely evaporate. To avoid creating a serious fire hazard, never wash an engine down with solvent while the engine is hot.) Rather than let the solvent evaporate, it's best to wash the solvent off, if possible, with warm water. Stoddard solvent, like kerosene, tends to leave a film when it evaporates.

If any particularly grimy areas remain unaffected by this cleaning procedure, reapply solvent, and attempt to dislodge the persistent grease and dirt with a bristle brush. *Do not use a wire brush.* Again, follow up with a water rinse.

During the final hosedown, be careful not to spray water directly into the engine's air intake, if the induction air filter is not in place. (This caution applies for all previous solvent rinses, too.) It's not really necessary to block off the air intake; just be careful where you aim your spray nozzle.

When you're finished rinsing, allow the engine to dry by evaporation; do not attempt to speed the drying process by starting the engine up, since this could result in a fire. Remove all plastic and tape from the magnetos, generator or alternator, and starter motor.

Before returning the plane to service or going on to perform other maintenance, take a moment to relubricate your throttle and prop governor control linkages and any other lubrication points that may have been affected by the solvent spray, in accordance with the recommendations given in the lubrication section of your aircraft service manual. If, as is often the case, your service manual doesn't specify any lubrication procedures to be followed after an engine washdown, simply apply a drop of lightweight engine oil (*new* oil, not dipstick oil) to exposed linkages wherever you find them. Also, wipe the propeller with a slightly oily rag, and give your cowling fasteners a shot of LPS #1 or WD40. This will help keep them from rusting up.

With your powerplant thus sanitized, you should have no trouble spotting and tracing the origins of oil leaks. You've lessened the chances of an engine fire developing or, once developed, spreading; you've made the engine easier to work on, because now you can see what you're doing, and your hands won't get black every time you touch something; and, to top it all off, the engine should now run cooler and smell cleaner. It's amazing what a gallon and a half of solvent can do!

HOW TO CHANGE YOUR OIL

Engine oil, like brake pucks, O rings, and spark plugs, wears out after so many hours of use. The engine-cleaning additives become saturated with contaminants, the antioxidant additives become oxidized, and even the oil molecules themselves (which start out as long, thin, spaghettilike entities) change with time, undergoing slow cleavage to shorter, less viscous molecules under prolonged exposure to high heat and pressure.

Of course, a good oil filter can, by removing all particles larger than 10 or 20 microns in diameter from the circulating oil, stave off some of these problems; that's why engine manufacturers recommend a longer oil-change interval for engines that are equipped with an oil filter. No oil filter, however, can effectively remove the lead oxides that are continually being supplied to the crankcase oil from piston blow-by—just as no oil filter can prevent the oil molecules themselves from shearing into smaller pieces at the piston ring–cylinder wall interface. Even the best of oil filters will eventually become clogged with impurities, so that the lead-laden crankcase oil must be replaced along with the oil filter.

How often should you plan on changing oil? The answer depends on many factors, including how often you fly, how effective your air filter is in keeping dirt out of the engine, how much lead is getting into your oil, the type of climate you're in (humid and dusty climates requiring more frequent oil changes), etc. Even the engine manufacturers will tell you that their oil-change guidelines are just that—guidelines. Your particular engine and operating conditions may demand oil-change intervals that are longer or shorter than the factory-recommended intervals (which are only based on average engines being flown under average operating conditions).

Avco Lycoming and Teledyne Continental both recommend that engines without oil filters (and believe it or not, there are plenty of brand new engines flying around without oil filters these days) have the crankcase oil replaced every 50 hours or less, depending on operating conditions. When the engine is equipped with a conventional full-flow oil filter, Avco Lycoming allows operators to adjust this oil-change interval upward by 25 to 100 percent, as long as the filter element is replaced every 50 hours. Similarly, Teledyne Continental recommends that its filter-equipped engines be transfused with new oil once every 100 hours, contingent upon the oil filter element being replaced every 50 hours. (However, when the filter is a king-size spin-on model, it need be replaced only once every 100 hours.)

Notice that there is no requirement to change crankcase oil and filter elements at the same time. There may be occasions on which you will change the oil filter but not the oil; and there may well be times when you'll want to change the oil but not the oil filter. Of course, it is nonetheless desirable, from the standpoint of convenience, to have filter replacements and oil changes coincide whenever possible.

You should also know that, although the engine manufacturers' oil-change recommendations are given in terms of hours of engine operation, it is never a good practice to go more than a few months between oil changes, regardless of how few hours you've flown during those months. (Oil tends to oxidize and form corrosive by-products when allowed to stand for weeks or months at a time.) Plan on changing your oil no less than once every 4 months, no matter what.

Before you actually set about changing your oil, you will, of course, want to consult your aircraft owner's manual or, better yet, the appropriate engine manufacturer's service bulletins, to determine what type of oil to use. (The engine makers' "approved lubricants" bulletins will be more up-to-date than your owner's manual with respect to the types and grades of oil currently available.) Unless you have reasons for doing otherwise, you'll probably want to choose an *ashless dispersant* (compounded) aviation oil of the appropriate viscosity grade for the range of ambient air temperatures you expect to encounter over the next 50 to 100 hr of flying. Straight (uncompounded) mineral oil should, because of its inferior antiwear, anticorrosion, antifoaming, and other properties, be avoided unless (1) your engine has been top- or major-overhauled within the past 50 hr or (2) your engine has been operating on straight mineral oil for several hundred hours. In the latter case, it is likely that considerable sludge has accumulated in the engine; a sudden switch to ashless dispersant oil could (owing to the oil's cleansing action) cause some of this sludge to come loose and possibly lodge inside one or more oil passages, with potentially disastrous results. Naturally, you'll want to follow the engine manufacturer's recommendations exactly when switching from mineral oil to ashless dispersant oil.

It goes without saying that *under absolutely no conditions can automotive oil be substituted for aviation oil*. Practically all automotive oils contain barium and calcium additives that can and will produce destructive preignition in aircraft engines.

If you've never changed your plane's oil before, the procedure itself is anti-climactically simple—simpler, even, than changing your car's oil. The first thing you'll want to do is start the engine and run it for 5 to 10 min on the ground or, better still, fly it around the traffic pattern. The purpose here is to get the oil warmed up, but not hot. Remember, you just want the oil to flow easily—you don't want to get burned. Next, you'll need to gain access to the oil-sump drain plug, which is a matter of removing a single access panel on some planes, and removing the entire lower cowl half on others. (Owners of single-engine Cessnas will find that, with a little practice, it's usually possible to get at the drain plug by unfastening one side of the lower cowl, prying the cowl back slightly, and reaching into the engine compartment carefully with one arm.)

Many engines (such as the 470-cu-in. Continentals) have two drain plugs, one on either side of the sump. Check both of them; usually, one will be of the quick-drain type. If your engine does not have a quick-drain sump valve, now's the time to get one. (Check with your FBO, or write Aircraft Spruce and Specialty Company, Box 424, Fullerton, CA 92632.)

If all else fails, have a mechanic show you where the oil drain point is on your engine. Once you've located it, put a 4-gal container under the plane, run a rubber or plastic hose from the container up to the sump drain plug, and either remove the drain bolt (if you don't have a quick drain) or push in on the drain valve and turn it so that it stays open. Allow about 10 min for the oil to drain.

That's one way to drain old oil out of an engine. Another, less troublesome way is to pump the oil out from above, using a hand-held cigarette-lighter-powered rotary oil extractor (such as those sold through J. C. Whitney and other automotive sources for about $20). Of course, before you can use one of these devices, you must make sure that the pump's oil suction hose is of small enough diameter to fit down your engine's oil dipstick hole; and you must make sure the suction hose is not blocked from reaching the low point in the engine's oil system. (Also, if your extractor requires 12-V direct current and your plane has a 24-V system, you'll want to plug the device into your car's cigarette lighter.) Providing these conditions are met, you should find the rotary extractor method to be a most pleasant and sanitary alternative to the drain-hose-bucket technique. With a little luck, you may even be able to suck a bit of sludge out of your sump this way.

Incidentally, not all planes have just one oil drain point. If you have a dry-sump engine, or if your oil cooler is mounted below sump level, you may find it necessary to drain old oil from both the sump and another, lower point. All the more reason to read your aircraft service manual (and/or consult a knowledgeable mechanic) before you get under way.

When all the oil has drained from your engine, replace the sump drain bolt and, after torquing it to manual specs, safety-wire it in such a manner that it cannot come loose. Or, simply twist and pull on the quick-drain valve to shut it. Likewise, secure any remaining drain points.

Used crankcase oil has few legitimate uses, so by all means dispose of your engine's drippings properly. The best thing to do is take it to an FBO or service station and combine it with their used oil. There's really no reason to keep the stuff around.

With all drain points secured and the old oil properly disposed of, you can begin adding fresh oil to the engine—assuming, of course, that you have already pulled and replaced the oil filter and/or the main oil screen, if you are going to. (If your engine requires further oil-system maintenance, stop and do it now, before adding new oil.)

Remember to maintain sanitary conditions while adding fresh oil to the engine. Use a clean spout or funnel, and wipe all the dust off the top of each new can of oil before opening it.

When you're done, check the oil dipstick to make doubly sure that the oil level is where it should be (everyone eventually makes the mistake of forgetting to secure the sump drain or some other drain point properly). Then run the engine on the ground for a few minutes, shut it down, and check for leaks. If none is found, you may at last make an entry in the engine logbook, stating the fact that on this date (state the date), at such and so a tach time (state the engine time), you drained the engine's oil, added 12 qt of Aeroshell W 40-weight oil (or whatever), ran the engine, checked for leaks, and found none (if that's what you found).

As much as you might be tempted to do so, don't put off this logbook entry till later. You might forget to make the entry altogether, or you might forget the tach time at which the oil was changed (in which case you won't be able to tell exactly when your *next* oil change is due). When it comes to making logbook entries of any kind, your motto should always be: Do it now.

OIL FILTERS AND SCREENS

Not all lightplane engines have oil filters. Sad to say, oil filters are, even in this enlightened day and age, offered as *optional* equipment on many aircraft piston engines. All conventional aircraft engines do, however, have either a full-flow oil filter or a removable oil screen (frequently *two* screens), or both.

Aircraft oil filters come in two basic types: the familiar automotive spin-on type, and another type that consists of a reusable can and lid enclosing a replaceable paper element (Figure 8-1). Both these filter types come in a short version and a long version. Which of the two versions your engine has depends, for the most part, on how much clearance exists between your engine's accessory case and the firewall. The manufacturers generally try to install long-version filters whenever possible, since these filters (owing to their larger size) offer greater filtration capacity and proportionally longer oil-change intervals than their smaller counterparts.

The filter types described above are often referred to as *full-flow* oil filters; this

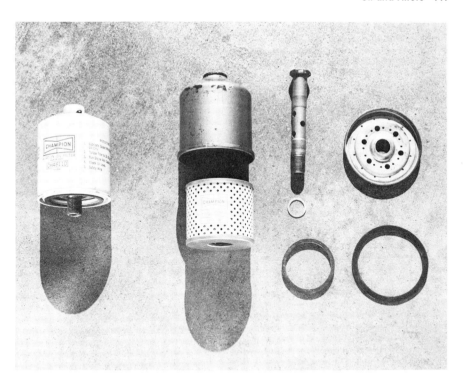

FIGURE 8-1 Spin-on aircraft oil filter (left), and cartridge-type "take apart" oil filter with associated gaskets (right).

is simply a short way of saying that the filter element is mounted in series with, and immediately downstream of, the engine oil pump, so that all circulating oil must go through the filter after it passes through the oil pump. (See Figure 8-2.) To guard against the possibility of oil starvation downstream of the filter in the event of filter clogging, all full-flow systems incorporate a pressure relief valve, either in the oil filter itself or in the filter mounting adapter, to allow oil to detour around the filter element under conditions of high oil pressure.

The alternative to the full-flow lubrication system is something known as a *bypass* filter system (Figure 8-3), in which the oil filter is mounted in parallel with the engine oil pump, rather than in series. In a typical bypass system, only about 10 percent of all oil coming from the oil pump gets diverted to the oil filter; the remainder of the oil goes directly to the engine's bearings and oil galleries. A chunk of metal or dirt thus might travel many times around the engine's oil system before being caught by the oil filter, in this system. Bypass systems are often used with special filters that tend to restrict flow and that, therefore, aren't well suited to use in a full-flow system. Very few aircraft engines employ bypass filtration of crankcase oil.

Before we get into the "how" of oil-filter maintenance, it's important to say a few words about oil *screens*. All present-generation aircraft piston engines have at least one main oil screen in the line leading from the oil sump, or oil tank, to the oil pump. It is a relatively coarse metal screen, designed to remove large

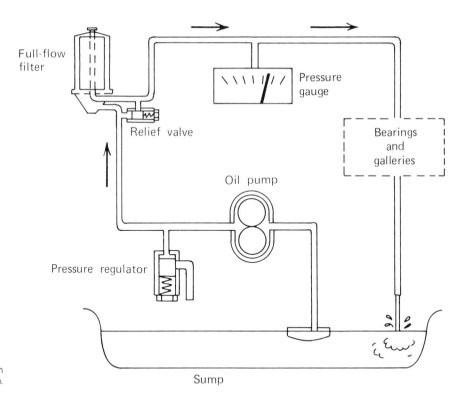

FIGURE 8-2 Full-flow lubrication system.

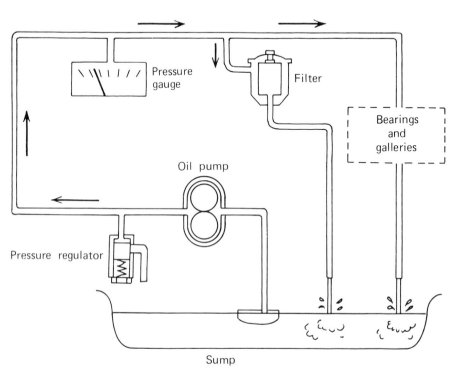

FIGURE 8-3 Bypass oil-filtration system.

impurities from circulating oil. This screen is called the *suction* screen, because it is located just upstream of the oil pump. On Lycoming engines, the suction screen is usually found at the bottom aft end of the oil sump, installed horizontally, although on a few models the screen is installed vertically, near the carburetor. (Have a mechanic point it out to you if there's any doubt in your mind where the suction screen on your engine is.) On most Continental engines, the suction screen is located deep inside the sump and does not come out for servicing, except at overhaul time. (An exception to this is the Continental O-300 series engine, which does have a removable, horizontally mounted suction screen.)

Along with the suction screen, most engines also have a *pressure* screen, located just downstream of the oil pump. The only engines that don't have a pressure screen are those that employ a full-flow oil filter (in which case the oil filter itself substitutes for the screen).

Depending on what type of engine you have, then, it's possible that you could have (1) a suction screen and a pressure screen, both removable for servicing; (2) a suction screen and a pressure screen, with only the latter removable; (3) a removable suction screen and a full-flow oil filter; or (4) a nonremovable suction screen and a full-flow oil filter.

In any case, if you do have a removable screen or screens, you should plan on inspecting and cleaning the screens at regular intervals, preferably at each oil change. If you have a full-flow oil filter, you should, as mentioned earlier, plan on replacing it at 50-hour intervals or however often your aircraft service manual suggests.

Servicing an oil screen (either suction or pressure) rarely takes more than a couple of minutes. Once you've let the oil drain out of your engine, simply cut the safety wire on the plug hex, noting, for future reference, exactly how the plug was wired to begin with. Unscrew the plug from the sump (or the engine accessory case, if it's a pressure screen), and carefully pull the plug straight out of the engine. A small, cylindrical screen will come out with the plug; this is what you're after.

Examine the screen thoroughly. In all likelihood, you'll see a few tiny slivers of metal, along with some carbon; this is normal. If the engine has been overhauled in the past 100 hours, it is not unusual to see as much as ¼ teaspoon of "sump solids" in the screen at each oil change. Some rules of thumb for categorizing—and determining the importance of—various types of oil-screen debris are given in Table 8-1. If you should discover a *lot* of metal in your oil screen, don't panic; but by all means do send the fragments to the engine manufacturer for analysis. Both Lycoming and Continental have their own metallurgical labs and are happy to analyze any screen trappings their customers care to send in.

After inspecting your oil screen, wash it in naphtha or Varsol, gasoline, etc., and dry it with compressed air. Then check the strainer cavity in the engine with your finger (to be sure there is no debris there) and replace the screen in the engine, using a new gasket. Your FBO should have plenty of these gaskets on hand. The screen should go almost all the way in, with finger pressure only. If

Table 8-1   Oil-screen and oil-filter particle-analysis guidelines

Type of contamination	Quantity	Suggested course of action
Small, shiny, nonmagnetic flakes of metal and/or hairlike magnetic slivers.	Fewer than 40 pieces (total)	Place aircraft back in service and recheck screen or filter after 25 hr.
As above.	40 to 60 pieces (total)	Clean screen, drain oil, refill. Run engine on ground for 20 to 30 min, then recheck screen. If clean, fly aircraft 1 to 2 hr and recheck again. If still clean, check once more after 10 hr.
As above.	½ teaspoon or more	Remove engine from service. Investigate to determine cause.
Chunks of metal, magnetic and nonmagnetic, the size of a broken lead-pencil point or greater.	Any quantity	Check sump for other pieces. Borescope cylinders to check for possible valve and/or ring and piston failure.
Nonmagnetic plating averaging approximately ¹⁄₁₆ in. in diameter. May have copperish tint.	¼ teaspoon or more	Ground aircraft and investigate. If cause cannot be found, mail particles to engine manufacturer for analysis.
Same as above, but minus copperish tint. Propeller action may be impaired.	¼ teaspoon or more	Ground aircraft. Mail material to engine manufacturer for analysis.
Nonmagnetic brass- or copper-colored material resembling coarse sand in consistency.	¼ teaspoon or more	Ground aircraft and investigate. If origin cannot be found, send particles to engine manufacturer for analysis..
Any piece of metal (of any kind) larger than a broken pencil point.	Any quantity	Ground aircraft and send particles to engine manufacturer for analysis.

you find you need a wrench to tighten it down immediately after starting the plug, the screen may be misaligned, and you should recheck it.

Finally, safety-wire the plug with MS20995-C41 lock wire. Be sure the wire wraps around the plug hex in a tightening direction, as explained in Chapter 3.

Changing an oil filter can either be quick and easy or unbelievably exasperating, depending on what kind of filter assembly you have (spin-on or can/stud/

NOTE

Do NOT substitute automotive gaskets
for any gaskets used in this assembly.
Use only approved gaskets listed in the
Parts Catalogs.

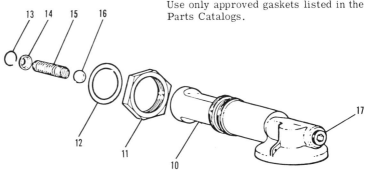

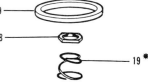

* Spring (19) used on earlier
filters only.

1. Stud
2. Metal Gasket
3. Safety Wire Tab
4. Can
5. Filter Element
6. Lower Gasket
7. Lid
8. Nut
9. Upper Gasket
10. Adapter
11. Adapter Nut
12. O-Ring
13. Snap Ring
14. Retaining Cap
15. Spring
16. Ball
17. Plug
18. Thread Insert
19. Spring

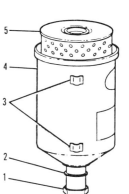

FIGURE 8-4 (Cessna diagram.)

cartridge), where it's located, and whether or not the filter is stuck. If you have an older-style can/stud/cartridge type of oil filter (Figure 8-4), replacement of the paper element can be accomplished as follows:

1. After gaining access to the filter assembly, remove all safety wire from the can and stud, noting (for future reference) how the wire was installed.

2. Unscrew the hollow stud, using a 1-in. open-end wrench or a socket wrench with a crow's-foot adapter. (It's a good idea to place an old coffee can under the filter at this point, to catch the drippings.) Remove the filter assembly from the mounting pad as a unit.

3. Invert the filter assembly. Discard the filter-to-engine gasket. Unscrew the nylon nut from the threaded end of the stud, and set the nut aside; then press downward on the end of the stud, pushing it out of the filter can.

4. Lift the lid or cap off the filter can, exposing the filter element. Throw away the gasket between lid and element.

5. Remove the old filter element from the can. (Don't throw it away yet; you'll want to open it up later to look for metal chips.)

6. Clean the stud, can, and lid in gasoline; then wipe them dry with a *clean* rag. Set the can in an upright position on a perfectly flat surface to check for distortion; if an out-of-flat condition greater than 0.010 in. exists at the rim, replace the can.

7. Lubricate the new copper washer, the two new rubber gaskets, and both ends of the replacement filter with *clean* engine oil. (Dry gaskets will cause erroneous torque readings in step 11.) Do not use any other lubricants.

8. Place the new element inside the can; place the new copper gasket on the stud; then insert the stud through the can and element.

9. Install the new gasket inside the flange of the lid. Place the lid carefully on the end of the can, and secure it there by screwing the nylon nut onto the stud until the nut contacts the lid. Use finger pressure only; the fiber nut is easily stripped if overtightened. Be sure the nut lies flush with (or slightly below) the lid's rim.

10. Install a new, oiled gasket on the outer surface of the lid. Inspect the mounting-pad gasket seat for gouges, deep scratches, etc. If surface imperfections are noted, consult a mechanic; replacement of the filter adapter (mounting pad) may be required.

11. Install the filter assembly on the adapter. (Rotate the can so that the safety-wire tabs are in the proper orientation for final rewiring.) Holding the can to prevent it from turning, tighten the stud to the torque specified on the side of the can or in the aircraft service manual.

12. Service the engine with the appropriate grade and amount of oil. Since the filter housing holds approximately 1 qt of oil, the engine will require at least one additional quart whenever the filter is changed.

13. Start the engine, and check for proper oil pressure. Allow the engine to warm up. Check for oil leakage at the lid–mounting pad junction and around the stud hex at the top of the filter housing. If leaks are evident, repeat steps 7 through 13, using fresh gaskets.

14. With the engine stopped, recheck the filter stud torque. Check the security of the adapter to the engine. If the adapter can be rotated by hand, disassemble it from the engine to check for damage.

15. Finally, safety-wire the stud to the can, and the can to the engine adapter, in accordance with service-manual recommendations, and make your log entry.

As you can see, the replacement of a can/stud/cartridge oil-filter element can hardly be considered a simple 5-minute affair. A great deal of time is spent assembling, disassembling, cleaning, and inspecting parts; and once the parts are put back on the engine, they must be checked rather carefully for leakage. (Cannister-type oil filters are well known, and widely cursed, for their ability to leak oil.) Little wonder that Detroit abandoned the use of take-apart filters on automobiles years ago.

Spin-on filters are removed and installed in much the same way on aircraft engines as on automobile engines; however, not all aviation spin-on filters are designed the same as automotive spin-ons. Aircraft spin-on filters come in long and short versions, with and without a male thread in the end, as well as with and without an internal bypass (pressure-relief) valve. Thus, it is extremely important that you obtain the correct part number spin-on filter for your plane's engine; not just any filter will do. (Consult the filter manufacturers' application charts and/or your aircraft parts manual prior to purchasing a replacement filter. Don't simply replace your existing filter with one just like it unless you *know* that the old one has the correct part number.)

Before removing your old spin-on filter from the engine, study the installation to see how the filter is safety-wired. Notice, in particular, where the wire attaches to the engine or the adapter. There's a good reason why the filter is wired the way it is, i.e., to a point on or near the engine itself: If it were wired to anything *not* directly attached to the engine, the violent shaking of the engine with respect to its surroundings during startup and shutdown would cause the safety wire to snap instantly.

Note, also, whether the filter is mounted in such a way that it points up, down, or straight out horizontally. If the filter is angled upward, you can count on its releasing about a quart of oil as you begin to remove it; consequently, you should plan on placing an old coffee can underneath the filter mounting pad to catch the spillage. If the filter is mounted horizontally, you can expect about half a quart of oil to come out as you begin unscrewing the filter. If the can is nearly inverted, most of the oil will, of course, stay in the filter, and you'll be able to keep things perfectly sanitary with a well-placed rag or two.

There's not much to say about the actual removal and installation of aircraft spin-on oil filters, except that if the filter is stuck to the mounting pad (as is often the case) you may well invent a few never-before-heard expletives before getting it off. Fortunately, most of the spin-on oil filters in use in aviation today incorporate a 1-in. steel hex on the top of the can, so that both a conventional wrench and an automotive-style oil-filter wrench can be used simultaneously to free a stuck filter—*if* access to the filter is good enough to permit the use of such implements. It is not unheard of for vacuum pumps and other accessories to have to be removed from the engine to allow sufficient access to the oil filter (Figure 8-5).

After you've removed the oil filter, it is a good idea —especially if the filter did not come off easily—to inspect both the filter and the mounting adapter to see that the male-threaded stud is in good shape and in its proper location. Male-threaded filters (such as the Champion CH48110) have been known to leave their studs in the mounting adapter upon removal, and the reverse has happened with female-threaded filters. In either case, the stud should be returned to its original location, if there is no damage to the threads.

To prevent sticking of the new filter, prelubricate its gasket, not with engine oil (as is usually done), but with Dow Corning DC-4 compound, applied sparingly but evenly. Unlike engine oil, DC-4 will not break down at high operating temperatures, thus cementing the filter to the pad. Champion specifically approves the use of Dow Corning DC-4 as an "antistick" agent for spin-on filters; however, Champion recommends that this compound not be used on the gaskets that accompany take-apart filters.

FIGURE 8-5 Aircraft oil filters are famous for their lack of easy access. This one (mounted at the rear of a Continental IO-520) is wedged so tightly beneath the vacuum pump (top, center) that wrench access to the hex at the top of the filter is almost impossible. Note that, because the filter is upright, a good deal of oil spillage can be expected when and if the filter ever comes off. The owner of this engine would be well advised to use a *short-reach* filter next time.

To install a new spin-on filter, simply lubricate the filter gasket (as explained above), wipe the mounting adapter surface with a clean rag, screw the new filter on by hand until the gasket contacts the mounting adapter, and then torque the filter to 18 ft-lb (or to the torque limit given in the instructions that came with the filter). In any case, *do not tighten the filter more than 1¾ turns after the gasket has contacted the mounting pad.* If you do, you may never get it off again.

Finally, run the engine a few minutes, check for leaks, and safety-wire the filter in place. (Don't forget to add an additional quart of oil to the engine, if need be.) That's all there is to it.

Obviously, the replacement of a spin-on oil filter entails considerably fewer steps (and thus offers significantly less opportunity for error) than the replacement of a can/stud/cartridge filter. For this reason alone, any aircraft owner-operator who intends to perform oil-filter changes on a regular basis ought to convert over to spin-on filters as soon as possible, if the aircraft does not already use spin-on filters. Some spin-on filters can be applied as direct replacements for some take-apart filters; it's possible you can switch over without buying any new mounting hardware at all. Even if your engine has no oil filter at all, though, you can have the engine converted to spin-on filter use for only about $35. It's worth it.

It should be mentioned that spin-on filters are not only easier to install than their can/stud/cartridge counterparts, but are less apt to leak, and they weigh about a pound less, thus contributing to reliability. (Any weight reduction on a right-angle adapter of any kind increases its reliability.) When it comes to simplicity, reliability, and ease of maintenance, spin-on filters are without peer.

Regardless of whether you are replacing spin-on-type filters or disposable paper elements, it is important that you save the old element at each filter change and open it up for closer examination, to determine whether your engine is shedding metal. What shows up in the filter may not show up in oil analysis (see below), and vice versa. Auto-parts stores often sell "can cutters" for spin-on filters at a cost of a few dollars; plan on getting one soon. Cartridge-type filter elements can be autopsied relatively easily with the aid of a stout knife. Use Table 8-1 as a guide for evaluating the contents of your oil filter element, as well as your oil screens.

OIL ANALYSIS   When you stop and think about it, blind adherence to a strict once-every 50 hours (or even 25 hours) oil-change schedule really offers no assurance at all that your engine is receiving optimum lubrication and, thus, optimum protection against rapid wear. In some engines, the crankcase oil becomes heavily contaminated with lead, carbon, dirt, and metallic wear particles within only a few hours after an oil change; in other engines, the oil may still be clear and relatively uncontaminated 100 hours after the last oil change. Obviously, in the former case it would be imprudent to go 50 or 100 hours between oil changes, whereas in the latter case an oil-drain interval of 50 hours would be exceedingly wasteful of time, money, and oil.

Each aircraft engine differs in its ability to pollute crankcase oil (according to operating conditions, the age of the engine, the efficiency of the air and oil filters, and many other factors). Thus, the ideal way to plan one's oil changes would be to monitor the actual contamination level of the crankcase oil, and change the oil when the level of contamination became excessive—no sooner, no later. Happily, it is possible to do just that, at a very nominal cost, using something known as *spectrometric oil analysis*.

The physical explanation of spectrometric analysis is somewhat complicated; we shall not go into the physics of the process here. Suffice it to say that with the aid of a device known as an *emission spectrometer* it is possible to determine (with part-per-million accuracy) the actual concentrations of various types of contaminants in a given sample of oil. Some contaminants of particular interest that can be detected and accurately measured by this technique are:

Iron (Fe) An indicator of cylinder-wall wear in engines with ordinary steel or nitrided steel cylinders.

Chromium (Cr) Produced through piston-ring wear in engines with steel cylinders, or cylinder-wall wear in engines with chrome-lined jugs.

Aluminum (Al) Primarily an indicator of piston wear, since all aircraft reciprocating engines employ aluminum pistons (and since there are no other large, aluminum moving parts in an aircraft engine).

Copper (Cu) Produced through valve-guide and bearing wear.

Lead (Pb) Produced mainly through combustion blow-by.

Silicon (Si) A principal component of all dirt. A high silicon count literally indicates dirty oil.

As you can well appreciate, spectrum analysis has potentially enormous value as a preventive maintenance tool. It not only tells you when and to what degree your oil has become contaminated with dirt, wear particles, etc., but it also tells you which parts of your engine are wearing out, and how fast. Many fleet operators (not only of aircraft, but of buses, trucks, and construction equipment) swear by the technique, claiming it allows them to optimize oil-change intervals (thus increasing uptime) and to detect potentially serious engine problems in their early stages, well before expensive repairs are needed. If an engine's bearings are wearing rapidly, say, it'll generally show up in oil analysis reports well before anything appears in the oil screens.

As good as oil analysis might sound, however, you should know that the technique is subject to a number of important caveats. First, it should be remembered that while wear-related problems are nearly always revealed by oil analysis, fatigue-related problems usually aren't. You could be flying with a crankshaft or a crankcase or a cylinder that's on the verge of cracking, and never see the slightest indication of any problem in your oil analysis reports.

Also, oil analysis is very sensitive to operator technique where sample taking is concerned. Results will vary considerably, depending on the type of apparatus used to collect the oil sample, the temperature of the oil at sample-taking time, and where in the sump the oil came from. (Bottom-of-the-sump oil, the first oil to come out of the engine when the sump drain is opened, tends to be rich in impurities.)

Still another of the technique's limitations is that it cannot be relied upon to give truly meaningful results until a data baseline, consisting of several oil analyses made over a 100- to 200-hr period, has been established for the engine in question. A one-shot oil analysis yields virtually no useful information. To get a reliable picture of the engine's state of health, you need the whole movie—not just one frame.

Still, in spite of its limitations, oil analysis represents a tremendously powerful diagnostic tool for the maintenance-conscious lightplane owner. Certainly, it's something to consider if you have any doubts at all about the state of health of your plane's engine.

For more information on spectrometric oil analysis, contact your nearest repair shop, or write to one of these labs:

Cleveland Technical Center, 13600 Deise Ave., Cleveland, OH 44110

Spectro, P.O. Box 16526, Fort Worth, TX 76133

Wear-Check, 87 Walton St., Atlanta, GA 30303

AIR-FILTER MAINTENANCE

Avco Lycoming has estimated that as little as one tablespoon of dirt, if allowed to enter an engine, will "cause wear to the extent that an overhaul will be required." Hence the need for frequent air-filter maintenance.

Most of us have grown accustomed to having mechanics do our air-filter servicing at 100-hour or annual inspections. Unfortunately, that's not good enough. Check your aircraft service manual, and you'll probably find that inspection of the induction air filter should be performed once every 50 hr or less, which means that if you fly 300 hr per year, your air filter should be serviced an average of once every other month. Read more closely, and you'll probably find that under dusty conditions, *daily servicing* of the air filter is recommended.

The first step in servicing an air filter, of course, is to remove it from the aircraft. Unfortunately, most aircraft service manuals do not tell you how to do this; they merely say, "Remove filter from aircraft." Some filters can be removed quite easily by turning several quick-disconnect fasteners at the front of the cowl; this is true for most single-engine Cessnas, for example. Other installations demand more patience. To remove the air filter from a Mooney M20C, it is necessary to take no less than 23 sheet-metal screws out of the cowling, and 4 machine screws out of the filter assembly itself. Getting the filter out of a pre-1964 Cherokee requires that you reach into the cowling *behind* the filter and disconnect the landing light before actually sliding the element out. With installations like these, is it any wonder that pilots often tend to neglect their air filters?

Once you've managed to remove the filter from the aircraft (perhaps with the aid of a knowledgeable mechanic), servicing it is a simple matter of following the instructions printed on the side of the unit. (Like oleo struts, air filters generally carry a decal or placard somewhere on them describing, in brief outline form, the relevant servicing procedures. See Figure 8-6.) Start by giving the element a thorough visual examination, paying particular attention to edges and corners. Obviously, if any holes or tears are evident, you won't want to waste time cleaning the filter. Buy a new one. And until the new one comes, keep your induction airbox blocked off to prevent dirt from entering it.

Some paper elements can be washed and/or blown out with compressed air; others can neither be washed nor blown out. If your filter falls into the latter category (check the instructions on the filter, or look in your aircraft service manual), simply tap the filter against a hard, flat surface to remove loose dirt. Wipe the filter housing with a clean cloth soaked in Stoddard solvent, check the gasket (if any) on the rear of the filter frame for damage, and inspect the induction airbox for debris such as dirt, paint chips, or bits of gasket material. Then reinstall the filter.

If your filter has a dry-type, washable element (again, check the filter decal or look in your service manual), either blow the filter clean with compressed air if it does not appear to be very dirty, or plan on washing it. To prevent damage to the element during compressed-air cleaning, use an air pressure of 100 psi or less, and keep the nozzle at least 2 in. away from the filter at all times. Blow in the direction opposite normal air flow, i.e., opposite the direction of the arrows on the sides of the filter frame.

To wash a dry-type filter, simply drop it in a bucket of detergent and water. Use only a mild household detergent, and don't use much. Let the filter soak for

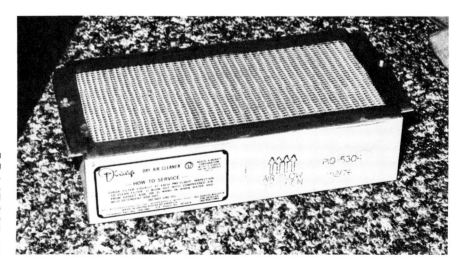

FIGURE 8-6 All air filters carry a decal or placard giving abbreviated servicing instructions. Most also have arrows on the side, as shown, to indicate normal airflow direction. Dry-type Donaldson air filters of the type shown here are standard equipment on most new aircraft. (This one is from a V35 Bonanza.)

FIGURE 8-7 Urethane foam filters (such as this one, installed on a Cessna 172) are becoming increasingly popular, owing to their high filtering efficiency and ease of maintenance. The metal mounting frame swings open at the front, allowing the operator to replace the foam element (which is usually quite inexpensive) with a minimum of downtime.

10 minutes or so; then agitate it back and forth for about 2 minutes to dislodge dirt deposits. Afterward, rinse the filter in clear water until the rinse water is clean, and then set the unit in a dust-free area to dry. (The element may become slightly distorted when wet, but don't let this bother you. It should return to its normal shape after it dries.) You may place the filter in a drying oven (180°F maximum) to speed the drying process. However, *do not* place the element directly over (or near) a light bulb; distortion of the element could result.

If your filter is of the flocked, wetted kind, wash it thoroughly in Stoddard solvent, allow it to air dry, and, once it is dry, dip it in clean SAE 50 engine oil. Allow the excess oil to drain off, and then reinstall the filter on the aircraft.

Until recently, nearly all light aircraft were equipped with either a dry-type paper air filter or a flocked, wetted filter. Within the past few years, however, a fairly large number of aircraft have been converted over to wetted urethane foam filters of the type developed by General Motors' AC Spark Plug Division and marketed by Brackett Aircraft Specialties (Figure 8-7). This filter, which was originally designed to increase the service life of helicopter engines in Vietnam, offers two main advantages over pleated-paper-type filters for airplane use: (1) Wetted foam is a more efficient filtering medium than paper; helicopter engine life is said to have tripled when foam filters came on the scene in Vietnam. (2) Servicing is much easier. Unlike paper filters, the foam filters sold by Brackett Aircraft Specialties (the STC holder) employ a permanently mounted metal frame that, regardless of cowling design, opens easily at the front to allow access to the replaceable element. This, and the fact that the throw-away foam elements cost less than half what ordinary paper-and-frame filters cost, has made the urethane foam filter exceedingly popular among maintenance-conscious owner-pilots and fleet operators everywhere.

Some day, you may want to convert your plane to urethane foam, if it is not using a foam-type air filter already. Until then, though, keep the following air-filter do's and don'ts in mind:

1. Do not wash a dry-type paper filter in solvent. Do use a mild detergent and water. Only wet-type (i.e., oiled) filters may be washed in solvent.

2. Do not wash a dry-type paper filter more than 10 times, nor blow it out with compressed air more than 30 times. When these limits have been reached, replace the filter.

3. Always reinspect a filter for signs of damage after washing or compressed-air cleaning. Elements are especially prone to damage when wet; and compressed air, improperly used, can ruin a filter.

4. Do not replace a filter on the aircraft if the filter-to-airbox gasket is in any way defective. Also, do not reinstall a filter until any paint chips, dirt, etc., that might have accumulated around the airbox opening have been removed.

5. Do not operate with a dirty air filter. Check the filter for dirt and damage before every flight; service no less than once every 50 hr. Replace the filter at least once a year.

Naturally, these rules are intended to supplement—not substitute for—the advice given in your aircraft service manual. So before you actually undertake any air-filter maintenance, be sure to read the applicable parts of your service manual. Otherwise, your work may not be legal—or safe.

FUEL SCREENS   As you might guess, aircraft engine designers, ever mindful of the effects of dirt and grit on an engine's moving parts, have taken precautions against the entry of contaminants into lightplane engines, not only via the air and oil, but also via the fuel. If you study the fuel system diagrams in your aircraft service manual, you'll notice that strainers, filters, and dirt traps dot the entire length of your fuel system, from the fuel tanks (where finger strainers are used to keep large bits of debris out of the gas lines) to the carburetor or fuel injector (where a fuel inlet screen, similar to, but larger than, the type found in automotive carburetors, is used).

Technically speaking, FAR Part 43 (Appendix A) allows you to clean all the screens in your plane's fuel system if you wish. In practicality, though, there are really only two screens worth looking at: the main fuel strainer (located at the lowest point in the fuel system) and the fuel inlet screen (in the carburetor or fuel injector).

Fuel strainers vary in design quite a bit from plane to plane, so obviously I cannot tell you exactly how to service your main fuel strainer. Lest you go away

FIGURE 8-8 Typical fuel-strainer installation. (*Cessna diagram.*)

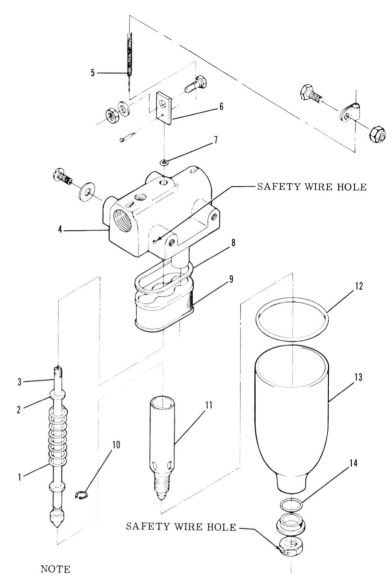

SAFETY WIRE HOLE

SAFETY WIRE HOLE

NOTE

Fuel strainers vary in methods of mounting and
strainer drain controls vary in routing for the
different models. On some models, a drain tube
is attached to standpipe (11) to drain fuel overboard.

1. Spring
2. Washer
3. Plunger
4. Top Assembly
5. Drain Control

6. Plate
7. O-Ring
8. Gasket
9. Filter

10. Retainer
11. Standpipe
12. O-Ring
13. Bowl
14. O-Ring

with the idea that cleaning a gascolator-type strainer is in the least bit difficult, however, I urge you to look at Figure 8-8, which shows a fairly typical fuel-strainer installation. To service a strainer of this type, it is merely necessary to do the following:

1. Turn the cockpit fuel selector valve to "off," and drain the strainer by pulling on the drain knob.

2. Clip the safety wire on the nut at the bottom of the strainer assembly; remove the nut and step washer from the bottom of the bowl. Also remove the bowl itself.

3. Carefully unscrew the standpipe and remove the filter screen and gasket.

4. Wash the filter screen and bowl in Stoddard solvent or its equivalent. Dry both with compressed air.

5. Using a new gasket atop the screen, reinstall the screen and standpipe. (Install the standpipe finger tight.)

6. Reinstall the bowl, step washer, and nut using new O rings.

7. Turn the fuel selector back to the "on" position. Open and close the strainer drain, and check for leaks. If none is found, safety-wire the bottom nut to the hole in the top assembly.

Servicing the fuel inlet screen in the carburetor or fuel injector requires a bit more finesse; unless you've done it before, you should arrange to have a qualified technician show you exactly where your inlet screen is and how to get at it. (Your aircraft service manual will not be of much help here.) Basically, you'll start by turning the cockpit fuel selector to "off" and then disconnecting the fuel line to the carburetor. Next, you'll unscrew the hex plug at the end of the screen and carefully remove the screen from the carburetor or injector; then you'll wash the screen in acetone, dry it with compressed air, and reinstall it in the carburetor or injector, using a new gasket. Afterward, you'll reconnect the fuel line using the thread lubricant and torque value recommended by the airframe manufacturer, turn the fuel selector back to "on," energize the engine's boost pump (if it has one), and check for leaks. (If a leak exists, do not attempt to correct it by over-tightening the fuel inlet connections; instead, suspect a bad gasket.) Finally, you'll safety-wire the inlet connection as per the advice of your mechanic.

Most aircraft service manuals advise that a check of the fuel inlet screen be made every 50 hr. If you aren't already performing this procedure yourself, plan on doing it in the future. Don't assume that it'll get done during your next 100-hr or annual inspection; this check is often overlooked at annual time. In an airplane—much more so than in an automobile—a clogged fuel inlet filter can ruin your whole day.

Automotive ignitions systems, as everyone now knows, have achieved a high degree of refinement in recent years. Today, thanks to solid-state electronic ignition, advances in spark-plug design, and an almost total switch to lead-free fuels, the average car owner can expect to get 30,000 to 40,000 miles between spark-plug changes (with perhaps only two or three gap adjustments and cleanings in the interim). Some motorists will go even longer on a set of plugs, without the slightest hesitation or concern.

Unfortunately, this somewhat relaxed attitude toward spark-plug maintenance has, to a great extent, carried over into the aviation sphere. Pilots have come to regard as axiomatic the idea that the spark plugs in an airplane, if serviced once a year by a mechanic at annual-inspection time, can be relied upon to perform flawlessly year round, without any maintenance on the operator's part. Pilots, in other words, have come to expect automotive spark-plug performance from aircraft spark plugs—a not entirely reasonable expectation.

The fact of the matter is, aircraft spark plugs need rather more frequent looking after than automotive plugs if they are to perform reliably and live to a ripe old age. Aircraft spark plugs are exposed to a much wider range of fuel-air mixtures than their automotive counterparts, just as they are also exposed to a great deal more lead (from leaded avgas) and oil (from seepage past piston rings and valves, the clearances in these areas being somewhat greater for air-cooled engines than for water-cooled ones). Thus, aircraft spark plugs are more prone to carbon, lead, and oil fouling than automotive spark plugs. Aircraft plugs are also, by virtue of their unique application, exposed to fewer of the kinds of abrupt power changes that could normally be expected (in a car engine) to thermally "shock" lead deposits away; thus, once formed, such deposits are very persistent. This, and the fact that spark gap is critical to optimum plug performance in a magneto-type ignition system (as opposed to an electronic ignition system, which can tolerate large gaps fairly well), make frequent spark-plug maintenance essential for light aircraft.

HOW OFTEN SHOULD SPARK PLUGS BE SERVICED?

Many aircraft service manuals list cleaning, gapping, and rotation of spark plugs as something to be performed every 100 hours or at annual-inspection time, whichever comes first. However, for some engines—perhaps the majority of aircraft

NINE
SPARK PLUGS

engines—this is not enough. One plug rotation every 100 hours may be fine for air-taxi operators who log that many hours in a month, or for people who fly brand-new engines equipped with platinum-iridium plugs. But for the rest of us, a plug maintenance schedule based on one inspection and rotation every 50 hours (or less, if fouling is experienced) makes more sense.

Let us not forget just why it is that spark plugs need to be pulled periodically in the first place. There are three basic reasons:

1. Electrode gaps tend to grow over time, owing to the constant arcing between the electrodes and the generally corrosive conditions prevalent in the combustion chamber. As the electrodes erode and the gap between them enlarges, ever-higher voltages are required to induce sparking; thus, the chance of connector-well flashover increases. Also, hard starting becomes a problem. The only answer is to regap the electrodes. Exactly how often you will have to do this is something only you can determine; the rate of gap growth varies greatly from plane to plane. But the point is, you *will* need to regap your plugs periodically, and it is better to check plug gaps too often than too infrequently.

2. Lead, oil, and carbon fouling of the electrodes can become serious problems (particularly on bottom-hole plugs) within a very short period of time on some engines under certain operational conditions. To avoid the possibility of misfiring, preignition, etc. (and subsequent engine damage), it is essential that such electrode deposits be removed periodically. What's more, it is important for long plug life to catch lead buildup in its early stages, since advanced lead fouling is often ineradicable.

3. To achieve long spark-plug life, it is important that plugs periodically be rotated top to bottom (and vice versa) in firing sequence on the engine, to prevent abnormal electrode wear caused by constant-polarity discharge. In case you didn't know it, every ignition lead coming from a given magneto fires with an electrical polarity opposite that of the lead firing before or after it. For any given ignition lead, the polarity stays constant; over time, this causes asymmetric electrode wear. If a plug fires repeatedly with positive polarity, the ground electrodes wear faster than the center electrode; conversely, if a plug always fires negatively, the center electrode tends to wear rapidly. To achieve balanced electrode wear and optimum electrode life, it is necessary to rotate the spark plugs on the ignition leads of each magneto at regular intervals. This can usually (but not always) be accomplished simply by rotating plugs between top and bottom holes and between even- and odd-numbered cylinders.

There are other reasons, of course, for periodically removing the plugs from your engine (such as to inspect the plugs for serious damage, signs of flashover, etc.), but the foregoing considerations are paramount in importance. If any of your plugs are beginning to crumble apart or short out, you'll know about it in short order. But the only way you are going to find out if your plugs' electrodes are wearing abnormally, or whether oil fouling is beginning to be a problem in cylinder number three (indicating incipient ring and/or valve problems), or whether lead oxide deposits are threatening to take 50 hr off the life of your plugs, is to pull and inspect (and then clean, gap, and rotate) your igniters religiously every 50 hours— or even more often if conditions warrant.

SPARK-PLUG REMOVAL

Removing spark plugs from an aircraft engine is neither difficult nor unsafe (even for a beginner), as long as certain rules are followed, and as long as the proper tools are used (see Chapter 2). You'll want to start, of course, by removing as much of the cowling as necessary to gain access to all the plugs. Next, simply walk up to a plug and use a ¾- or ⅞-in. open-end wrench or an adjustable-end wrench to begin loosening the terminal nut at the top of the plug.

Incidentally, if you find that a ⅞-in. wrench does the job here, it means that you have all-weather ignition leads and plugs, so called because the plugs' shielding barrels have been designed to accept a resilient grommet that forms a watertight seal to keep moisture out of the barrel. All-weather plugs have ¾-in.-diameter barrel threads with a pitch of 20 turns per inch, and a hex diameter of ⅞ in. If you find that the terminal hex on each plug takes a ¾-in. wrench, it means your spark plugs' barrel threads are of the ⅝-in.–24 variety and your ignition leads are of the older, nonleakproof type. (Have non-all-weather leads converted over to all-weather leads at your next engine overhaul.)

All right. Once you've got the terminal hex started, hold the ignition elbow steady with one hand (Figure 9-1) to prevent it from twisting while you loosen the terminal nut with your other hand. Then, very carefully so as not to exert side pressure against the cigarette, pull the lead assembly straight out of the shielding

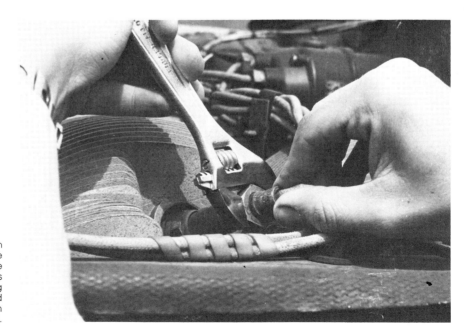

FIGURE 9-1 The first step in removing a spark plug (once access has been gained to the plug) is to loosen the plug's terminal hex. While this is being done, the ignition elbow should be grasped and prevented from turning.

barrel. Try not to touch the spring or cigarette with your fingers; the salts on your skin are highly conductive and could (if deposited on the terminal-sleeve assembly) cause a short circuit to ground.

If you encounter difficulty in getting the all-weather-type cigarette to pull out, twist it slightly as if to unscrew it. The seal should break easily.

To remove the spark plug, place your deep socket on the plug, being sure it is completely bottomed on the plug hex. Attach a long handle (the longer, the better) to the socket, steadying the socket with one hand to prevent it from cocking over and damaging the plug, and apply pressure to the wrench handle. (*Note:* Do not use a torque wrench for this step. The extreme forces that are usually necessary to unscrew a plug will throw the wrench's calibration off.)

When the plug has begun to rotate freely, remove the wrench handle and continue to unscrew the socket by hand. As you reach the last couple of threads, carefully withdraw the socket and grab the plug in your hand, being very careful not to let the plug fall to the ground. *If you drop a plug, throw it away.* A dropped plug, even if it is not already cracked, may fail in flight later; it cannot be reused.

Place the free plug upright in a plug tray or some other safe place; note its cylinder number and position. Continue removing plugs in this manner until you have removed all the spark plugs you intend to work on.

THE PRELIMINARY INSPECTION

Obviously, you won't want to waste time cleaning and gapping any plugs that are too worn out or damaged to be reused, so now's a good time to stop and give all your plugs a thorough preliminary inspection for wear and damage. Inspect all threads for damage; the shell hex for rounded corners or other signs of mutilation;

FIGURE 9-2 This plug (a Champion RHB32E) is worn beyond limits; the electrodes have eroded to 50 percent of their original size. (Notice the characteristic "football" shape of the center electrode.) The sooty appearance of the center ceramic suggests carbon fouling due to overly rich operation.

the center-electrode ceramic for signs of chipping or cracking; the firing ends for severe damage (e.g., copper runout); and the electrodes for severe wear. Any of these conditions should be considered cause for retirement of the plug in question, with the exception of thread damage, which, if minor, can be repaired by an A&P.

Should any electrodes be found missing, or if copper runout is evident at the center electrode, you should tentatively assume that preignition and/or detonation has occurred in the cylinder from which the plug came. Quite possibly, you're looking a top overhaul in the face. Have a mechanic examine the cylinder with a borescope.

How worn must the electrodes be before you have to toss a well-used but otherwise sound plug into the garbage? According to the spark-plug manufacturers, a plug should be retired from service any time the ground or the center electrodes wear to 50 percent or less of their original thickness. (This holds for fine-wire as well as massive-electrode plugs.) Generally speaking, when a massive center electrode goes out of round by 0.030 in. or more, you can be sure the plug is shot. (Refer to Figure 9-2.)

WHAT PLUGS TELL YOU ABOUT ENGINE WELL-BEING

It has rightly been said that the firing ends of a set of spark plugs can tell you as much or more about the health of an engine as any other single item or observation. This being the case, you'll probably want to stop at this point, and arrange your plugs in a tray by cylinder (and by cylinder position: top or bottom), so you can get a clear picture of how healthy your engine is.

The first thing to check for is uniformity among the plugs. The firing ends should all have more or less the same light brown or grayish color, with no sriking differences between top and bottom (or odd- and even-numbered) plugs. As a rule, bottom plugs will tend to be a bit "wetter" (i.e., oilier) than top plugs; this is normal. On any fairly new engine, however, all the plugs—even the bottom-hole plugs—should be dry.

Any plugs that look markedly different from their neighbors could be a sign of problems. For example, if one pair of plugs from the same jug were to have a powdery, whitish appearance compared to all the other plugs, you would have evidence of a lean-running cylinder (perhaps the result of an induction-air leak, or a plugged injector nozzle). If, on the other hand, all your even-numbered plugs were to exhibit this whitish appearance, you would know that one side of your engine is running leaner than the other side. If *all* of your plugs are clean and white, you've been running your engine a bit on the lean side; quite possibly, your carburetor or fuel injector needs adjustment.

Suppose the plugs from one cylinder, or perhaps one bank of cylinders, are not white, but sooty black in appearance. This is carbon fouling, and it indicates that the cylinders in question are running overly rich. Such fouling, if it occurs uniformly on all plugs, can be eliminated by the proper use of the mixture control, both on the ground and in the air. Quite often, it indicates an overly rich idle-mixture setting, which should be readjusted by a mechanic.

FIGURE 9-3 Moderate electrode wear and fairly severe oil fouling are evident on this massive-electrode Champion. The presence of this much oil on a plug means that crankcase oil is finding its way into the combustion chamber, via either worn rings (and/or worn cylinder walls) or leaky valve guides.

As mentioned above, a certain amount of oil on an engine's bottom plugs (especially if the engine is more than 50 percent of the way toward its next major overhaul) is considered normal. Oil on an engine's top plugs, however, is a sign of trouble. Generally, it means advanced ring and/or cylinder-wall wear. (If you are considering buying an airplane whose engine is at or near its TBO, pull all the top plugs after your first demo ride; they'll tell you the whole story, as far as engine wear is concerned.) If oil consumption is on the high side, the top plugs are wet and cylinder compression isn't what it used to be, an overhaul is just around the corner.

Some of the types of firing-end problems mentioned above are depicted in Figures 9-2 to 9-4. If your plugs don't appear to fall into any of these categories with regard to electrode deposits, or if you're just not sure whether they're normal in appearance, by all means show them to a mechanic.

SPARK-PLUG CLEANING

If your plugs pass their preliminary inspection for wear and damage, you'll want to subject them to a thorough cleaning regimen before checking their gaps and reinstalling them in the engine. However, if the plugs are already dirt- and deposit-free, you can skip this step. Only after your plugs have been thoroughly cleaned can their electrodes (which may be partially worn away by the cleaning process) be gapped, and the plugs themselves subjected to electrical testing.

First things first: If the firing ends of your plugs look at all greasy or oily, wash the ends off with Varsol, Stoddard solvent, unleaded gasoline, or dry-cleaner's naphtha. The accepted procedure is to place the plugs in a tray, firing ends down, set the tray in a container filled 2 in. deep with solvent, and then remove the plugs

FIGURE 9-4 The gray-white or "ashen" appearance of this platinum-electrode plug suggests a lean operating environment. The near-total absence of combustion deposits tends to confirm the diagnosis. Generally speaking, the cleaner and whiter a plug is, the leaner the cylinder.

after 30 min. Whatever you do, *don't* submerge your plugs completely in solvent; you don't want the fluid to enter the shielding barrel. Also, don't use any solvent other than the four just mentioned. These four solvents are the only ones specifically recommended for plug degreasing by AC and Champion.

After your plugs have been degreased as above, blow-dry them with compressed air or dry them in an oven no warmer than 200°F.

When the firing ends are dry, any combustion deposits should be removed by light abrasive blast cleaning. You can either take your plugs to a mechanic and have the necessary cleaning done for you (at a cost of anywhere from 75 cents to $2 per plug), or you can find a shop that's willing to let you use their plug-cleaning machine (which is not as difficult as it might sound, particularly if you check with the smaller one- and two-mechanic shops first). Or—and this is a possibility well worth looking into—you can invest in your own plug-cleaning equipment (and quite possibly write if off on your taxes). J. C. Whitney, the auto-parts house, offers several different types of plug blast cleaners ranging in price from $20 or so on up to $100. There's nothing that says you can't use one of these units to clean your airplane's spark plugs. (*Note:* If you do decide to invest in your own plug cleaner, be sure to use only aluminum oxide abrasive in it. Silicon-type abrasive powders are not recommended.)

The main thing to remember about cleaning spark-plug electrodes by the abrasive-blast method is that you don't want to hold the "blast" button down too long. Three or four 5-second blasts is about the limit if you want to keep your electrodes from being eroded away. This is particularly true for fine-wire spark plugs. (It is said that more spark plugs are worn out on abrasive blast-cleaning machines than in engines. I don't doubt that this is true.)

If lead buildup (in the form of little brown globules adhering to the center-electrode ceramic) is moderate to severe, abrasive blasting alone isn't going to do the trick. Here, once you've given the electrodes a light blast cleaning, you're going to need to go after the deposits deep inside the firing-end cavity, using a sharp tool of some sort. Champion and AC each market their own vibrating-prong tool for this; if you can arrange to use one of these devices, by all means do so. Otherwise, get a hacksaw blade and grind it on the nonserrated side so that the blade tapers to a long, sharp point; then use the pointed blade to poke around inside the end cavity of each lead-fouled plug, dislodging as much of the brownish crust as you can.

Of course, if you inspect your spark plugs often enough to catch lead buildup in its early stages, and if you operate your engine so as to minimize lead fouling (see below), you should never have to go to these lengths to clean your plugs. Light abrasive blasting will be all you'll ever need.

After the firing ends of your spark plugs have been blasted and, if necessary, vibrator cleaned, blow them out thoroughly with compressed air. (You don't want any abrasive material left over from cleaning to fall into your engine later on.) Then check the condition of the 18-mm shell threads, and, if need be, clean them with a wire brush to remove caked-on carbon, grit, etc. If you elect to use a power-driven brush for this step, be exceedingly careful not to let the brush touch the electrodes.

Depending on how long it's been since your plugs have received a thorough cleaning, it may be advisable at this point to clean the terminal well of each spark plug (Figure 9-5). This is easy to do: Simply insert a cotton swab or a clean piece of sponge or felt, moistened with methanol, Stoddard solvent, or methyl ethyl

FIGURE 9-5 For optimum plug performance, it is essential that the connector well area be cleaned periodically. (Champion recommends Bon Ami for this purpose.) After scouring the terminal wall area with a small, clean, damp piece of felt coated with Bon Ami, flush with methanol, MEK, or Stoddard solvent, and blow dry.

ketone, into the barrel of each plug, and rotate the swab several times. If solvent alone does not appear to be doing the job, you can use Bon Ami as an abrasive cleanser. But whatever you do, don't use any other abrasive products, and never use carbon tetrachloride as the cleaning solvent. When you are finished, remove all traces of cleanser, and blow the plugs out with compressed air.

GAP ADJUSTMENT   As mentioned earlier, different operators using different types of plugs in different operating conditions inevitably experience different rates of electrode wear, so it is impossible to predict how often you will have to gap your plugs. (The enthusiasm with which you blast clean your plugs will have a lot to do with this.) In any case, you will probably find that your plugs do not need to be regapped very often—which is just as well, considering the somewhat extraordinary measures that must be employed to adjust the gap of an aircraft-type plug.

Because of their distinctive two- and three-pronged electrode designs, aviation spark plugs are not easily gapped as automotive plugs. Special equipment is, in fact, required, and that equipment is not cheap. Champion's CT-415 tool for gapping massive-electrode plugs was selling at close to $40 at the time this book was being written.

There are ways to get around the high cost of gapping equipment. One way is to have your plugs gapped by a shop, at nominal cost. Another way is to do the work yourself, using someone else's equipment. Still another possibility is to chip in with some friends and buy the necessary equipment (thereby, perhaps, taking the first step toward the creation of a maintenance cooperative or tool-buying collective).

Actually, there's still another way around the high cost of gapping tools, and that's to switch over to fine-wire (exotic-metal) plugs. The equipment needed to adjust the gap of platinum or iridium electrodes is considerably less elaborate and less expensive than the corresponding equipment for massive electrodes. AC markets a tool in the $15 to $20 range that not only gaps fine-wire electrodes but serves as a feeler gauge, too. If you're not already using fine-wire plugs, however, you may not want to go this route, since (1) the conversion from massive-electrode plugs to platinums or iridiums will cost you hundreds of dollars more than it would cost you simply to purchase the necessary massive-electrode gapping gear, and (2) because of the brittleness of platinum and iridium, fine-wire electrodes tend to break rather than bend. Even with the proper equipment, fine-wire electrodes are difficult (some would say impossible) to adjust.

If you end up regapping your plugs yourself, be sure to work in accordance with the following "accepted industry practices":

1. Always adjust electrode clearances with the feeler gauge *removed* from the gap. Otherwise, a side load may be applied to the center electrode.

2. Move the outer electrodes only—never the center electrode. The ceramic body may crack if the center electrode is moved.

FIGURE 9-6 In checking electrode gaps, the usual practice is to use two feeler wires to judge the nominal gap of the electrodes. For a nominal gap of 0.016 in., the 0.015- and 0.019-in. probes of the Champion CT-450 gap gauge are used. (For a nominal gap of 0.019 in., the 0.018- and 0.022-in. wires would be used to establish the "go" and "no go" limits.)

3. Do not attempt to open a gap that has been closed too much during a previous adjustment; abnormal stresses may be set up in the electrode. (If you find that you have closed a gap too much, take the botched plug to an experienced mechanic for reworking. There are ways of salvaging such a plug.)

Electrode gaps are fairly critical in today's engines, so if you aren't sure what the proper range of gaps is for your plugs, consult your aircraft service manual or call the factory. (If you're installing brand new plugs and you've got the right type for your engine, the new plugs will come with the correct gap; that gap will be stated on the package label.) The correct way of checking electrode gaps is shown in Figure 9-6.

ELECTRICAL TESTING

Unless your plugs have been subjected to rough handling during servicing, or you have some other reason for suspecting that they may not perform normally when put back into service, you do not absolutely have to subject your spark plugs to electrical testing (or "bomb testing") every time they're out for servicing. Nonetheless, testing your plugs for proper function in a bomb-test apparatus now and then can't hurt. It'll certainly put to rest any fears you might have about the plugs' airworthiness after cleaning.

Bomb-testing is something either you or your mechanic can do, using the shop's equipment or your own. (The term *bomb* as used here simply refers to the fact that the apparatus tests individual spark plugs under pressure to simulate actual engine operating conditions.) The procedure is simple: All you do is screw the spark plug into the machine finger tight. (Some air leakage past the plug threads is desirable, to permit the escape of ionized air.) Then connect the high-voltage lead to the spark-plug shielding barrel, open the air valve to allow compressed air to enter the pressure chamber (135 psi for an electrode gap of 0.016 in., or 115 psi if the plug is gapped to 0.019 in.), press the tester switch, and observe the plug to see that it is sparking properly. If the plug sparks continuously under pressure, it is deemed serviceable; if it sparks intermittently or not at all, it is dispatched to the garbage pail.

PLUG REINSTALLATION The reinstallation of spark plugs in an aircraft engine calls for a good deal of common sense; it is easy to make mistakes, and the mistakes can, in some cases, be quite costly. So proceed slowly and with due caution.

First, remember that you are *not* going to put the plugs back into the same holes whence they came, nor into just any hole, randomly. As mentioned before, it is necessary, to minimize constant-polarity electrode wear, that you *rotate your plugs in firing order* on the cylinders when reinstalling them. In other words, you'll want to study your magnetos and rotate the plugs in sequence on the various ignition leads. (Have you kept track of which plug came from which hole in which cylinder? This is where a plug tray becomes virtually indispensable.)

Before you install any plugs, check the cleanliness of the individual cylinder openings. Any obviously unsanitary bushings should be cleaned out. Steel or brass bushings are best cleaned using a thread chaser. (Grease the notches in the side of the tool before you begin; this will keep debris from falling into the combustion chamber.) If your cylinders employ Heli-Coil inserts (look for a small tang at the top of the threaded opening), *do not* use a thread chaser. Instead, clean the inserts as best you can with a lightly greased toothbrush. (A thread chaser may cause damage to, or backing out of, the Heli-Coil insert, resulting in some rather expensive cylinder repairs.)

The next thing to do, assuming you are dealing with reconditioned plugs rather than new ones, is to put new copper gaskets on the plugs. (Brand new plugs come with brand new gaskets.) Old gaskets should not be reused, since they are likely to have become brittle and misshapen through use. True, the chances of a reused gasket forming a bad seal are small, but the consequences of an imperfect seal (plug seizure, thread damage, preignition) are sufficiently grave to negate any benefits to be gained by recycling old gaskets. New gaskets cost, at most, 10 cents apiece. Use them. And use only one gasket on each plug. If one of your cylinders employs a gasket-type thermocouple, substitute the thermocouple for the regular 18-mm gasket on that cylinder, for that particular spark-plug hole.

Now is the time to apply antiseize compound or a little engine oil to the threads of your plugs, if you intend to do so. (Again, I'm assuming you are working with reconditioned plugs. New spark plugs come prelubricated.) Apply antiseize compound very sparingly; start the application at least one full thread away from the firing end (Figure 9-7), and *do not* allow any of the compound to come in contact with the electrodes. Graphited antiseize compounds will cause permanent fouling of spark plugs.

Double-check to be sure your plugs are the correct type for your engine (remember, the plugs that came out of the engine may not necessarily be the kind that are supposed to be there). Then install the plugs in your engine. Start by screwing each plug all the way down by hand, until the base of the shell contacts the copper gasket. Again, be absolutely certain that there is one—and only one—gasket on each plug. It's easier than you think to install a plug with no gasket on it at all. If you find that the plug won't turn all the way down by hand, something is wrong. Either the bushing is dirty, some threads are damaged, or you've managed to cross-thread the plug. Recheck everything and try again.

Use extreme care when screwing spark plugs into cylinder bushings, to avoid cross-threading the plugs. Cross-threading can result in expensive cylinder repairs. Take it slow and easy, and don't start using your torque wrench until you know each plug is in right.

With all the plugs in their proper holes, resting against their gaskets, it is now a simple matter to snug up each plug with a torque wrench. Place your ⅞-in. deep socket over the first plug (bottoming it on the shell hex), attach the torque handle, and, as smoothly as possible, tighten the plug to the proper torque range (30 to 35 ft-lb for Lycoming engines, 25 to 30 ft-lb for Continentals). Proceed in like fashion all the way around the engine, until the plugs are tight (Figure 9-8).

The torque limits given above apply to all 18-mm plugs, regardless of reach, heat range, or electrode design. However, for older engines using 14-mm spark plugs, the proper torque range is 20 to 25 ft-lb, regardless of engine type.

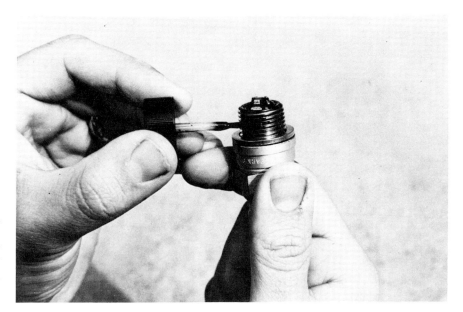

FIGURE 9-7 Later plug removal will be facilitated by the use of thread antiseize compound, applied sparingly and carefully to your reconditioned plugs' threads immediately before reinstallation. Start the application at least one full thread away from the firing end, as shown.

FIGURE 9-8 When installing (or for that matter, removing) plugs, it is essential to plant one hand firmly on the socket as shown, to prevent it from cocking over and damaging the spark plug. Here, a plug is being torqued down after having been installed as far as possible by hand. (*Note:* A torque wrench should not be used to remove spark plugs.)

Before placing the ignition leads back in the plugs, take a moment to wipe each cigarette with a clean cloth moistened in methanol, MEK, acetone, or unleaded gasoline (Figure 9-9). (Dirty terminal connectors can short out.) Then, without letting your skin touch the cigarette itself, carefully insert each connector assembly into each plug barrel, using a straight-line motion.

Finally, screw each connector nut into place finger tight, holding the ignition elbow so it doesn't turn. Use a wrench to tighten each nut an additional ⅛ turn. Do not tighten any more than this.

FINAL TESTING Spark-plug servicing does not end with the installation of the cleaned and gapped plugs in the engine. The only sure way to find out whether your servicing operations were successful and did not damage any of the plugs is to run the engine and perform an ignition system check.

After taxiing to the runup area, perform a normal mag check, noting not only the rpm drop on either magneto but also (in particular) the sound and feel of the engine on either magneto. Rough single-mag operation (a shuddering feeling or a quite noticeable vibration, accompanied by a large rpm drop) tells you that one or more spark plugs are cutting out. An attempt should be made to find the cause.

If you have a multiprobe EGT (an exhaust-analyzer system), you will be able to tell immediately which cylinder has the bad plug on single-mag operation, just

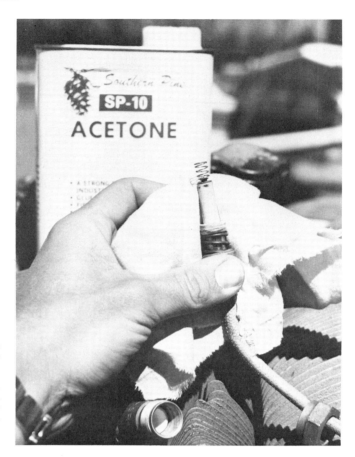

FIGURE 9-9 Cigarettes can be hazardous to your health when they are allowed to become dirty. Before reinstalling terminal connectors, wipe them down with acetone or methanol to remove carbon, oils, salts, and other impurities that might cause shorting out inside the spark-plug terminal well.

by rotating the selector switch to each jug in turn. Having isolated the problem cylinder and having determined which magneto gives rough operation, you should be able to tell exactly which of the two plugs in the questionable cylinder is defective, by tracing the lead wire from the magneto in question to the appropriate cylinder and spark plug.

If you do not have a multiprobe EGT, and you suspect that you have a faulty plug somewhere but you aren't sure where, you can pinpoint the defective igniter's location by simply running the engine a minute or two on the rough mag, shutting the engine down, and performing a "cold-cylinder" test. (The older generation of mechanics would do this simply by spitting on each exhaust pipe. The pipe that doesn't hiss is connected to the cold cylinder.) Thus, if continuous left-mag operation produces a cold number three cylinder, and if you know that the left magneto in your plane fires the bottom plugs in the odd-numbered cylinders, then you know that the bottom plug in your number three cylinder is bad.

Actually, it's probably a good idea to avoid performing the above test if you can, since (1) it is not good practice to continue to run an engine whose cylinders are not all firing, and (2) prolonged single-mag operation will cause fouling of the nonoperating spark plugs. A far better approach is to monitor EGT indications, or simply pull and inspect all the plugs associated with the rough mag.

In any case, after you've performed a runup check and determined that everything is working properly, you may make your logbook entry and return the plane to service.

HOW TO REDUCE FOULING AND INCREASE THE LIFE OF PLUGS

Most mechanics agree that the single most important causative factor in premature spark plug retirement is lead oxide accumulation. When spark plugs accumulate lead, they have to be serviced (i.e., blast cleaned) more often; and when plugs are serviced often, they tend to wear rapidly. In 300 hr of operation, a plug may be subjected to as many as 15 blast cleanings—enough to take hundreds of hours of life off any set of electrodes.

Of course, if lead deposits are not removed often, the buildup of lead oxides can proceed so rapidly that the plug may, in less than 100 hr, become fouled beyond all hope of reconditioning. Then, the next thing you know, you're shelling out $50 to $150 for new plugs again. And again. And again.

Fortunately, it doesn't have to be this way. As it turns out, there are any number of operational tricks that you can employ to reduce lead fouling (and other types of fouling, as well) in your engine. Avco Lycoming, in Service Letter No. L192, recommends that the following 10 procedures, in particular, be adhered to:

1. Use the manufacturer's spark-plug recommendation chart to make sure the proper spark plugs are installed in the engine. Do not simply install plugs with the same part number as those removed; a previous mechanic may have installed plugs of the wrong heat range, reach, etc.

2. Do not accept an overly rich idle-mixture setting. Have a mechanic adjust the carburetor or fuel injector, if necessary.

3. After a flooded start, slowly run the engine to high power to burn off harmful lead deposits; then return the engine to normal power.

4. Avoid closed-throttle idling whenever possible. Set the engine at 1200 rpm; this will produce a spark-plug nose-core temperature of 800°F or more (the minimum temperature at which the lead-scavenging agent contained in leaded avgas will function). Below 1200 rpm, nose-core temperatures of 800°F or more (and thus proper lead scavenging) are not possible. (*Note:* At 1200 rpm, the engine will run cooler and smoother, and the alternator or generator will produce more output.) The foregoing does not apply to taxiing; during taxi, accept whatever rpm is required.

5. Use normal (factory recommended) leaning techniques under cruise conditions *regardless of altitude*, and relean as necessary following the application of alternate air or carburetor heat.

6. Avoid fast low-power letdowns from cruising altitude. Plan ahead. Descend with power. (However, do not use cowl flaps as speed brakes.) Avoid overrich conditions in the descent.

7. Avoid closed-throttle landing approaches whenever possible. Instead, use a small amount of power. (Remember, carburetors and fuel injectors are set slightly rich at closed throttle.)

8. Keep engine operating temperatures in the normal operating range. Many people think lower temperatures are better, but this is not always so. Use normal power and proper leaning to keep cylinder-head temperatures in the normal operating range at all times. In winter, use an oil-cooler baffle to keep the oil temperature "in the green."

9. Swap top and bottom spark plugs every 25 to 50 hr. Top plugs scavenge better than bottom plugs.

10. Before engine shutdown, go to 1800 rpm for 15 to 20 seconds, reduce to 1200 rpm, and then shut the engine off immediately with the mixture control.

Since all the makers of leaded aviation gasolines go out of their way to add ethylene dibromide, a potent lead-scavenging compound, to avgas in just the chemical proportions needed to fully remove the lead products formed in combustion, one might reasonably ask why it is that lead fouling should occur at all in aircraft engines. The answer is twofold: (1) For ethylene dibromide to scavenge (or carry away lead products) efficiently, spark-plug tip temperatures of 800°F or more must be maintained, and, as pointed out in item 4 above, such temperatures simply are not attained during low-rpm operation. (2) Tetraethyl lead, the antiknock compound that gives low-lead gasoline its name, quite often does not travel the same path through the induction system that ethylene dibromide does. Some cylinders receive a fuel-air charge with a high ratio of tetraethyl lead (TEL) to ethylene dibromide, while others receive fuel with a low TEL to scavenger ratio.

Maldistribution of TEL and/or ethylene dibromide comes about as a result of differences in volatility between the two substances. Ethylene dibromide has a boiling temperature of about 265°F; the corresponding temperature for TEL is approximately 390°F. Gasoline, of course, is a mixture of many different, chemically distinct substances and thus has no single boiling temperature. However, most of the hydrocarbons in gasoline have a boiling point close to or less than that of ethylene dibromide. Because of this relatively wide spread in boiling temperatures, some degree of *fractionalization* of fuel components occurs in an engine's induction system. In fact, under conditions of rich mixture and low induction air temperature, less-volatile fuel molecules, rich in TEL, may go almost entirely to one or two cylinders, while ethylene dibromide (because of its greater volatility) is distributed more evenly. The result is relatively rapid fouling of the spark plugs in those cylinders exposed to the greater amount of lead.

Obviously, one way to deal with the problem of TEL maldistribution in the induction system is to raise the temperature of the induction air, thereby aiding vaporization and mixing of the fuel components. On carbureted engines, this can be accomplished with judicious use of carburetor heat. The proper use of cowl flaps also helps, as does turbocharging.

Merely raising the temperature of the induction air is not the whole answer, however, for there is also the problem of airflow. In a carbureted powerplant, under conditions of reduced induction airflow, it is possible for tiny droplets of liquid fuel to form in the intake manifold—tiny droplets that, because of TEL's reluctance to vaporize, can be extremely rich in lead content and very low in scavenger content. Once ingested into the cylinder, these droplets tend to fall to the lowest point in the combustion chamber; thus, they accumulate on the bottom spark plug and form beads of lead oxide there during combustion.

Nor are fuel-injected engines immune to this problem. In the typical continuous-flow system, the fuel-air charge is admitted to the combustion chamber (via the open intake valve) during only about one third of the cylinder's operating cycle. The other two thirds of the time, the spray of fuel goes into the intake port with the intake valve *closed*. Thus, it is often possible, particularly under low-cylinder-head-temperature conditions, for liquid fuel (again, high in TEL content) to find its way into the combustion chamber, after having accumulated in the intake port. The result is severe, rapid lead fouling of the bottom spark plug.

It's easy to see how proper leaning, along with operation of the engine so as to keep cylinder temperatures well into the green, can go a long way toward increasing the effectiveness of ethylene dibromide as a lead scavenger *where it is present*. What proper leaning and proper CHT management cannot do, however, is eliminate lead fouling when (as is often the case) there is a *high ratio of TEL to ethylene dibromide* in one or more cylinders. Obviously, if there's not enough scavenger in the combustion chamber to carry off all the lead, it doesn't much matter how you lean the engine; you're still going to have leftover lead in a few cylinders. The question is what, if anything, can be done about this.

The answer is to add more scavenger to your fuel. Then why aren't the oil companies doing this for us already? They are, in the case of leaded automotive gasolines. The reasons the refineries don't blend an excess of scavenger into aviation gasolines are (1) ethylene dibromide is expensive, (2) even more important, the bromine in ethylene dibromide is chemically very active (i.e., corrosive), and (3) bromine compounds are severely toxic. The extra cost, the corrosion risks, and the health risks that would be posed by the increased use of ethylene dibromide would almost surely outweigh any advantages to be gained in reduced spark-plug maintenance.

Of course, ethylene dibromide is not the only lead-scavenging agent around. Tricresyl phosphate (TCP) also scavenges lead effectively, and it is not as corrosive nor nearly as toxic as ethylene dibromide. What's more, thanks to the recent efforts of Alcor, Inc. (which bought the relevant patents and formulas from Shell Oil Company some years back), TCP concentrate is now widely and inexpensively available on the aviation market. It is also FAA approved (for non-turbocharged engines only). Thus, if you want to add more lead scavenger to your fuel, you can now do so legally, at a cost of about a penny a gallon. And you *should* do so, if you have been having problems with lead fouling.

It is probably safe to say that the regular use of TCP in one's fuel, combined with strict adherence to the 10 antifouling recommendations listed above, will virtually guarantee the elimination of lead fouling from one's spark plugs. This is not to say that spark-plug deposits will not be formed; they will. But they won't be formed as rapidly. And, if TCP is used regularly, they won't be as electrically conductive as they would otherwise be.

Obviously, lead fouling is a complex phenomenon. Suffice it to say, there are effective techniques for dealing with spark-plug fouling, the most dependable of which, perhaps, is simply to add extra lead scavenger to your fuel. By applying these techniques diligently, you can expect to double or even triple spark-plug life, thereby reducing your plane's maintenance costs by $50 to $100 per year (maybe more, depending on what inflation does to spark plug prices over the years ahead).

We have seen how some aircraft accessories (spark plugs, for instance), while appearing to be very similar to their automotive counterparts, actually differ substantially from those counterparts in both internal design and maintenance requirements. This, happily, is not the case with lead-acid storage batteries. In aircraft as in automobiles, a battery is a battery is a battery.

To be sure, aircraft batteries are somewhat smaller (and thus carry lower ampere-hour ratings) than their automotive equivalents; their posts are designed a bit differently (to accept ring-tongue cable connectors and wing nuts); and their cells have spillproof vent caps (to prevent acid leakage in severe turbulence). But the chemistry, the cell voltages, and the construction methods used with aircraft batteries are, for the most part, the same as those used for car batteries. This, in turn, means that the basic maintenance requirements for the two battery types are the same.

The various airframe manufacturers' service manuals differ somewhat with regard to recommended battery servicing intervals; however, the Beech 33/35 *Shop Manual* is fairly typical in its recommendation that batteries be removed from aircraft for servicing once every 30 days or 100 hours, whichever comes first. Beech also states, in this manual: "If the ambient temperatures are above 90°F or the time between engine starts averages less than 30 minutes, the time between servicing should be reduced." Heat and inactivity are a battery's worst enemies.

Requiring operators to service their batteries once every 30 days or less may at first sound a little extreme, but actually Beech is right. Pilots *should* service their batteries at least once a month. Many auto makers, after all, recommend that owners check their car's battery at each service station fill-up, or once a week—and yet car batteries are (almost without exception) stouter and more forgiving of abuse than airplane batteries.

The point is this: If you are not already checking your airplane battery for water level, terminal corrosion, and state of charge once every 30 days, you are doing yourself and your plane's electrical system a disservice. Conversely, if you go out of your way to treat your battery right, you can expect to increase substantially your MTBBF (mean time between battery failures), thus keeping battery-related maintenance costs and downtime to a minimum.

ROUTINE SERVICING OPERATIONS

Routine servicing of an aircraft lead-acid battery consists in (1) ascertaining the state of charge of the battery, to determine if recharging is necessary, (2) adding water to the cells as needed, and (3) cleaning up any corrosion that may have accumulated on or near the battery. For safety reasons, and to allow a thorough inspection for corrosion, each of these checks is performed with the battery removed from the airplane.

Speaking of safety: It is absolutely *essential* that adequate safety precautions be taken when working around any lead-acid (wet-cell) battery. Like car batteries, aircraft storage batteries contain electrolyte with an extremely high (30 percent) sulfuric acid content. If allowed to contact skin or clothing, the electrolyte can and will produce serious burns in a matter of seconds; consequently, one should never attempt to perform any kind of battery maintenance without adequate eye and hand protection. Wear glasses and gloves, and old clothing if possible, when working around batteries. Keep a supply of baking soda on hand to neutralize spills, and try not to go far from a source of running water. Should your best efforts to prevent accidental burning fail, *immediately flush spilled acid from skin or eyes with copious amounts of water.* Continue flushing for approximately 5 min. Do not use eye drops or other medication on any burned area unless so instructed by a physician or paramedic. In case of a large spill or a severe burn, call a doctor at once.

In addition to the obvious health hazard posed by the acid in a lead-acid battery, there is also, of course, a very serious explosion hazard to consider. All lead-acid batteries generate hydrogen and oxygen gases, which, as you'll recall, are widely used as rocket fuels; and all batteries, by virtue of their role in life, are capable of making sparks. Thus, a "live" battery is an explosion waiting to happen. For this reason, it is never a good idea to perform battery maintenance in any kind of enclosed or poorly ventilated area (such as an airplane tail cone). *Keep sparks, flames, cigarettes, etc., away from batteries at all times, and always work in a well-ventilated area.* And again, wear eye protection. To do otherwise is not merely careless, but reckless.

Unlike automobile batteries, which are generally quite accessible, airplane batteries are unfortunately quite often hidden in remote parts of the airframe. This helps explain, perhaps, why so many pilots neglect this all-important accessory. In some planes (high-performance Cessna singles, for example), the battery is mounted in the tail cone aft of the baggage compartment, behind a plastic bulkhead. In other planes (including various Piper models), the battery is cleverly concealed beneath a rear passenger seat. Some aircraft mercifully carry their batteries high on the firewall, within easy view and reach (most Cessna 150s and 172s fall into this category).

Once you've managed to determine the location of your plane's battery, removing it is relatively easy. Begin by unclipping the top of the battery box (Figure 10-1) and setting it aside. Be sure to set it in a safe place if it is wet with electrolyte. Next, look closely to see which of the battery posts is the negative terminal, and loosen the wing nut on that terminal. Temporarily remove the wing nut; then lift the lead wire off the post, and replace the nut. As a precaution, place a piece of masking tape over the end of the negative lead wire.

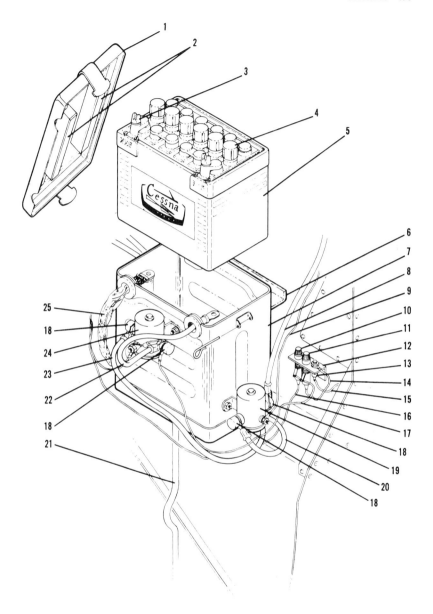

FIGURE 10-1 Typical battery-box installation. (*Cessna diagram.*)

1. Battery Box Lid
2. Insulator
3. Wing Nut
4. Filler Cap
5. Battery
6. Mounting Bracket
7. Battery Box
8. External Power Contactor Line

9. Contactor Control Wire
10. Clock Fuse
11. External Power Fuse
12. Mounting Bracket
13. Diode
14. External Power Fuse to Diode
15. Diode Wire
16. Clock Wire
17. Fuse Wire

18. Cover
19. External Power Contactor
20. Starter Contactor Cable
21. Drain Tube
22. Positive Battery Lead
23. Starter Contactor Power Cable
24. Battery Contactor
25. Negative Battery Lead

Remember that aircraft batteries are negatively grounded—which means that, to minimize the chance of spark formation, you should always *disconnect the negative lead first and reconnect it last* (when the time comes to reinstall the battery).

With the ground cable thus disconnected, you may proceed to disconnect the positive lead wire. (Again, unscrew the wing nut, lift the cable off, and replace the nut.) At this point, the battery should be completely detached from the airframe. All you have to do to remove it is grab the little rope handle atop the battery case and lift it straight up out of its box (assuming you have a strong enough forearm).

Upon removing the battery from the plane, give it a thorough examination for damage and wear. Among other things, look for cracks in the polypropylene outer case, loose posts, severely corroded posts, and worn vent-cap gaskets. Wetness on the top of the case means either that someone overfilled the battery with water or the battery is being charged too rapidly. Sprinkle baking soda on any wet areas, and wipe up the residue with a sponge. Be careful not to let any soda enter the battery itself, since this will damage the cells.

If, by chance, you happen to notice a slimy goo on the battery's posts or the top of the case, don't be alarmed. The battery is not melting. The goo is petroleum jelly, applied as a preservative by whoever serviced the battery last.

If you intend to check the specific gravity of the cells (and you really should), do it now, before you add any water to the cells. Begin by washing your hydrometer in clean water if it is dirty. Then, beginning with the cell closest to the positive terminal, say, take a sample of electrolyte with the hydrometer and note where the meniscus meets the calibrated side of the float. Write down your specific-gravity reading.

If your battery has seen heavy service or is more than a year old, it would be a good idea to check the charge level of all six (or all twelve, for a 24-V battery) of the battery's cells, and compare the readings. According to the FAA (See AC No. 43.13-1A, Chapter 11, Section 8), "When a specific gravity difference of .050 or more exists between cells of a battery, the battery is approaching the end of its useful life and replacement should be considered."

After you have obtained and recorded specific-gravity readings for the electro-

TABLE 10-1 ELECTROLYTE SPECIFIC GRAVITY VERSUS CHARGE LEVEL (AT 80°F)

Hydrometer reading	State of charge (percent)
1.280	100
1.250	75
1.220	50
1.190	25
1.160	Dead

**TABLE 10-2 SPECIFIC-GRAVITY TEMPERATURE
CORRECTIONS**

| Electrolyte temperature | | Amount to be added to |
°F	°C	specific gravity*
140	60	+0.024
130	55	+0.020
120	49	+0.016
110	43	+0.012
100	38	+0.008
90	33	+0.004
80	27	0
70	21	−0.004
60	15	−0.008
50	10	−0.016
40	5	−0.020
30	−2	−0.024
20	−7	−0.028
10	−13	−0.032
0	−18	−0.036
−10	−23	−0.040

*For example, if the electrolyte gives a specific-gravity reading of
1.200 at 100°F, the corrected reading (for 80°F standard conditions)
is 1.200 + 0.008 or 1.208.

lyte in all the battery's cells, compare your readings to the values shown in Table
10-1. Ideally, your specific-gravity readings should be within 0.050 of one another,
and all should be between 1.250 and 1.280. (The higher the concentration of
sulfuric acid in the electrolyte, the higher the liquid's specific gravity and the
greater the state of charge of the battery. Pure water has a specific gravity of 1.000.)

If the average of all your specific-gravity readings is below 1.220, which indicates a 50 percent charge, plan on putting the battery on a charger before reinstalling it in the airplane (see below).

Note, incidentally, that the specific-gravity values shown in Table 10-1 are
valid only for an electrolyte temperature of 80°F (27°C). If your electrolyte is
significantly warmer or cooler than this, you will need to adjust your specific-
gravity readings up or down as shown in Table 10-2, to correct for density errors
caused by thermal expansion or contraction of the electrolyte. Measure the electrolyte temperature with a thermometer, if need be.

After you have checked the specific gravity of each cell, you may proceed to
add water to the cells as necessary to bring the electrolyte level approximately ⅜
in. above the tops of the plates. (Obviously, if you were to add water before
checking the specific gravity, you'd dilute the acid in each cell and throw your

TABLE 10-3   EFFECT OF SPECIFIC GRAVITY ON FREEZING POINT OF BATTERY ELECTROLYTE

Specific gravity	Freezing point	
	°F	°C
1.300	−90	−70
1.275	−80	−62
1.250	−62	−52
1.225	−35	−37
1.200	−16	−26
1.175	−4	−20
1.150	+5	−15
1.125	+13	−10

readings way off.) Use distilled water, if possible, and add no more water than necessary. The slightest excess will be expelled out the vent caps when the battery undergoes charging in the airplane, thereby creating a serious corrosion hazard.

On the subject of corrosion: Be sure to inspect your battery box and surrounding structures, including control cables, for corrosion damage before reinstalling the serviced battery. Corrosion detection is one of the more important reasons for servicing a battery every 30 days; sulfuric acid fumes have a way of working very quickly on exposed metal surfaces. If you find any corrosion, first neutralize the area with baking soda; then flush thoroughly with clean water, wipe the surface dry, and blow out crevices with compressed air. Corroded aluminum should be cleaned down to the bare metal with aluminum wool, powdered pumice, and/or nylon scouring pads. Steel can be cleaned up with steel wool. In any case, be sure to flush the scoured area with clean water and blow all crevices dry. Then, finally, follow up with a good coat of acid-resistant black paint (Randolph 344 or equivalent, military specification TT-L-54).

Carefully inspect the area where the battery vent tube exits the airframe and, here again, remove any surface corrosion that might be present. Anything more advanced than mild surface corrosion should be brought to the attention of a mechanic at once. Also be sure to check the vent tube for obstructions. If the vent tube is blocked, unblock it. (If you don't, you may find yourself in the position of the Citabria pilot whose battery vented into the fuselage, ultimately causing a control cable to dissolve and elevator control to be lost during a stall-spin maneuver. Fortunately, this true-life incident ended happily when the pilot regained control of the plane with the elevator trim and landed.)

It should be noted that, in some aircraft, the battery vent line connects to a jar containing a piece of felt saturated with a strong bicarbonate solution. If you find such a jar, remove and rinse the felt pad, soak the pad in a solution made by mixing 4 oz of baking soda in 1 qt of water, and replace the pad in the vent jar.

BATTERY RECHARGING Any time you find that your battery's electrolyte has a specific gravity of less than 1.220 (50 percent charge), you should put the battery on a charger before returning it to service. This is particularly true during cold-weather operation, when the danger of battery freezing is at its highest. As you can see from Table 10-3, the temperature at which battery electrolyte will freeze is markedly influenced by the solution's specific gravity. The lower the specific gravity, the higher the freezing temperature. Under low-ambient-temperature conditions, merely adding water to a cell can dilute the electrolyte to such an extent that immediate recharging is required to prevent freezing.

Instructions for recharging your battery will, in most cases, be printed or molded on the battery itself. One popular 35-amp-hr aircraft battery contains the following information, molded into the side of the case:

FULLY CHARGED SP. GR. 1.270
RECHARGE REQUIRED WHEN SP. GR. REACHES 1.225
START CHG. 4 AMP   FINISH CHG. 2 AMP
MAXIMUM TEMPERATURE ON CHARGE 120°F

In the absence of such specific charging instructions, plan on using a charging current (in amperes) equal to or less than 7 percent of your battery's ampere-hour rating. In other words, if you have a 25 amp-hr battery, do not exceed 1.75 amp of current during charging.

How long should you keep your battery on the charger? The charge time (i.e., the time it takes the battery to come back up to full charge) will vary, depending on how badly discharged the battery was to begin with, how much charging current is being applied, and how hot or cold the battery is. As a rule, an aircraft battery is considered to be fully charged when three consecutive hydrometer readings taken an hour apart show no change in specific gravity. When this point is reached, the battery should be taken off the charger, to prevent overcharge damage.

The foregoing information applies mainly to batteries that have reached a low state of charge through short-term overloading or discharging (as, for example, when radios are used too long on the ground, or when the master switch is left on overnight). The recommended charging procedure for a battery that has gone dead through spontaneous self-discharge (that is, through lack of use) is somewhat different. When a battery is allowed to stand in a parked plane unused and unre-charged for weeks at a time, a phenomenon known as *sulfation* occurs: The lead sulfate that forms on the cells' plates during normal self-discharging accumulates to such a degree that a visible white crust begins to appear on the plates, insulating them from the surrounding electrolyte. In time, the plates may become so en-crusted with sulfate, and so well insulated from the electrolyte, that no amount of recharging will restore activity to the cells. When that happens, you throw the battery away and buy a new one.

Recharging a sulfated battery can be tricky. If sulfation has proceeded to the point where all the plates are affected, the battery's internal resistance may be so high that it will accept only a small fraction of the charging current offered to it. On the other hand, if even the slightest excess of charging current is applied to the battery, plate spalling (the shedding of large pieces of active plate material) may occur, causing a buildup of plate residue at the bottom of each cell and a shorting of the elements. To guard against the latter possibility, it is necessary to charge the battery at a slower-than-normal rate for a longer-than-normal period of time. Common practice is to charge a sulfated battery at half the factory-recommended charge rate for 50 to 100 hours. (Yes, 50 to 100 hours.) Generally, if this doesn't bring the battery back to life, nothing will.

Regardless of what recharging technique you use, and whether the battery is sulfated, run down, or merely waterlogged, you should always observe the following rules when recharging any battery:

1. Loosen (but do not remove) the battery's vent caps to facilitate the release of gas.

2. See that the battery is placed in a *well-ventilated* area, away from electric motors and other spark hazards. (Lead-acid batteries liberate significant quantities of explosive gases during recharging.) Do not recharge a battery while it is mounted in the plane.

3. To reduce the chance of sparking and explosion, be sure the charger is "off" whenever you connect or disconnect the battery.

4. Periodically check the specific gravity of the cells to determine when charging should be discontinued.

5. Do not allow gassing cells to go dry. Check fluid levels from time to time, and add distilled water as needed.

6. Monitor the battery temperature; never let it exceed 120°F (extremely warm to the touch). Decrease the charging current or temporarily discontinue charging if the battery is heating rapidly or gassing violently.

7. Do not overcharge. Continuous charging over a long period of time, even at a low rate, can cause plate damage.

To the foregoing list of precautions, I would add one other: Double-check the battery before turning the charger on, to be sure it is connected properly. If the battery is hooked up backward (with the red wire to the negative post and the black wire to the positive post), its polarity will be reversed during charging. Upon reinstallation in the plane, damage to radios or other equipment will result.

HOW TO ACTIVATE A NEW BATTERY

Almost all new lead-acid batteries for aircraft are sold in the dry-charged state (that is, minus electrolyte). Thus, before you can install one in your plane, you'll have to activate it according to the instructions that come with the battery.

The first thing to do is remove the vent caps and eliminate any sealing devices that may have been used to seal the openings. Next, take the battery down to your local FBO or any service station, and ask to buy some battery electrolyte. (The instructions with the battery will tell you exactly what strength of electrolyte to buy.) Sulfuric acid is sulfuric acid, so it doesn't much matter where you buy the electrolyte. You could even buy the pure acid and some distilled water and mix up the electrolyte yourself, if you wanted to—although, for safety reasons, I don't recommend you actually try this.

You'll need approximately a quart and a half of electrolyte to fill a standard 12-V, 25-amp-hr aircraft battery, and a little over half a gallon for a 35-amp-hr 12-V battery. You can double these figures for 24-V aircraft batteries. As you add the electrolyte to the cells, *gently* rock the battery from side to side; this will help trapped air escape from the labyrinthine plate-separator assemblies. Bring the fluid level just above the tops of the plates. Do not overfill the cells.

Next, you'll need to give the battery a short-duration high-current charge—a "boost" charge—to fully activate it. Ask your mechanic or a service-station attendant if you may put your battery on the shop's charger for several minutes. Charge the battery at 15 amp for 10 min (or as stated in the instructions that came with the battery).

Keep an eye on the battery during the boost-charge period. If vigorous bubbling occurs in the cells, reduce the charging current immediately. Continue charging until an electrolyte specific gravity of 1.250 (minimum) is reached, concurrent with an electrolyte temperature of at least 60°F. (It's best to warm the battery to room temperature before beginning the boost charge, if the battery has been sitting in a cold room. Cold batteries don't charge well.) After boost charging, check the level of electrolyte in all the cells, and adjust as necessary by adding more electrolyte.

At this point, the battery is ready to be put into service. But from now on, when the cells need replenishment, add pure water—not electrolyte.

HOW TO INSTALL A BATTERY   The procedure for installing a new battery in a plane is the same as that for reinstalling an old battery. Start by ensuring that the top of the battery is dry, the cells are adequately filled (not overfilled), and the terminal posts are free of corrosion. If the posts are fuzzy, take a wire brush to them.

Unless you are 100 percent certain that the battery was charged or recharged correctly, it is a very good idea to check the battery polarity with a voltmeter before going any further, to be sure the polarity has not been inadvertently reversed. As mentioned above, a battery's polarity can be changed by hooking it up backward on a charger.

Likewise, when you lower the battery into its box in the airplane, be sure that the terminal posts are oriented so as to face the proper lead wires (+ to red, and − to black). At the very least, you can expect to blow all the diodes in your alternator if you connect the battery backward. A good precaution, as noted earlier, is to keep masking tape over the ends of the lead wires until the battery is actually ready to be hooked up.

FIGURE 10-2 A battery should never be allowed to get so low on water that dry plates and separators can be seen when the vent caps are taken off, as is the case here. Sulfation occurs quickly where plates are exposed to air.

With the battery facing in the correct direction, make sure it is securely in place; use wooden shims, if necessary, to brace the battery. Then untape the positive (red) lead wire, slip it over the positive battery post, and tighten the wing nut down on that post. Then do exactly the same for the negative (black) lead wire. (Always connect the ground wire *last*.) Check to be sure the connections are tight. Loose cables can add resistance to the electrical system, thus causing hard-start or no-start conditions and/or preventing the charging system from supplying sufficient current to fully charge the battery in flight. You should also know that the battery acts as a large capacitor, absorbing stray voltage spikes, so loose cable connections can be a source of radio interference.

Finally, after (not before) the wing nuts are cinched down tight, coat them and the ends of the lead wires with petroleum jelly, to retard corrosion. Then strap the lid back on the battery box, get out your airframe log, and make your log entry. (Some manufacturers actually recommend that operators keep a *separate* logbook just for the battery, as you might keep a separate log for, say, the propeller. You may not want to go to this extreme, but you should certainly keep some sort of record of the maintenance performed on your battery. Don't simply skip it.) Record not only the date, tach time, and nature of the work performed, but specific information regarding charge level, water consumption per cell, etc. The more specifics you can think of to record, the better.

Incidentally, if you've just installed a new battery in the plane and you want

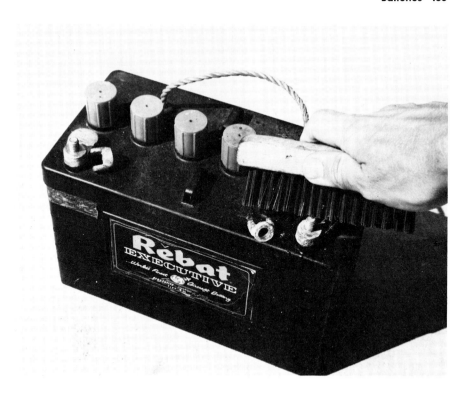

FIGURE 10-3 Whenever a battery's posts have begun to corrode, they should be cleaned with a wire brush.

to be sure the battery holds its charge, you probably should fly the plane for an hour or so, to ensure that the battery is fully activated and to see that all ammeter indications are normal. Afterward, be sure to note this "test flight" in the airframe or battery logbook.

TIPS FOR LONG BATTERY LIFE

The key to attaining extended battery TBRs (time between replacements) is to maintain the optimum amount and concentration of electrolyte in each battery cell at all times. Failure to do this will result in early battery replacement.

Keeping the electrolyte at exactly the proper level (usually ⅜ in. above the tops of the plates) in each cell of a lead-acid battery is exceedingly important, since damaging and ineradicable sulfate deposits form quickly at the air-metal interface whenever plate material is exposed to air. Any time you can peer into a cell and see dry or partially dried out plates and separators, chances are some sulfation damage has already occurred (Figure 10-2). At this point, nothing can be done; prevention is the only answer.

Checking the cells once every 30 days or 100 hours (as recommended by airframe manufacturers) is not the best way to maintain electrolyte at the proper level in each cell. Instead, you should keep a careful logbook record of the amount of water consumed by the various cells over time. By starting with relatively frequent servicing intervals (once every 3 weeks, say) and monitoring water usage

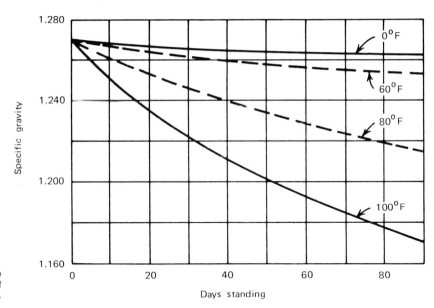

FIGURE 10-4 Self-discharge behavior of a lead-acid battery at various temperatures.

accurately to determine each cell's consumption pattern, you should quickly be able to determine the optimal service interval for your battery in your plane, and that way avoid ever running a cell dry. As Beech notes in one of its manuals, "Accurate water consumption data is a valid barometer to use for adjustment of servicing intervals."

Also important for long battery life is maintaining the electrolyte at a high specific gravity (1.250 to 1.270). In the winter, this is generally easy to do; once charged, a battery tends to stay charged unless deliberately drained. In the summer months, however, when a lead-acid battery's self-discharge rate is considerable (Figure 10-4), electrolyte specific gravity tends to diminish rapidly unless the plane is flown often or the battery is taken out of the plane once a week and recharged. And once the electrolyte specific gravity begins to decrease, sulfation is just around the corner.

This point cannot be stressed enough: If a battery is not recharged regularly, *sulfation will take place.* Once present, sulfation is very difficult (if not impossible) to eliminate; thus, every effort should be made to prevent sulfation at the outset. The only way to do this is to keep the battery charged.

From the foregoing, it should be obvious that the aircraft voltage regulator plays a critical role in determining the service life of a lead-acid battery. If the regulator is set too low, the battery may never reach a fully charged state; sulfation will begin during the first relatively long period of inactivity. If, on the other hand, the regulator output is too high, water will be lost from the cells via hydrolysis at a rapid rate, exposing the plate assemblies to air and thus to sulfation. Also, under rapid-hydrolysis conditions, the concentration of sulfuric acid in the electrolyte can increase to the point where the acid will soften the plates and shorten plate life.

Aircraft voltage regulators can, to some degree, compensate for the temperature effect (i.e., the fact that batteries require greater charging current at cold temperatures); however, this compensation is frequently imperfect enough to warrant seasonal readjustment of the regulator output. This is something you ought to consider if you've been having problems (or suspect you may be having problems) with undercharging in the winter and overcharging in the summer. But don't attempt to make any regulator adjustments yourself; instead, take it up with a qualified mechanic.

Getting long life out of a battery isn't difficult, as long as you (1) keep the cells filled, (2) keep the battery fully charged, and (3) avoid exposing the battery to excessive heat or vibration. While there may not be a whole lot you can do about the last item (particularly if your battery is mounted on the firewall, where heat and vibration are present in abundance almost all the time), control over the first two items is entirely in the pilot's hands. Whether your battery lives to a ripe old age or dies before its time is thus largely up to you.

Oddly enough, most of us do not think of the cockpit as one of an airplane's high-maintenance areas, at least not in the same way that we might think of the engine, say, as a high-maintenance area. What makes this odd is the fact that instrument, radio, upholstery, and other inside-the-cockpit repairs account for a very sizable proportion of the total maintenance requirements of the average 10- to 20-year-old lightplane. For many aircraft, in fact, cockpit repair work constitutes an expense of several hundred dollars per year, making such work second in economic importance only to unscheduled engine maintenance.

Make no mistake: The cockpit *is* a high-maintenance area. However, there is a great deal that pilots themselves can do inside the cockpit to (1) save money on hired-out repairs, (2) lessen the need for such repairs (and associated downtime) in the future, and (3) at the same time, make the cockpit a little nicer place to be—particularly with regard to instruments, avionics, upholstery, and soundproofing.

ELEVEN
INSIDE THE COCKPIT

UPHOLSTERY

According to Appendix A of FAR Part 43, preventive maintenance includes (among other things) "repairing upholstery and decorative furnishings of the cabin or cockpit interior when the repairing does not require disassembly of any primary structure or operating system or interfere with an operating system or affect primary structure of the aircraft." In addition, pilots are allowed to replace "seats or seat parts with replacement parts approved for the aircraft," again so long as no primary structures or operating systems are molested.

In plain English: You may repair or reupholster the furnishings inside your cockpit, with the FAA's complete blessing, so long as you do not tamper with primary structures in the process.

Of course, the performance rules that govern all maintenance [FAR 43.13 (a) and (b)] apply where reupholstery work is concerned; in addition, all the materials you use must (according to FAR 23.853) be flame-resistant. The best way to ensure compliance with the latter requirement is simply to obtain samples of the fabrics, paddings, and other materials you intend to use, and apply a hot flame (from a propane or other torch) to each in turn. Upon removing the flame, note whether the sample material continues to burn. If it self-extinguishes, you can consider it to meet the requirements of FAR 23.853; if it continues to burn, the material flunks the test.

Unless you have some experience as an upholsterer, it would probably be best for you to redo your plane's interior using custom-made reupholstery kits, rather than by cutting and stitching the materials yourself. Such kits are available through several sources, the best known of which is Airtex Products, Inc., 259 Lower Morrisville Rd., Fallsington, PA 19054. Airtex offers customized replacement aircraft interiors for virtually all types of general aviation aircraft, from trainers to light twins. Their kits are specifically made for do-it-yourselfers; they come in a wide variety of fabric types; and all materials in the kits meet applicable FARs. If you're serious about doing reupholstery work on your plane, you ought to write for the Airtex catalog.

Because cabin layouts and methods of attaching upholstery vary tremendously from plane to plane, even within a single model series, a comprehensive treatment of the subject of aircraft reupholstery cannot be included here. Rather, I would like to offer a few comments and caveats of a more general nature concerning some of the problems one is likely to encounter in refurbishing or replacing the seats, carpeting, side panels, and headliner in the typical lightplane.

Seat   Before you can reupholster a seat, you must remove it from the plane. As a matter of fact, before you can work on any of an airplane's interior furnishings, the seats must generally come out. Fortunately, this is rarely a problem, since aircraft seats—unlike many other vital accessories—are specifically designed to be easily removed. As always, though, some airplanes rate higher than others in this regard.

In general, front seats may be removed very quickly by simply unscrewing or otherwise removing the stops at the ends of the seat tracks, sliding the seats forward until the front brackets lift off the tracks, and sliding the seats backward until the rear brackets slip off the rails. (Afterward, it's a good idea to replace the seat stops in the tracks so that they won't get lost.) On older aircraft, front-seat removal can be a bit trickier, but it should never take you more than a few minutes to figure out how to remove the seats, no matter what type of plane you have. They really are made to come out quickly.

Rear seats are generally held down by bolts. Getting the seats out is just a matter of locating all the bolts and unscrewing them—a job that usually requires a very small wrench, owing to the severely limited amount of working space available. (You'll see what I mean when you try it.) Be careful, when removing double-wide (bench-type) rear seats, not to let seat legs or hold-down brackets scrape the cabin walls; sometimes the fit is rather tight.

If you are going to reupholster the seats completely, you'll have to strip them down to the frame. Take a good look at the nylon webbing material that covers the seat frame. This material is usually stretched around the frame one layer thick and glued to itself on the bottom side. For greater strength and durability, you might want to consider stretching some of this material across *both* sides of the frame (after all, this is what you're sitting on), and then proceed to build up the seat with foam, seat covers, etc.

If your seats are merely a little faded and you are hesitant to spend the money necessary to reupholster them, you may want to consider dyeing the existing fabric. Republic Aerosol Company, Compton, CA 90224, offers a series of aerosol-can-type fabric sprays specifically designed to "renew faded fabrics." (One 13-oz can costs about $2; ask your paint store for Republic Fabric Spray.) Obviously, this approach is not suitable for all fabric types; leather and vinyl cannot be refurbished this way. But if your seats do have fabric covers and the covers are of a solid color, spray dyeing is something to consider.

Carpeting Carpets are generally the easiest part of an aircraft interior to redo. Getting the old carpets out, however, can sometimes be quite a challenge. In some airplanes, it is practically necessary to rip the carpeting out, which is a perfectly acceptable technique if you intend to install a precut carpet kit. If, on the other hand, you plan to make your own replacement carpet, you're going to need the old carpet as a pattern from which to cut the new one. In that case, you'll want to avoid damaging the old carpet as you remove it from the plane.

The carpeting in many Piper airplanes is glued to a cardboard or honeycomb-type floorboard which, in turn, is glued to the cabin floor. In some cases, the carpeting is glued directly to the aluminum floor. (Piper makes limited use of snap-down carpet panels.) Getting the glued-down carpets out demands skillful use of a mallet and putty knife. In the process of removing the old carpets, you may well end up damaging the floorboards, so when you order new carpets for your Cherokee (or whatever), order new floorboards too.

Unlike Piper, Cessna installs nearly all its carpets with snaps or screws (because the cabin floor of a Cessna contains numerous inspection covers, all of which must be easily accessible to the mechanic at annual time). Consequently, it is never necessary to rip the carpet out of a Cessna. However, making a new carpet for a Cessna can be tricky unless you have access to a machine that installs snaps—and then you must be careful to install the snaps in exactly the right spots. A custom precut carpet kit is usually your best bet.

Side Panels Wall panels are generally easy to replace. They consist of a cardboard or fiberboard backing material to which is attached a decorative finish. The whole assembly is held to the wall by snaps or (more commonly) numerous tiny screws and washers. Wall panels, again, are something you can make yourself; you can also buy pre-fabricated wall-panel sets from Airtex or other sources. The sets offered by Airtex are, in most cases, better than the original factory-installed wall panels, owing to Airtex's use of Durapanel mounting stiffeners in place of the usual cardboard or fiberboard. The Durapanel stiffening material consists of layers of thin polyethylene separated by polyethylene fluting, similar to corrugated cardboard in design. It will not absorb moisture, warp, rot, expand, or contract; also, the Durapanel material is lighter than fiberboard and will not take a set when bent.

The trick in reinstalling wall panels is to locate all the little screw holes for all those tiny mounting screws. This is almost impossible to do by feel or by luck. The thing to do is find a large sewing needle, nail, or other pointed object, stick it through a hole in the wall panel, and fish around until the needle's pointed end encounters the corresponding screw hole in the fuselage. Then remove the needle and immediately insert a screw. Do this all the way around the wall panel, and you'll have it installed in about one-tenth the time it would otherwise take you to locate all those miniscule holes.

Headliners   Headliner replacement is among the most tedious of all cockpit reupholstery tasks. Before you can remove a headliner, you must detach all plastic trim panels, hat racks, map lights, courtesy lights, sun visors, trim-tab controls, and any other impedimenta attached to the headliner. The headliner itself will be held in by screws, contact cement, Velcro tape, metal bows, or a combination of the above. (On older Cessnas, the edges of the headliner are held in place by metal teeth that grab the headliner fabric. Piper, as usual, prefers glue.) Naturally, while you're working your arms will be above your head, and your head will probably be tilted back at a neck-kinking angle. Also, you'll be using back muscles you didn't know you had.

The hard part in installing a new headliner is getting everything to line up properly, so that no wrinkles show when you're done. One way to get around this bugaboo is to order a headliner kit from Airtex. The material in the Airtex kits is heat shrinkable, so that if there are any unsightly wrinkles in the headliner when you're finished, you can easily remove them with a hot iron or a hair blow dryer.

SOUNDPROOFING   Although today's lightplanes tend to be a bit quieter than their ancestors of 20 or 30 years ago, it is still nonetheless true that general aviation aircraft are comparatively noisy inside. What's more, a plane actually tends to become noisier over the years, as door seals shrink and crack, window caulking dries out, vents fail to close, etc. Fortunately, this tendency toward increasing loudness can be arrested (or even reversed, in some cases) through preventive maintenance.

Each aircraft cabin is unique in its particular constellation of bothersome frequencies and resonances. Usually, though, if the cabin is fairly well sealed against air leaks, the windshield and side windows constitute the most important entry points for noise coming into the cockpit: the next most important entryways are the firewall and the belly skins. In a cockpit that is not well sealed, gaps around doors, vents, etc., can contribute more noise than any other single source.

Obviously, if your cockpit is not well sealed, you ought to go to work first on door gaps, stuck vents, etc., before becoming involved in more costly and more complex soundproofing operations. To determine where the loudest noise entry points in your cabin are, take a 3-ft piece of rubber hose (inside diameter about ½ in.) with you the next time you go flying. While in cruise flight, probe the cockpit with one end of the hose as you hold the other end to your ear. Using the hose as a stethoscope, you'll quickly be able to locate the real problem areas in your cockpit.

Cracked and dried-out door seals are a common source of cockpit noise. (To the ear, a door with a bad seal is not much different from a door that isn't shut tight.) Replacing these seals is easy. Take a chunk of the old seal material to your local auto-parts store or body shop and buy about 10 feet of the same type of material; also buy some contact cement. Next, completely strip all the old rubber from the edge of your plane's doors. To speed this process, you may want to use a needle and syringe to apply methyl ethyl ketone, very sparingly, just between the seal and the door. The MEK will quickly dissolve any traces of old glue, allowing you to peel the rubber seal from the door easily. (The MEK will also dissolve paint and Plexiglas, though, so proceed with caution. Have a rag handy to wipe up excess solvent.)

Incidentally, while you're removing the old door seal, note exactly where it is positioned along the door edge; you'll want to lay the new seal down in exactly the same position, unless you want to take a chance on the door not closing properly after you're done. Of course, if you want a tighter-shutting door, you can move the new seal inboard of where the old one was (i.e., closer to the fuselage), but again, be careful. If you change the seal location more than $1/16$ in. (or a few millimeters), you may well end up with a door that doesn't function correctly.

With every trace of the old seal gone from the door, you can begin laying the new seal down very carefully, using a suitable contact adhesive (3M makes several good ones). Allow the cement to cure thoroughly before trying the door. To prevent the new seal from drying and cracking, periodically apply Oakite 6 compound or a similar preservative to the rubber.

Vent noise can be quite unpleasant in some aircraft; high-wing Cessnas, in particular, often have very noisy wing-root (pull-tube) vents. The thing to do here is go to the supermarket and pick up some plastic (not metallic) scouring pads of the type used to wash pots and pans. Stuff these blobs of plastic into the air-vent openings in the plane's wings. The plastic mesh slows—but does not block—the flow of air into the cabin, thereby reducing vent hiss considerably.

Exhaust noises can, in many cases, be made much more tolerable with the addition of extensions to the exhaust pipes. Lately, it seems that more and more exhaust extension kits have been coming onto the market; for an update on the situation, check the latest issue of *Trade-A-Plane*. (If no kit is available for your aircraft, don't give up on the idea of designing one yourself. In many cases it is not difficult to obtain one-time approval for such mods from the local FAA maintenance inspector.)

Any time the wall panels, floorboards, or headliner are out of your plane for refurbishing is a good time to consider adding extra cabin soundproofing in these areas. Ordinary fiber glass insulation is one of the more commonly used materials for this purpose; also, 3M makes an excellent adhesive foam product (Scotch Foam Y370) that can be applied behind wall panels, underneath carpeting, etc., to reduce noise and vibration. For information on soundproofing kits, contact Airtex.

A word of caution: Don't install so much sound-deadening foam, tape, etc., that you end up altering the center of gravity of the plane. (It's possible to do this: Some foil-backed foam and tape products weigh a half pound or more per square foot.) The use of aluminum tape, lead inlays, etc., will require the filing of an FAA Form 337: Major Repair and Alteration.

If you're really serious about reducing the sound level inside your cabin, the single most effective (and expensive) thing you can do is install thicker windows. Quarter-inch-thick acrylic windows are now available for a wide variety of aircraft, through sources listed in *Trade-A-Plane* and elsewhere. A ⅜-in.-thick windshield is available for Barons and Bonanzas, from Beryl D'Shannon Aviation Specialties, Inc., Rt. 2 Box 272, Jordan, MN 55352. Except for this, ¼ in. is the maximum Plexiglas thickness available for cockpit windows.

Naturally, the installation of thicker windows will increase the empty weight of your plane, probably by no more than 2 to 5 lb, and decrease the plane's useful load correspondingly. Be sure to remember this if you decide to install thick windows.

Of course, if you aren't willing to replace your windows, and you don't have the time to add extra padding behind your wall panels, headliner, carpet, etc., a $1.98 set of earplugs will do an acceptable job of reducing cockpit noise. They won't add much to the resale value of your plane, however.

AVIONICS Avionics manufacturers have devoted a great deal of study, in recent years, to the problem of how to increase the reliability of aircraft radios. As a result, virtually all types of aircraft radios, from marker beacons to DMEs, are now a good deal more reliable than they once were. Navcoms that 10 years ago might have had a mean time between failures (MTBF) of several *hundred* hours can today boast MTBFs in the *thousands* of hours.

At the same time, however, light aircraft have begun to carry and depend more heavily on ever-greater quantities of sophisticated electronics equipment, and the repair costs associated with that gear have gone up substantially (by virtue of its sophistication). Thus, paradoxically, although aircraft radios have, over the years, become a great deal more reliable, the average pilot is spending more on radio repairs today than ever before.

All this points to the increased importance and desirability of keeping radios in good shape. From a preventive maintenance standpoint, there are several things pilots can do in this regard—starting with keeping all black boxes dry and cool.

Windshield leaks are a common source of radio problems. Many (if not most) airplane windshields leak a bit in rainy conditions, and when rain water contaminates radios, bad things happen. In addition to causing out-and-out short circuits, water corrodes relay and switch contacts and deteriorates insulation. (A few drops of standing water can, over time, thoroughly wreck a poorly sealed RF or IF transformer.) To avoid water-related problems, make it a point to trace cockpit leaks to their source and fix them. (3M Strip Calk is good to use around windows.) Also, if your plane is stored in a particularly humid area—humid enough, say, for mildew to form in the cockpit—consider placing bags of desiccant on the seats between flights, to keep the cockpit air dry.

Heat, like water, has an extremely deleterious effect on electronic equipment; here again, airplane cockpits can be somewhat less than hospitable environments. On a warm (85°F) day, passive solar heating can raise the cockpit temperature of a parked arcraft to 160°F (71°C) or more. By comparison, TSO requirements for many types of avionics call for continuous-operation capability at only 131°F (55°C), with short-term high-temperature operation to be demonstrated at 160°F. Some deterioration of power-transistor performance can be observed, typically, at temperatures as low as 77°F (25°C); failure occurs at approximately 257°F (125°C). What this means, very simply, is that when you climb into your cockpit on a hot day and turn on all your radios, you are operating them in an environment that *exceeds* TSO requirements for high-temperature reliability. It is not an environment conducive to long radio life.

Several things can be done to protect your avionics from the ravages of heat. The first and most important is to install a windshield sunscreen, if the aircraft is not routinely hangared. (Even if it is routinely hangared, you should carry a sunscreen for those occasions when the plane may have to be tied down outside at strange airports.) A good sunscreen will keep cabin air temperatures within a few degrees of the outside air temperature at all times, thereby prolonging not only radio life, but instrument and upholstery life as well. Custom-made sunscreens are available through a variety of sources, or you can fabricate your own screen using heat-reflective "space blanket" material obtained through a local hardware or department store.

Something else you can do to minimize the risk of heat damage to your black boxes is to keep them turned off until you need to use them. Owing to the way radios are often stacked, adjacent radios tend to absorb each other's heat. (Since heated air rises, the number one navcom—top dog in the pile—generally suffers the most in this regard and is often the first unit in the stack to fail.) This being the case, it only makes sense to turn on but one com set and, say, the transponder, and keep all other boxes *off* until cruising altitude (i.e., cool air) is reached.

Air conditioning can, of course, be expected to lessen the likelihood of heat damage, but only if the radios in a warm cabin are left off long enough for the air conditioning to begin to be felt. Allow 5 to 10 min after the start of air conditioning for the black boxes to become thoroughly cold.

If you don't have (or don't want to spend) the money necessary to install air conditioning, you may well want to consider the installation of an inexpensive electric fan behind the panel, to circulate cooling air around the radio chassis. Any avionics shop can install such a cooling fan for you, if your mechanic doesn't want to tackle the job.

From a preventive maintenance standpoint, keeping radios *dry* and *cool* are without question the most important things you can do to enhance avionics reliability. They are also, in effect, the only things you can do to increase the serviceability of modern-day digital avionics (aside from turning radios off prior to engine startup and master-switch manipulations, to guard against voltage-spike* damage). If, however, your panel contains mostly pre-digital-era electronics (a surprising number of panels do), there may be a couple more things you can do to extend the life of your radios.

After a radio containing tubes (and that includes not only older navcoms, but more recent transponders and DMEs too) has been in service 10 years or more, you can expect some of those tubes to start becoming a bit senile. Unlike solid-state components, tubes wear out as they are used; the exact extent of the wear depends on how severely the tubes are stressed by their circuits. Different tubes have different life expectancies. Those with the shortest life expectancies are gen erally found in pulse equipment (transponders and DMEs).

Once an old navcom has been in service 9 or 10 years, it is not a bad idea to remove it from the panel every year or two to check its tubes. Removing the navcom from its tray usually isn't difficult; look for a pair (or two pairs) of mounting screws on the unit's face. Loosen these screws just enough so you can pull the radio out by grabbing it firmly by the channel-selector knobs. Then, once you've got the radio started—and you may find it takes a surprising amount of tugging to do this—grab it by the sides and carefully slide it all the way out of the panel (Figure 11-1). Check the back of the box to make sure the plug-in connectors are all intact.

With the radio thus removed, carefully place it in a padded box or case and take it to the local electronics-supply store, or any store that has a tube-testing machine. Then, following the instructions on the machine, plug in and test your radio's tubes one by one, returning them to their proper sockets when you're done. Don't forget to test all the tiny Nuvistor tubes scattered throughout the chassis. Some radios contain as many as two dozen of these tiny thimblelike metal tubes (Figure 11-2). If you need help, ask the store manager.

If you find a tube that's bad, you'll be faced with a dilemma: You will have to choose between buying a new tube and installing it yourself (which, under existing FARs, is not exactly legal), or paying a licensed avionics technician to buy and install the new tube for you (which would be legal but expensive). Such are the choices confronting the maintenance-conscious pilot.

Before you reinstall that old navcom in your panel, take a moment to make one other maintenance check: (again, this applies only to relatively ancient equip-ment): Inspect the frequency-selector wafer switches for cleanliness. If the contact areas are not shiny, and they probably won't be, buy a spray can of contact cleaner (Figure 11-3) at any electronics store, along with a package of cotton swabs, and thoroughly clean the contact points on those wafer switches. Direct a short burst of spray onto the back side of each wafer; then, using the end of a cotton swab, rub the contact areas until all the surface oxidation has been cleaned away. When you're done, the metal contacts should shine.

---

*Voltage spikes—transient uncontrolled increases in system voltage—can occur when the master switch or starter switch is engaged; this can be very damaging to unprotected electronic circuits.

FIGURE 11-1 In most cases, removing a black box from its tray requires only that you loosen one or two screws at the front of the radio (often with the aid of a very long, skinny screwdriver) and pull. Loosen the screw or screws just enough to free the radio—not enough to allow the screws to fall out and get lost. The retaining screws for this vintage ARC navcom are located at the upper right and left corners of the box, opposite the volume knobs.

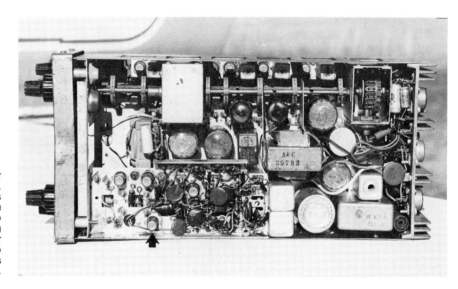

FIGURE 11-2 A surprising number of tube-equipped, hard-wired, pre-digital-era navcoms (like this old ARC 300) are still in use. If you own one, it pays to check the tubes from time to time—including all those tiny, thimble-like Nuvistor tubes, which may number in the dozens. One of the many Nuvistors is indicated by an arrow here.

After several years in service, switch contacts invariably accumulate a good deal of surface oxidation, which tends to act as an electrical barrier; obviously, it makes sense to remove this oxidation layer periodically. (Commercial contact cleaners dissolve such oxidation while leaving behind a very thin oil layer, which acts to protect the metal from further oxidation.) If contacts are not periodically cleaned in this fashion, it's just a matter of time until dirt and oxidation accumulate to the point where the contacts fail to function properly. Then, the next thing you know, you're taking your radio (which has mysteriously "lost" several frequencies) to the shop and complaining about the high cost of avionics repairs.

With your wafer switches cleaned and your tubes all checked out, you can reinstall the radio in the panel. Be sure all connectors achieve firm contact before

FIGURE 11-3 Radio Shack and others sell spray-can cleaners that you can use (with the aid of cotton swabs) to clean switch contacts in your radios. Older radios, especially, need their contacts cleaned often.

retightening the mounting screws at the front of the set; also, be especially sure to recheck all antenna connections. (Double-check to see that the master switch is off the whole time, too.) When you are confident that everything has been reinstalled properly, turn the switches on and verify that the set works. If it doesn't, check the circuit-breaker panel, recheck the antenna connections, recycle all switches, and try again. If it *still* doesn't work, you've got problems.

Owing to the nature of the failure modes that affect solid-state devices, there is only so much that any operator can do in the way of preventive maintenance, and we have covered most of the applicable techniques here. Before leaving the topic of avionics, however, I would like to mention some of the things you can do *after* a black box has failed or begun to deteriorate in performance, to ensure its quick return to service.

The main thing you can do to save time, money, and aggravation on avionics repairs is communicate your needs clearly to the service technician. Before taking a radio to any repair shop, you should prepare a written brief containing answers to all the following questions:

1. Is the set completely dead, or does it work intermittently?

2. Exactly which channels, if any, are out?

3. If the set works intermittently, does it usually fail immediately after being turned on, or several minutes later?

4. If later, how much later? Have you noticed a definite pattern?

5. Are you ever able to make the set regain function? How?

6. Does turning other equipment (navcoms, rotating beacons, etc.) on or off affect the behavior of the faulty set?

7. For a communications radio, can you transmit?

8. For an ADF, can you still tune and receive stations properly? Does the needle point to the station? Does the press-to-test button work?

9. For a nav unit, is your VOR error the same near the station as it is when you are further out?

10. If the VOR head is out, are you still able to pick up the nav-station signal and identify it?

11. Have you tested VOR indications in all quadrants and determined the amount of error (in degrees) for various bearings? Is the error always on the "plus" side? The "minus" side?

12. Have you tried the set on the ground with the engine on and off? Does operating the engine make any difference? Does the set behave differently on the ground than in the air?

13. Is the aircraft battery in good health? (How much water has it used in the past two months?) Have you noticed any starting problems?

These are just some of the things a good repair technician will want to know before examining a faulty radio. (This list of questions was, in fact, obtained from a large midwestern avionics shop; I did not make it up.) You should, however, anticipate other questions as well, by telling the technician whether any previous maintenance (and what kind) has been performed on the box in question, whether the alternator or some other component of the electrical system has recently been worked on, etc. The more things you can tell the repair technician about the defective radio's present behavior pattern, its past service history, and the circumstances under which it went kaput, the less time will be wasted diagnosing the problem (at $25 to $50 per hour), and the sooner you can be back in the air with a fully functional radio.

You should not always assume that the radio itself is at fault. Quite often, what appears to be a bona fide radio problem actually turns out, on closer examination, to be purely an airframe or installation problem. This is particularly true of newer-generation avionics. For example, if one navcom in a dual installation fails, it is common practice (and a good idea) to switch the tray locations of the two sets and observe whether the problem travels with the set or appears to be location-specific. Any problem that disappears when the radio is moved to another tray obviously involves installation.

Many a transponder has been declared inoperative when the antenna (which is generally mounted on the belly of the plane, not far aft of the crankcase breather line) became thoroughly covered with oil and dirt, thus blocking reception.

Before assuming that a particular problem resides within a particular piece of avionics gear, check all electrical connections for security, inspect antennas and antenna cables for condition, check the battery for charge level, and recycle all switches and circuit breakers. And even then, don't assume anything. Avionics technicians are discovering new failure modes every day.

INSTRUMENTS   Offhand, one would not think that the pilot's role in instrument maintenance could be very great, since A&P mechanics themselves are forbidden to calibrate or repair instruments. And, in fact, where actual hands-on maintenance is concerned, the pilot's role is indeed limited *once a breakdown has occurred*. Prior to the time an instrument fails, however, there is actually a great deal a pilot can do in the way of hands-on preventive maintenance. Most pilots are totally unaware of their privileges and duties in this area.

Flight instruments are surprisingly reliable, considering the delicacy of their internal mechanisms; any lack of reliability is often due to the extreme amounts of vibration to which panel-mounted instruments are subjected. To deal with the vibration problem, most manufacturers of modern-day aircraft have incorporated rubber shock mounts (similar to the engine shock mounts, but much smaller) in the mounting of at least the gyro instruments, if not the entire flight-instrument panel. As with engine mounts, though, the miniature Lord mounts used to secure instrument panels tend to shrink, harden, and crack over a period of years, so that they eventually need to be replaced. If they are not replaced every few years, engine and prop vibrations (which, of course, tend to increase in magnitude as the engine and *its* mounts get older) are felt more and more strongly by the instrument panel, until, finally, the gauges themselves begin to suffer.

The next time you are inside your plane (on the ground, with the engine off), take a look at the shock-mounted portions of your panel. The panel should not visibly sag, and when you place your fingers around its edge near the bottom, you should feel no "slop"; i.e., you should not be able to move the panel around easily. If the panel sags or can be worked up and down easily, chances are you need new shock mounts. The diagnosis is confirmed if, in cruise flight, you can see your instrument needles quivering.

If your panel shock mounts pass this preliminary test but are more than 2 years old, now is a good time to rotate them. Like engine mounts, rubber instrument-panel mounts tend to compress more on one side than on the other, and they thus take a "set" when allowed to remain in one position for years at a time. To counteract this tendency, it is a good idea (with both engine mounts and panel mounts) to rotate the rubber biscuits 180° in place and/or move them to other mounting locations every couple of hundred hours. This is not often done during annual inspections, although it should be.

It is worth noting, by the way, that if extra gauges have been added to your panel over the years, your present shock mounts may not be adequate for their task. As Cessna points out in one of its service manuals:

> Service life of instruments is directly related to adequate shock-mounting of the panel. In some cases, particularly when additional instruments have been added in the field, the original shock mounts are inadequate to support the increased weight of the panel. Installing additional shock mounts, when the instrument complement is increased, is a practical fix to prevent rapid deterioration of the mounts at the original locations.

Some instruments require a good deal more than just adequate shock mounting, as far as preventive maintenance goes, to ensure their continued proper functioning. The vacuum-operated gyro instruments, for example, are particularly fastidious with regard not only to the amount of air that passes through them, but also the cleanliness and temperature of that air. Feed a gyro instrument dirty air, and it will soon gum up. Feed it too much or too little air, and it will indicate incorrectly. Offer it air that's too cold [40°F (4°C) or lower], and it may not operate at all. (The lubricating oils in a gyro can thicken enough at cold temperatures to prevent gyro spinning.)

To keep your vacuum instruments (the gyro horizon, directional gyro, and, in older aircraft, the turn-and-bank indicator) in optimal working condition at all times, it is necessary for you to (1) replace system filter elements regularly and (2) monitor suction-gauge readings frequently to ensure that your gyros are getting just the right amount of air. Inattention to either of these items can spell trouble for gyros.

In many pre-1970 aircraft, the vacuum lines leading from the engine-mounted vacuum pump terminate at the instruments themselves; thus, to keep the gauges from becoming contaminated with dust, smoke, etc., individual filter elements are installed in each instrument. In most newer aircraft, by contrast, suction tubing runs from the vacuum pump to gyro instruments to a suction gauge, and thence to a central air filter mounted underneath the panel. Air (cockpit air, incidentally) is thus evacuated first through the main filter under the panel, then through the suction gauge, then the gyro instruments, and finally to the vacuum pump. The latter type of system is depicted in Figure 11-4.

It should be noted that in some aircraft having a central (or "system") air filter, individual filters are still used in the gyro instruments themselves. This is somewhat rare, however.

Most airframe manufacturers recommend that individual instrument filter elements be replaced every 100 hr or whenever erratic gyro responses are observed, whichever comes first. For central air filters, the usual recommended replacement interval is 500 hr. Because of the exceedingly delicate nature of a gyro instrument's internal workings, it is very important that filter elements be replaced promptly at the recommended intervals, especially if the aircraft is operated in a dusty environment, and *especially* if cigarette smoke is often present in the cockpit. Tar and nicotine have a way of shortening gyro life. (Don't laugh. Some A&Ps swear they can tell whether a DC-6 has been used to carry freight or passengers, just by

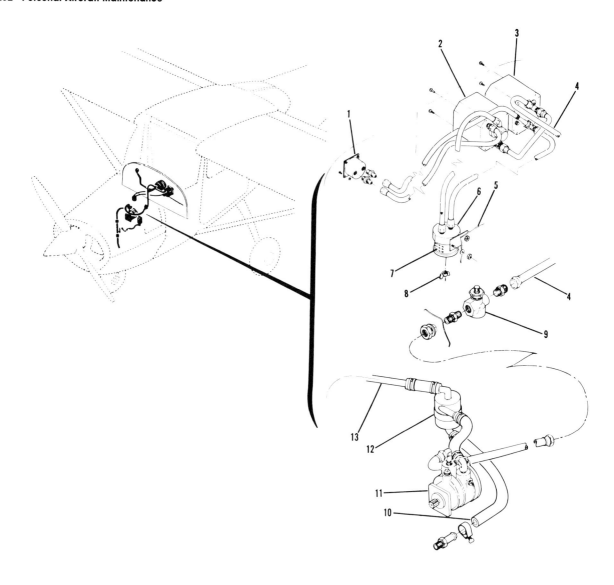

FIGURE 11-4 Typical vacuum-system installation. (*Cessna diagram.*)

1. Suction Gage
2. Gyro Horizon
3. Directional Gyro
4. Hose
5. Firewall
6. Filter Bracket
7. Filter Element
8. Wing Nut
9. Relief Valve
10. Hose (Oil Return)
11. Vacuum Pump
12. Oil Separator
13. Hose (Overboard)

looking at the rivets on the outside of the fuselage. The passenger aircraft, it is said, can be distinguished from the freight hauler on the basis of tiny brown stains streaking downwind from the fuselage rivets, where the lower outside air pressure sucked nicotine out of the interior of the aircraft over years of high-altitude flight.)

The second important point is to monitor suction-gauge readings closely, to determine whether the vacuum instruments are receiving the proper flow of air. In every vacuum-instrument-equipped plane, somewhere between the vacuum pump and the gyro instruments themselves (usually on the cabin side of the fire-wall), there's a device known as a *suction relief valve*. Its purpose is to prevent system suction from becoming too great at high engine rpm. This valve is usually covered with a screen or filter of its own (often foam rubber), to prevent the vacuum pump from ingesting foreign matter when the valve opens. When the suction-relief-valve screen clogs, system suction increases; depending on the magnitude of the increase in suction, your gyro instruments will either become much more sensitive (something you may enjoy) or completely insane (something you won't enjoy at all).

Of course, the suction-relief-valve screen rarely clogs all at once, instantly and totally. Rather, the screen tends to accumulate dirt gradually, causing a slow, insidious rise in system suction levels. The only way to keep track of such changes, obviously, is to monitor suction-gauge readings on every flight. If the relief-valve screen is filling with dirt, you'll generally see it in your suction-gauge readings well before your instruments go berserk. (Check your service manual for information on how often to clean or replace the suction-relief-valve screen in your airplane.)

One problem that can affect not only vacuum instruments (gyro horizon, DG, turn-and-bank) but also pitot-static instruments (airspeed, altimeter, rate-of-climb) is that of leaky hoses and hose connections. Granted, this is not apt to be a very common problem in newer aircraft; however, some planes have been flying 20 years or more on the original factory plumbing, and in these aircraft, leaks can be expected to crop up at any time.

Leaks in vacuum-system lines can often be detected in suction-gauge readings before they have grossly affected gyro performance. A leak at any point in the vacuum system will generally show up as an abnormally low suction-gauge indi-cation. The suction gauge thus serves as a kind of low-key annunciator for vacuum-system leaks.

The pitot system, unfortunately, has no equivalent to the suction gauge; a leak either manifests itself as a faulty instrument indication or goes unnoticed. There is, however, a simple way of testing the pitot system for small leaks that may be on their way to becoming big ones. All you do is attach a stout piece of rubber tubing, several feet long, to the end of the pitot tube out on the plane's wing. Clamp the tubing down securely so that there are no leaks at the point of attach-ment. Then, with someone else in the cockpit, slowly begin rolling the free end of the tubing up, as you would roll up a tube of toothpaste, until the airspeed indicator reads in the cruise-airspeed range. Clamp the tubing tightly, and wait 5 to 10 min. If the indicated airspeed drops more than about 50 mph during this period, you can reasonably assume that there is a leak somewhere between the rubber tubing and the airspeed indicator. (*Note:* at the end of the leak test, release the pressure in the system slowly. Otherwise, damage to the airspeed indicator may result.)

If you suspect a leak in any instrument system, begin by retightening all hose connections along the length of the system. Also, inspect all tubing for signs of chafing, cracking, etc. Replace any tubing that looks questionable. (According to FAR Part 43, Appendix A, pilots may replace "any hose connection except hydraulic connections." This includes instrument hoses.)

If you do decide to replace any instrument tubing, remember to consult your service manual for information regarding the types of thread lubricants to use and *not* to use. (Thread lubes are usually not permitted in vacuum systems employing a dry-type vacuum pump.) Also, avoid disconnecting more than one instrument at a time; it's easier than you think to forget which hose goes where. And maintain sanitary conditions. Instruments are very sensitive to dust, moisture, tar, nicotine, etc.; so be sure, after disconnecting any instrument, to place dust covers over all exposed fittings.

One more thing: Should the need arise to blow out an instrument hose (to remove condensation or obstructions), always disconnect both ends of the hose in question. As an added precaution, blow from the instrument end out.

For more information on the subject of instrument maintenance, check your service manual and consult the troubleshooting charts in Appendix A.

✢   ✢   ✢

Obviously, a great deal more could be written on the subject of cockpit maintenance, and, indeed, on every type of maintenance discussed in this book. Dozens of volumes could (and, I think, should) be published on the various subtopics that we have lumped together as "aircraft maintenance." This book is really little more than a prefatory note to dozens of unwritten volumes.

Whether I have succeeded in making clear the murky waters of lightplane maintenance is something only the reader can decide. If nothing else, I hope that I have demystified the field of aircraft maintenance and debunked a number of widely held myths regarding the inadvisability of pilots taking maintenance into their own hands—thereby in some small measure contributing to the reader's own sense of self-confidence in this area.

There may be a better, less costly way to increase one's enjoyment of flying than to get involved in preventive maintenance—but if there is, I haven't heard of it.

APPENDIX A
TROUBLE-SHOOTING CHARTS

BATTERY

Trouble	Possible cause	Remedy
Dead battery	Standing too long	Place battery on charger; continue charging until electrolyte reaches a specific gravity of at least 1.250 (at 80°F); fly plane more often
	Master switch was left on	Recharge battery
	Battery is worn out (won't recharge)	Buy new battery
	Improper charging rate setting	Have voltage-regulator output adjusted by a competent technician
	Excessive discharging	Avoid using electrical equipment when alternator output is low (e.g., during taxi); use external power for starting when outside air temperature is below freezing
	Short circuit to ground	Check wiring
	Contaminated electrolyte	Replace battery
	Broken cell partitions	Replace battery
Short battery life	Heavy discharge	Reduce electrical load when alternator output is low
	Insufficient electrolyte	Replenish electrolyte on a regular basis (by adding distilled water)
	Sulfation due to disuse	Charge the battery for 50 to 100 hr at half the regular charging rate; if gravity readings do not increase, discard battery
	Contaminated electrolyte	Replace battery

BATTERY *(Continued)*

Trouble	Possible cause	Remedy
Cracked cells	Battery froze	Replace battery; keep new battery charged (*Note:* Always charge battery for 30 min minimum following the addition of water in freezing weather.)
	Hold-down bracket is loose	Install new battery and secure firmly
Excessive water consumption	One cell only: cracked cell	Replace battery
	All cells: charging rate is set too high	Have charging rate adjusted downward
Corrosion inside container	Spillage from overfilling cells	Flush battery box with soda solution (*Caution:* do not allow soda to enter cells.)
	Charging rate is set too high	Have charging rate adjusted downward
	Clogged vent lines	Clean out or replace lines
Reversed battery polarity	Cables were connected backward on charger during servicing	Slowly discharge battery completely (do not install in plane); recharge correctly and test for proper polarity

ALTERNATOR OR GENERATOR

Trouble	Possible cause	Remedy
Generator output is low	Excessively worn brushes	Replace brushes
	Dirty commutator	Clean commutator with Varsol-moistened cloth
	Scored or pitted commutator	Turn down or replace unit
	Brushes are not properly seated (mainly a problem with new or rebuilt units)	New brushes must be seated to at least 75% of the contact surface before generator is placed in service; this is done by running the generator with *no load* for at least 15 min
	Loose or high-resistance electrical connections	Check wiring; clean and tighten all connections
	Improper voltage regulator setting	Have voltage regulator checked and adjusted
Generator operates in normal speed range, but ammeter reads off scale	Generator field is magnetized in wrong direction	Flash the field by momentarily connecting a jumper between the "Generator" and "Battery" terminals of the voltage regulator
Alternator output is low	Faulty wiring	Check wiring; clean and tighten connections
	Faulty diode	Replace alternator diode(s)
	Faulty winding	Replace winding
Alternator output is high	Voltage regulator is out of adjustment	Have regulator adjusted
	Faulty wiring	Check wiring
	Defective voltage regulator	Replace unit
Alternator circuit breaker pops when master switch is turned on	Short between alternator and bus bar	Find and repair as necessary
	Damaged diode	Replace alternator diode(s)
Alternator diodes fail repeatedly	Reverse-current damage	Check battery polarity (incorrect charging can reverse a battery's polarity); check battery wiring
	Excessive engine vibration	Check engine mounts (see also "Rough idle" below)

STARTER MOTOR

Trouble	Possible cause	Remedy
Starter cranks very slowly	Battery is low (specific gravity below 1.220)	Recharge battery
	Starter switch and/or relay contacts are burned or dirty	Replace defective parts
	Bad cable connections	Inspect and clean all connections
	Worn, dirty, or burned commutator	Have commutator turned down; do not operate starter more than 30 sec continuously without allowing it to cool
	Worn, dirty, or improperly lubricated starter	Check starter brushes (replace if worn to half of original length), brush spring tension, brush lead terminals, condition of bearing; recondition motor as needed
Starter fails to operate at all	Low battery	Recharge or replace battery
	Defect in wiring	Check continuity; replace wiring as needed
	Defective master switch	Throw master "on" and check operation of lights, radios, etc.; replace switch if defective
	Defective starter switch	Check switch continuity; replace as needed
	Defective starter motor (all above items check out negative)	Check for worn, binding, or improperly seated brushes, excessive brush side play, shorted armature, dirty commutator, grounded or open field circuit; overhaul unit as required
Noisy starter	Worn pinion	Replace starter drive
	Dirty Bendix drive	Wash with petroleum-base cleaning solvent
	Worn or broken teeth on crankshaft gear	Turn engine over by hand, examining crankshaft gear; replace gear, if necessary
Starter runs but will not crank engine	Damaged starter pinion or crankshaft gear	Replace defective parts
	Defective overrunning clutch	Replace defective parts

FLIGHT CONTROLS

Trouble	Possible cause	Remedy
	AILERONS	
Resistance to control-wheel movement	Cables are too tight	Adjust cable tension
	Pulleys are binding	Observe pulleys as ailerons are operated; replace binding pulleys
	Cable has jumped pulley	Replace cable on pulley
	Defective U joints (if used)	Replace defective parts
	Rusted chain	Check chain(s); replace if rusted
Lost motion in control wheel	Worn rod ends	Check visually; replace worn parts
	Loose cables	Check and adjust cable tension
	Broken pulley(s)	Replace broken part(s)
	Defective bellcranks	Replace defective parts
	Loose chain(s)	Adjust chain tension
Control wheel not level with ailerons neutral	Improperly adjusted chain or cables	Adjust rigging per aircraft manual
	Improperly adjusted pushrods or pullrods.	If other components of system are properly rigged, rods are out of adjustment; adjust as necessary
Dual control wheels not coordinated	Chain is not properly adjusted on sprocket	Adjust chain
	ELEVATORS	
Binding or jerky motion in elevator control	Cables are slack	Adjust cable tension
	Cables are not riding on pulleys correctly	Check cable routing
	Lubrication is needed	Lubricate entire system
	Defective control T, Y, or U pivot bearings	Check pivots for free movement with no load; replace defective parts
	Clevis bolts are too tight	Adjust to relieve binding
	Defective elevator hinges	Move elevator by hand to check hinges; replace defective parts

FLIGHT CONTROLS (*Continued*)

Trouble	Possible cause	Remedy
AILERONS		
Elevator fails to attain prescribed travel	Cables are unevenly tightened	Rig per aircraft manual
	Stops are incorrectly set	Adjust per aircraft manual
RUDDER		
Binding or jerky movement of rudder pedals	Rudder is contacting tail cone	Check clearance at tail cone; readjust tail cone if necessary
	Pedals require lubrication	Apply general-purpose oil to lube points as needed
	Nosewheel steering rods are not properly adjusted	Adjust per aircraft manual
	Cables are too tight, cables are misrouted, binding or defective pulleys, etc.	Inspect entire system; adjust cable tension, reroute cables, and/or replace defective parts
	Defective rudder hinge bushings or bearings, or bellcrank bearings	Replace defective parts
Incorrect rudder travel	Bent pushrods or pullrods (if used)	Replace defective parts
	Incorrect rigging	Rig per aircraft manual
Lost motion between pedals and rudder	Insufficient cable tension	Adjust cable tension

LANDING GEAR

Trouble	Possible cause	Remedy
Nosewheel shimmies	Shimmy dampener is worn or defective	With the nose of the plane off the ground, grab the nose wheel and turn it back and forth rapidly to check damping action; repair or replace dampener as necessary
	Shimmy dampener lacks fluid	Service unit per aircraft-manual recommendations
	Shimmy dampener or bracket is loose	Replace hardware as necessary
	Tire is out of balance	Check balance; add weights to inside of tire or replace tire
	Worn wheel bearings	Replace worn parts
	Worn torque-link bolts or bushings	Replace worn parts
	Nose strut is loose in attaching clamps (Cessna fixed gear)	Tighten clamp bolts
Tires wear unevenly or excessively	Incorrect tire inflation	Maintain proper tire pressure; check at least once per week
	Excessive brake use	Get off the brakes
	Wheel(s) are out of alignment	Check and correct per aircraft-manual instructions
	Dragging brakes	Jack wheel and spin to check for excessive friction; inspect brake components; replace defective parts (see also "dragging brakes" below)
	Axle nut is too tight	Jack wheel, check for excessive friction with brake removed; if bearings are dragging, back off on axle nut (do not allow sideplay to develop, however)
	Defective or cheaply made tires	Buy a better brand or grade of tire
	Bent axle(s)	Replace defective part(s)
	Loose torque links	Check clearances; rebush or replace parts
Airplane leans to one side	Incorrect tire inflation	Adjust tire pressure
	Oleo strut requires air or fluid	Check oleo for proper extension; service with air and/or oil as needed

LANDING GEAR *(Continued)*

Trouble	Possible cause	Remedy
Airplane leans to one side *(Cont.)*	Hard-landing damage	Check for wing and fuselage deformation, popped rivets, etc.; repair damage
	Landing-gear attaching parts are not tight	Jack plane and check all parts for security
	Landing-gear spring is excessively sprung (Wittman-type gear)	Replace gear leg
	Incorrect shimming at inboard end of gear (Wittman-type gear)	Install shims per aircraft manual
Oleo strut(s) will not hold air pressure	Filler plug is not tightened properly	Check seals, apply thread lube, and retighten plug assembly per aircraft-manual specs
	Dirt inside valve core at top of strut	Service strut with air and check for leakage (with a suitably calibrated pressure gauge) over a period of several hours; replace valve core if necessary; keep valve stem capped at all times to prevent dirt entry
	Defective strut seals	Replace defective seals
Dragging brakes	Damage or accumulated dirt is restricting free movement of brake parts at disc	Check parts for freedom of movement; clean, repair, and/or replace parts as needed
	Brake pedal is binding	Adjust as necessary
	Parking brake does not release fully	Adjust as necessary
	Worn or defective piston return spring in master cylinder	Replace defective part
	Restriction in hydraulic lines and/or at compensating port in master cylinder	Jack wheel and loosen brake line at brake housing to relieve trapped pressure (wheel should then turn freely); drain and clean brake lines, then fill and bleed system; if problem persists, overhaul master cylinder
	Worn, scored, or warped brake discs	Replace discs and linings on both wheels (to ensure symmetric braking)

VACUUM SYSTEM

Trouble	Possible cause	Remedy
High suction-gauge readings	Suction relief-valve screen is clogged	Clean or replace screen
	Relief valve is inoperative	Reset valve; replace if defective
Low suction-gauge readings	Relief valve is out of adjustment	Adjust or replace valve
	Leaks or restrictions between instruments and relief valve	Disconnect and blow out lines; replace defective tubing
	Restriction in air-oil separator or pump discharge line	Clean air-oil separator in Stoddard solvent and blow dry; blow out lines
Normal suction-gauge readings; sluggish or erratic gyro instrument response	Instrument air filters are clogged	Replace filters
Suction-gauge readings fluctuate	Sticking relief valve	Clean valve with Stoddard solvent; if sticking persists, replace valve
	Defective suction gauge	Substitute known-good gauge
Oil comes over in pump discharge line (belly of plane may be coated with oil)	Clogged air-oil separator	Clean in Stoddard solvent; blow dry
	Oil-return line is obstructed	Blow out line or replace
	Excessive oil flow through pump (wet-type vacuum pump)	Pump oil-return rate should not exceed 120 cc/hr at 50 psi oil pressure; if necessary, replace pump oil-metering collar and pin

INSTRUMENTS

Trouble	Possible cause	Remedy
MAGNETIC COMPASS		
Excessive card error	External magnetic interference	Locate interference and eliminate, or relocate instrument
	Compass is not properly compensated	Compensate instrument
Excessive card oscillation	Improper instrument mounting	Align instrument
	Insufficient liquid	Replenish alcohol in instrument
Sluggish card	Weak magnets	Replace instrument
	Excessive pivot friction or broken jewel	Replace instrument
	Instrument is too heavily compensated	Recompensate instrument
Liquid leakage	Defective sealing gaskets	Replace instrument
	Broken cover glass	Replace instrument
DIRECTIONAL GYRO		
Excessive drift in either direction	Dirty air filter (high vacuum)	Inspect system filter; replace as needed
	Excessive vibration	Test with vibrometer; if amplitude is more than 0.004 in. (0.1 mm), examine panel shock mounts
	Insufficient vacuum	Check for proper adjustment of vacuum regulating valve; examine lines for leaks, breaks, etc.; retighten all connections
	Worn, dirty, or defective mechanism	Replace instrument
Dial spins continuously in one direction	Operating limits have been exceeded	Reset instrument with aircraft in level flight
	Defective mechanism	Replace instrument
GYRO HORIZON		
Horizon bar fails to respond	Dirty air filter (high vacuum)	Replace system filter

INSTRUMENTS *(Continued)*

Trouble	Possible cause	Remedy
Horizon bar fails to respond (*Cont.*)	Insufficient vacuum	Check adjustment of vacuum regulating valve; inspect lines for leaks, poor connections, etc.
Horizon bar does not settle	Insufficient vacuum	Check adjustment of vacuum regulating valve; inspect lines for leaks, poor connections, etc.
	Excessive vibration	Test with vibrometer; if amplitude is more than 0.004 in. (0.1 mm), examine panel shock mounts and replace if necessary
	Defective mechanism	Replace instrument
Horizon bar oscillates or vibrates excessively	Dirty air filter (high vacuum)	Check system air filter and replace if necessary
	Vacuum regulating valve is improperly adjusted	Adjust valve per aircraft manual
	Defective mechanism	Replace instrument
	Excessive vibration	Test with vibrometer; if amplitude is more than 0.004 in. (0.1 mm), examine panel shock mounts and replace if necessary
TURN COORDINATOR		
Gyro fails to start	At low temperatures: oil is too thick	Allow time for oil to warm up
	Clogged instrument filter (vacuum-type instrument)	Examine and replace instrument filter (if necessary)
	Circuit breaker has popped (electrically powered instrument)	Reset circuit breaker
	Low vacuum (vacuum-type instrument)	Check vacuum pump and system plumbing for integrity; readjust vacuum regulating valve as necessary
Instrument does not indicate level with plane in level flight	Bar is incorrectly set on its staff	Replace or repair instrument
	Gimbal-and-rotor assembly is out of balance	Replace or repair instrument

INSTRUMENTS *(Continued)*

Trouble	Possible cause	Remedy
Instrument sluggish in returning to level	Oil or dirt between damping pistons and cylinders	Replace instrument
	Excessive clearance between rotor and pivots	Replace instrument
AIRSPEED INDICATOR		
Instrument fails to operate	Pitot line is clogged	Check pitot tube; remove and clean if necessary (cover impact tube between flights to avoid contamination); blow out line, retighten connections
	Pitot line is broken or improperly connected	Replace line and/or retighten connections
	Damaged instrument	Replace intrument
Pointer vibrates	Excessive panel vibration (test with vibrometer)	Replace panel shock mounts
	Tubing is vibrating	Check tubing security
Pointer wavers	Leak in pitot or static lines	Tighten connections and/or replace lines as necessary
	Leak in lines connecting ASI, altimeter, and rate-of-climb indicator	Tighten connections and/or replace lines as necessary
	Damaged instrument	Replace instrument
ALTIMETER		
Instrument fails to operate	Static line is plugged	Open alternate air source; if instrument still fails to function, blockage exists in line from airspeed indicator to altimeter; if alternate air restores function, obstruction is in main static source line (blow line clear)
	Defective mechanism	Replace instrument
Incorrect indication	Hands are not set correctly	Reset hands
	Leaking diaphragm	Replace instrument
	Shift in mechanism	Replace instrument

INSTRUMENTS *(Continued)*

Trouble	Possible cause	Remedy
Pointer oscillates	Static is irregular	Check static lines for obstructions or leaks; blow out lines and/or retighten connections as necessary
	Leak in altimeter case	Replace instrument
	Leak in static connections to other instruments	Check plumbing from altimeter to other instruments; blow out lines and/ or retighten connections as necessary

RATE-OF-CLIMB INDICATOR

Trouble	Possible cause	Remedy
Does not indicate zero in level flight	Aging diaphragm	Return pointer to zero with reset knob while tapping instrument lightly
Instrument inoperative	Clogged static line (condensation, insects, etc.)	If alternate static source returns function, blockage is between rate-of-climb indicator and other instruments; if not, blow out all lines
	Static-line leak(s)	Replace line(s) and/or retighten connections as necessary
	Defective mechanism	Replace instrument
Pointer oscillates	Clogged static line	Blow out line
	Leak in static line	Repair leak
	Leaky instrument case	Replace instrument

TACHOMETER

Trouble	Possible cause	Remedy
No indication	Flexible shaft is broken	Replace shaft; lubricate per manufacturer's recommendations
	Defective mechanism	Replace instrument
Pointer oscillates excessively	Rough spot on or sharp bend in driveshaft	Check cable housing for kinks, bends with a radius of less than 6 in., and damage; repair, replace, and/or reroute shaft.
	Excessive friction in instrument	Replace instrument

MANIFOLD PRESSURE GAUGE

Trouble	Possible cause	Remedy
Gauge reads 29 to 30 in. at all times	Broken pressure line	Replace line
	Faulty mechanism	Replace instrument
Needle operates sluggishly	Foreign matter is lodged in pressure line	Blow out line

INSTRUMENTS *(Continued)*

Trouble	Possible cause	Remedy
Needle operates sluggishly (*Cont.*)	Leak in line	Have pressure line inspected; correct leaks
	Dirty mechanism	Replace instrument
Excessive gauge error with engine stopped	Condensate or fuel in pressure line	Blow out line
	Leak in line	Correct leak
	Leak in vacuum bellows	Replace instrument
	Loose pointer (or shifted pointer)	Replace instrument
High manifold pressure readings at idle	Air leak in induction system	Correct leak
	Improperly adjusted carburetor or fuel-injection system	Adjust carburetor or fuel injector
	Hydraulic lifters are bleeding down too fast	Replace lifters
	Incorrect hydraulic lifters installed in engine	Install correct P/N lifters
Excessive needle vibration	Excessive panel vibration	Replace panel shock mounts
	Tight rocker pivot bearings	Replace instrument

CONSTANT-SPEED PROPELLER

Trouble	Possible cause	Remedy
Blades fail to change pitch	Control cable is broken or disconnected	Reconnect or replace cable as necessary
Blades will not cycle through full pitch range	Excessive blade friction	Overhaul prop
	Defective pitch-change mechanism	Overhaul prop
	Defective or sludge-clogged governor	Repair or desludge governor as necessary
	Sludge buildup in crankshaft	Have crankshaft desludged
	Governor is improperly rigged	Check rigging; rerig as necessary
	Control cable is kinked	Replace cable (if kink resulted from routing-bracket failure, replace bracket also); do not rotate vernier prop control with knob at full-in or full-out position
Inability to attain full rpm on takeoff (or during ground operation at full throttle)	Governor high-rpm stop is set too low	Adjust stop properly
	Incorrect governor or propeller was installed	Check P/N of prop and governor; install correct prop and governor
	Defective governor	Overhaul governor
	Engine is not attaining full power	Check ignition and induction systems for proper operation and adjustment; check muffler for broken baffles, which may be blocking exhaust outlet (strike muffler with rubber mallet and listen for rattling baffles)
	Tachometer reading is incorrect	Check tachometer accuracy; replace tachometer if defective
Full-throttle rpm too high	Wrong governor setting	Reset governor
	Defective governor	Overhaul governor
	Incorrect propeller installed	Check P/N; install correct propeller

CONSTANT-SPEED PROPELLER *(Continued)*

Trouble	Possible cause	Remedy
Engine rpm will not stabilize	Sludge in governor pilot valve or relief valve	Have governor desludged
	Backlash in governor control system	Rerig system as necessary
	Air is trapped inside propeller actuating cylinder	Purge trapped air by cycling the prop repeatedly before takeoff
	Excessive friction in pitch-change mechanism	Lubricate or repair propeller as necessary
	Fluctuating engine oil pressure	Ground aircraft and examine engine
	Defective governor (sticky or bent pilot valve, burrs on pilot-valve lands, sticky relief valve, etc.)	Repair governor as needed
Oil leakage at mounting flange	Damaged engine to prop O-ring seal	Replace seal
	Nuts are not torqued correctly	Check torque, and retighten nuts if necessary
	Foreign matter is lodged between engine and prop mating surfaces	Clean mating surfaces
Oil leakage between hub and cylinder (McCauley)	Defective gasket	Replace gasket
	Mounting screws are not tight	Retighten screws
Grease leakage at hub grease fitting (Hartzell)	Loose or defective fitting	Replace or retighten fitting
Oil or grease leakage at any other place	Defective seals, gaskets, threads, etc., and/or improper assembly	Repair or replace parts (or overhaul propeller) as necessary

ENGINE

Trouble	Possible cause	Remedy
Engine will not start (starter motor cranks engine)	Engine is flooded (gasoline odor may be apparent near front of plane)	Continue cranking with throttle *full open* and mixture in "idle cutoff" (if fire ensues, continue cranking); when engine catches, return throttle to idle and place mixture control in "full rich" position
	Insufficient prime (most likely on a cold day with a cold engine)	Use primer and throttle in accordance with operator's-manual recommendations
	Throttle is open too far	Set throttle for 800 to 1000 rpm for starting unless engine is flooded
	Fouled plugs	Clean and/or replace plugs
	Magneto impulse coupling is not working (impulse click is not heard when prop is pulled through in the normal direction by hand)	Check mags for binding or broken impulse springs; check torque on coupling retaining nut
	Inoperative vibrator ("shower of sparks" type ignition)	Listen for buzz of vibrator during start attempt (lack of buzz indicates defective vibrator or open circuit)
	Low voltage at vibrator input ("shower of sparks" type ignition)	Check voltage between vibrator "in" terminal and ground terminal while starter is engaged (voltage must be at least 8 V in 12-V system, at least 13 V in 24-V system)
	Retard points are not closing ("shower of sparks" type ignition); engine may kick back	Check points for proper adjustment; check electrical connections at mag and vibrator
	Magnetos are not properly timed to engine	Check timing and adjust per aircraft-manual specs.
	Magneto internal timing is not adjusted properly (E gap may have drifted due to point or follower wear)	Check timing; replace worn or defective parts and/or adjust timing as necessary

ENGINE *(Continued)*

Trouble	Possible cause	Remedy
Engine will not start (starter motor cranks engine) *(Cont.)*	Vapor lock (most likely on a hot day with a hot engine)	Consult engine operator's manual for appropriate remedial action
	Induction air leaks	Inspect induction system; correct leaks
Engine starts but dies	Propeller control is set in low-rpm position	Select high rpm
	Water in fuel	Drain main strainer bowl and recheck all sumps
	Engine is flooded (black smoke appears as engine starts and dies)	Open throttle fully and continue cranking with mixture in "idle cutoff"; when engine catches, reduce throttle and apply full rich mixture
	Insufficient prime	Reprime in accordance with operator's-manual recommendations (if air temperature is below freezing, continue to prime while cranking)
	Fouled plugs and/or improper electrode gap	Clean and gap plugs
	Defective engine-driven fuel pump	Replace pump
	Defective fuel-injection system	Have system serviced
	Defective carburetor	If engine will operate while being primed but quits when priming is discontinued, carburetor is defective; replace unit
	Leaking primer	Replace or repair primer
	Induction air leaks	Repair leaks
Rough idle	Faulty ignition system	Check condition of spark plugs, ignition harness, and magnetos
	Primer is leaking or not properly locked	Lock securely or repair as necessary
	Low fuel pressure	Adjust fuel pressure higher; if pressure cannot be adjusted, repair or replace fuel pump
	Cracked engine mount or defective bushings	Repair or replace defective parts
	Idle mixture is too rich	Adjust idle mixture per aircraft-manual recommendations

ENGINE *(Continued)*

Trouble	Possible cause	Remedy
Rough idle *(Cont.)*	Vapor is forming in fuel line	Turn boost pump on
	Plugged injector nozzle(s)	Perform a cold-cylinder test to locate affected nozzle(s); wash nozzles in acetone and blow dry
	Uneven cylinder compression	Perform differential compression check; rework bad cylinders
Engine surges	Incorrect prop governor was installed	Replace governor with correct part
	Defective prop governor	Replace governor
	Crankcase breather is clogged	Remove obstructions from breather line (in winter, preheat may be necessary before engine startup to melt ice in breather)
	Injector nozzle(s) are dirty	Remove and clean dirty nozzles
	Defective oil pump	Check to be sure the pump is not sucking air; replace pump if it is defective
	Carburetor is out of adjustment	Repair or replace carburetor
	Propeller blades are not cycling freely	Lubricate or repair propeller as appropriate
	Waste gate is binding intermittently (turbocharged engines)	Attempt to free waste-gate butterfly with penetrant oil; if this fails, replace unit
	Air in oil lines or waste-gate actuator (turbocharged engines)	Bleed the system (continued running of the engine may correct the problem)
Engine fails to develop full power	Incorrect grade of fuel or contaminated fuel	Drain fuel system; service with appropriate grade and type of fuel
	Broken baffles in muffler have blocked exhaust outlet	Tap muffler with a rubber mallet and listen for rattling baffles; replace defective muffler
	Fouled spark plugs	Clean or replace plugs
	Throttle lever is not rigged properly	Check for full travel at the carburetor (or injector); rerig as necessary
	Low cylinder compression	Perform differential compression test; rework bad cylinders

ENGINE *(Continued)*

Trouble	Possible cause	Remedy
Engine fails to develop full power *(Cont.)*	Restrictions in induction system	Eliminate restrictions
	Crankshaft-to-camshaft timing is incorrect	Remove accessory housing and correct timing
	Dirt buildup on compressor wheel (turbocharged engines)	Inspect and clean wheel
	Waste gate is out of adjustment (turbocharged engines)	Adjust to correct open and closed limits
	Waste gate is stuck open (turbocharged engines)	Remove actuator and free waste-gate butterfly (in the future, apply penetrating oil to each end of butterfly shaft every 25 hr)
	Oil pressure too low to close waste gate (turbocharged engines)	See "Low oil pressure" below
	Waste-gate butterfly is warped (turbocharged engines)	Replace unit
High oil consumption	Improper grade of oil	Change oil; use only the grade and type of oil recommended by the engine manufacturer
	Glazed cylinder walls	Remove and deglaze cylinder walls by honing
	Worn cylinder walls and/or piston rings	Top spark plugs will usually be wet with oil; rework affected cylinders
	Worn valve guides	Replace guides
	Excessive oil leaks	Find and repair leaks
	Clogged air-oil separator	Clean air-oil separator in Stoddard solvent
	Loss of oil out of crankcase breather	Avoid overfilling engine with oil
	Oil is passing through turbocharger seals	Check to see that crankcase breather line is unobstructed (high crankcase back pressure will force oil through turbo seals); if breather is unobstructed, overhaul turbocharger

ENGINE *(Continued)*

Trouble	Possible cause	Remedy
High oil pressure	Improper weight of oil	Change oil; follow engine manufacturer's recommendations when choosing oil
	Oil is cold	Allow oil temperature to reach normal levels before advancing throttle
	Oil-pressure relief valve is out of adjustment	Adjust valve properly
	Incorrect spring was used in pressure relief valve	Replace spring with correct part
	Oil passage from relief valve to sump is clogged	Clean out passageway
	Oil-pressure pickup point has been moved on engine	Relocate pickup point to proper position
Low oil pressure	High oil temperature	Check for plugged oil-cooler lines, obstructed oil cooler, inoperative cowl flaps, incorrect engine baffling, etc.; service engine with proper grade and amount of oil
	Insufficient oil	Add oil
	Pressure relief valve is out of adjustment	Adjust valve properly
	Inlet side of oil pump is obstructed	Check oil suction screen and clean, if necessary
	Debris is lodged in oil-pressure relief valve	Remove, disassemble, and clean valve; check oil screens for signs of metal
	Damaged oil-pressure relief-valve seat	Repair or replace seat
	Oil-pressure pickup point has been moved	Relocate probe in accordance with engine manufacturer's recommendations
	Engine internal damage	Repair damage; check for worn gears, crankcase cracks near oil galleries, loose or missing oil-gallery plugs, and defective piston cooling squirt passages

ENGINE *(Continued)*

Trouble	Possible cause	Remedy
High oil temperature	Excessive combustion blow-by (usually the result of worn or stuck rings)	Perform a top overhaul
	Improper grade of oil	Change oil; follow engine manufacturer's recommendations when selecting oil
	Oil cooler or plumbing is clogged	Remove and clean oil cooler and/or associated plumbing
	Insufficient cooling airflow	Check oil cooler for obstructions and remove same
	Thermostatic bypass (vernatherm) valve is not operating properly	Replace valve and/or valve base
	Defective temperature gauge	Replace gauge
	Improper engine leaning	Observe proper leaning procedures as spelled out in operator's manual
	Induction air leaks	Find and repair leaks
	Carburetor or fuel injector is improperly adjusted (too lean)	Have carburetor or fuel injector adjusted properly
High cylinder-head temperature	Engine is running too lean	Check for induction air leaks; check carburetor or fuel injector for proper adjustment; observe proper leaning procedure
	Mixture control is improperly rigged	Check travel at carburetor or fuel injector; rerig as necessary
	Improper mag-to-engine timing	Adjust timing per aircraft-manual specs
	Plugged fuel nozzles	Clean nozzles
	Cooling baffles are improperly installed	Ensure that all required baffles are installed in accordance with aircraft manufacturer's recommendations
	Preignition and/or detonation	Use proper grade of gasoline; ensure that the correct type of spark plugs are used; follow engine manufacturer's operating recommendations

ENGINE *(Continued)*

Trouble	Possible cause	Remedy
Split in manifold pressure (twin-engine aircraft)	One air filter is obstructed (problem will be most noticeable at high altitude)	Replace obstructed filter
	Alternate air door is leaking on one engine	Rerig or replace door (door may appear to close on the ground but vibrate open in flight)
	Propeller blade angles out of adjustment	Adjust blade angles to appropriate limits
	Controllers are out of adjustment (turbocharged engines)	Adjust controllers to proper limits
	Incorrect hydraulic lifters were installed	Install correct parts
	Hydraulic lifters are bleeding down too rapidly (manifold pressure difference may disappear at power settings above 30 in.)	Replace or rework lifters as required
Poor idle cutoff	Mixture valve is corroded to valve seat (carbureted engines)	Clean and lap valve and seat
	Improperly rigged mixture control	Rerig control
	Valve in flow divider is sticking (fuel-injected engines)	Remove and clean valve
	Loose fuel line at flow divider or nozzles (fuel-injected engines)	Tighten all connections; ensure that nozzles are not cross-threaded in cylinders
	Dirt is blocking air-bleed hole of nozzles (fuel-injected engines)	Remove and clean nozzles

APPENDIX B
MAINTENANCE PUBLICATIONS OF INTEREST TO PILOTS

Sooner or later, if you decide to become serious about performing more of your plane's maintenance, you'll want to obtain and read additional literature on the subject of aircraft inspection and repair. The good news is that additional literature *is* available, if you know where to look. The bad news is that not much of it is up to date, or relevant to small aircraft, or written in such a way that pilots can use it. Even the U.S. Government—which has a way of surfeiting citizens with circulars, handbooks, and leaflets on every imaginable topic—has so far done a rather poor job of addressing the need for information in this area. This could change in a few years, however.

For now, suffice it to say that the pilot in search of accurate, up-to-date printed information on the subject of aircraft maintenance must be content to search through mountains of chaff in order to find a handful of wheat (some of which, in any case, will not be very digestible). The object of this appendix is to make the winnowing process a bit easier.

BOOKS In contrast to the automotive market, which can boast hundreds of "do-it-yourself" repair titles, general aviation has very few maintenance books written specifically for pilots. The best ones are listed below. (*Note:* The FAA's maintenance handbooks, which are technically advisory circulars, are listed under "Government Publications" near the end of this appendix.)

CRANE, DALE: *Preventive Maintenance for Pilots and Aircraft Owners*. Basin, Wyoming: Aviation Maintenance Foundation, Inc., 1976. (Available for $6.95 plus 75¢ postage from AMFI, P.O. Box 739, Basin, WY 82410.)

Although this book contains much useful background information and many fine photos, only 15 of the volume's 99 pages are devoted to actual hands-on maintenance. Long on theory, short on practice.

DOSSEY, CLIFF: *Lightplane Owner's Maintenance Guide.* Blue Ridge Summit, Pennsylvania: Tab Books, 1977. ($4.95 plus 50¢ postage from Tab Books, Blue Ridge Summit, PA 17214.)

A good general introduction to battery care, spark-plug maintenance, aircraft recovering and painting, and inspection techniques. Marred by cursory treatment.

SNYDER, AL, AND WELCH, WILLIAM A.: *Lightplane Construction and Repair.* Blue Ridge Summit, Pennsylvania: Tab Books, 1968. ($3.95 plus 50¢ postage from Tab Books, Blue Ridge Summit, PA 17214.)

Primarily of interest to the restorer or rebuilder working under FAR 43.3(d). Contains much good, detailed how-to information on aircraft metalwork, welding, dope and fabric, etc.

SPENCER, RUTH, AND SPENCER, WARREN: *Aircraft Dope & Fabric.* Blue Ridge Summit, Pennsylvania: Tab Books, 1970. ($3.95 plus 50¢ postage from Tab Books, Blue Ridge Summit, PA 17214.)

A copiously illustrated, highly authoritative (and highly readable) "layman's guide" to what is fast becoming a forgotten art.

PERIODICALS

Although *Flying, Private Pilot,* and the other newsstand aviation magazines occasionally publish articles relating to aircraft maintenance, the periodicals listed below are (as of this writing) the only ones that *consistently* publish maintenance-related material. (Subscription prices are, of course, subject to change.)

American Bonanza Society Newsletter. American Bonanza Society, Reading Municipal Airport, Box 3749, Reading, PA 19605. (Eleven times a year; $15 per year.)

Bonanza owners (and others) will find much excellent technical information on the care and feeding of Bonanza airframes and Continental engines in this newsletter. Highly recommended.

Avco Lycoming Flyer. Avco Lycoming Williamsport Division, Williamsport, PA 17701. (Published irregularly; free on request.)

Without a doubt one of the best maintenance publications for pilots in the world. Each issue is chock full of authoritative articles, news bits, and featurettes pertaining to engine operation and maintenance. Worth reading regardless of what kind of aircraft or engine you fly.

Cessna Skyhawk Association Newsletter. P.O. Box 761, Camden, SC 29020. (Eleven times a year; $12 per year.)

Similar in format and editorial scope to the *American Bonanza Society Newsletter,* except that Cessna 172s (rather than Beech Bonanzas) are the main topic of discussion. The same folks who put out this newsletter also publish the *Cessna Skylane Society Newletter,* also $12 (and 11 issues) per year. Both the CSS and CSA letters contain a great deal of hard-to-come-by maintenance information.

International Aviation Mechanics Journal. American Maintenance Publishers, P.O. Box 890, Basin, WY 82410. (Monthly; $9.50 per year.)

> The official organ of the Aviation Maintenance Foundation, based in Basin, Wyoming (largest aviation mechanics' organization in the country). Concentrates mainly on nonpreventive types of maintenance. As valuable for its advertisements as for its editorial content.

Light Plane Maintenance. P.O. Box 399, Maywood, CA 90270. (Fifteen times a year; $60 per year.)

> At present, the only plane-owner's publication in the United States devoted exclusively to preventive maintenance. A good source not only of how-to information, but also of information on new products and procedures, discount parts outlets, STCs, service bulletins, and airworthiness directives (both old and in the making). Contains no advertising.

CATALOGS

Mail-order suppliers frequently offer a better variety of goods, and in some cases better *prices* on those goods, than fixed-base operators—particularly for tools, AN hardware, cleaning supplies, dopes, thinners, paints, and certain other items. Because of this, and because mail-order catalogs are themselves often surprisingly good sources of technical information, I have listed the names and addresses of several of the largest, most reputable mail-order aircraft supply firms below. I urge you to send for their catalogs, which are free unless otherwise noted.

Aircraft Components, Inc., 700 North Shore Drive, Benton Harbor, MI 49022

> A good source of tools, brake parts, discount avionics, and miscellaneous pilot's supplies. Moderate discounts given on many items, including batteries and tires.

Aircraft Spruce and Specialty Co., P.O. Box 424, Fullerton, CA 92632

> The Aircraft Spruce catalog (now well over 200 pages in length) contains a wealth of technical information on AN hardware, composite materials, aircraft-quality wood, metals and their designations, etc., and would be well worth the $3.00-per-copy price even if it were not refundable on your first $25 purchase (which it is). Almost anything you want in the way of standard aircraft tools and replacement parts can be found here.

Aircraft Supply, Allegheny County Airport, West Mifflin, PA 15122

> Overhaul-exchange accessories (alternators, starters, magnetos, vacuum pumps, etc.), windshields and windows, instruments, and recovery supplies in addition to the usual line of replacement parts (batteries, tires, and so forth).

Cooper Aviation Supply Co., 2149 East Pratt Boulevard, Elk Grove Village, IL 60007

> Primarily a source of dopes, thinners, primers, solvents, paints, waxes, caulks, glues, penetrants, tapes, tubing, and fabrics—plus a few other odds and ends.

J. C. Whitney & Co., P.O. Box 8410, Chicago, IL 60680

> No, J. C. Whitney (the famous auto-parts house) does not sell aircraft parts; nor am I suggesting that you use automotive parts on your plane. The fact of the matter is, though, that J. C. Whitney's marvelously complete catalogs list dozens of tools that you can use on cars and planes (tire pumps, battery chargers, oil-filter wrenches, brake bleeders, and other devices too ingenious to mention), almost all of them at much lower prices than you can find anywhere else—if you can even *find* some of these items anywhere else! No plane owner should be without a J. C. Whitney catalog. If you don't have one, get one.

Univair Aircraft Corp., Route 3, Box 59, Aurora, CO 80011

> Like a good tool, a Univair catalog, once borrowed, usually doesn't come back. It's that useful. Univair supplies virtually all the standard hardware items and accessories found in the other catalogs (most of this stuff isn't even listed in Univair's spiral-bound catalog, for space reasons). What Univair really specializes in—and what you'll mostly find in their catalog—is parts and accessories for old and/or out-of-production aircraft. Univair holds the Type Certificates for the Stinson 108, the Swift, and the Ercoupe (along with the Aeromatic and Flottorp lines of propellers); and what they don't stock, they manufacture themselves. (That includes many "out of print" service manuals, which Univair perpetually reprints.) "All parts for some, some parts for all" has been the company's motto for many years. When you see their catalog, you'll know why. The catalog price is $2, nonrefundable.

Wag-Aero, Inc., Box 181, 1216 North Road, Lyons, WI 53148

> Wag-Aero's catalog is primarily of interest to the homebuilder or restorer; however, other aircraft owners will find it useful for its seasonal "specials" on tires, tubes, batteries, and instruments. Some truly great prices are offered year-round on muffler overhaul work through Wag-Aero's exhaust-component repair facility, otherwise known as Aero Fabricators (FAA Repair Station No. 3474). Send $1 for a catalog.

MANUFACTURERS' PUBLICATIONS

Manufacturers' maintenance publications fall into three categories: service manuals (and associated parts catalogs), service bulletins, and auxiliary service publications. Each category is (or should be) of interest to pilots.

The nature and scope of aircraft service manuals was discussed in Chapter 1; that information will not be rehashed here. The important things to remember are: (1) The airframe manufacturer's service manual is the primary source of airframe and engine maintenance information for your plane. The engine manufacturer's shop manuals will tell you virtually nothing about how to maintain your engine, since its manuals are devoted entirely to disassembly and reassembly, overhaul, and testing. (2) Service manuals are not static entities; they are constantly being updated, corrected, and improved. Therefore, be sure (when you buy a service manual for your plane or any of your plane's systems) that you are getting periodic revisions along with the basic manual. Usually, there'll be a "revisions starter" card in the front or back of the manual, which you can send in to the factory to get your name on the mailing list to receive future revisions. Be sure to mail that card in.

Keeping up with scores of service manuals and the many sporadic revisions associated with each has driven many an FBO service manager berserk. To cut down on the obvious logistic problems occasioned by the use of paper manuals and revisions, many general aviation manufacturers have gone to microfiche (microfilm-card) reproduction of service publications. So far, as of this writing, Piper is the only major general aviation manufacturer to have completely dropped the publication of paper manuals in favor of microfiche (or Aerofiche, as it is known in the trade); you cannot buy a paper manual for any Piper airplane made after 1973. Most other airframe manufacturers, however, have begun to *offer* Aerofiche manuals along with their paper manuals, and it seems likely that before long, these other manufacturers will follow Piper's lead in abandoning paper-format manuals altogether. If you intend to obtain a paper service manual for your plane, now's the time to do it.

As for how to order service manuals and parts catalogs: Most manufacturers prefer that customers order manuals through their established dealer networks. Some, however (Cessna and Mooney in particular), will take orders directly. Prices tend to fluctuate often and drastically; contact your nearest dealer for details, or write directly to the factory for an up-to-date publications catalog. Appropriate addresses are given below.

The situation with regard to service bulletins (or service letters, service instructions, etc.) is somewhat different from that for service manuals, in that (1) *all* service bulletins are issued in paper form, rather than microfiche, and (2) bulletins of an urgent or mandatory-compliance nature are sent to registered owners of affected aircraft free of charge, in most cases. (The only exceptions to this are the engine manufacturers' bulletins. Neither Avco Lycoming nor Teledyne Continental has a policy of automatically mailing service bulletins to affected owners, although their bulletins are frequently relayed to owners via the airframe manufacturers.)

Not all factory bulletins are of an urgent or mandatory-compliance nature, of course; it is probably fair to say, in fact, that most are not. The only sure way to keep up with both kinds of bulletins—the only reliable way to keep abreast of *all* product-improvement mods, changes in recommended operating procedures, etc.—is to subscribe to factory bulletins on a year-to-year basis. (This is particularly important in the case of engine service bulletins, which, urgent or not, you might not otherwise receive, except perhaps in the form of an airworthiness directive later on.)

In addition to subscribing to next year's service bulletins, I strongly suggest that you also consider investing in a complete back file of old (but still active) bulletins for your plane and your engine. The engine manufacturer's bulletin back-files in particular are tremendously valuable sources of information regarding performance mods, routine maintenance, special inspection tips, factory warranty policies, engine break-in, approved spark plugs, approved lubricating oils, etc.

Except for Beech and Piper, all the airframe and engine manufacturers will accept orders for service-bulletin subscriptions and backfiles direct from customers. (*Note:* Single service bulletins will be sent free of charge to owners on request. Just write and state your needs.) For price information, contact your nearest factory representative, or write to the appropriate manufacturers and request their Publications Catalogs.

Some of the best, most interesting service information comes not from the airframe manufacturers or from the big two engine manufacturers, but from a variety of accessory manufacturers that supply critical components to general aviation—manufacturers such as AC, Champion, Cleveland Wheels and Brakes, and B. F. Goodrich, to name but a few. For detailed service information on aircraft tires, wheels, and spark plugs, you can't beat the publications put out by the tire, wheel, and plug manufacturers themselves. (These are the "auxiliary service publications" mentioned at the beginning of this section.) Obviously, a complete listing of all the general aviation subsystem manufacturers and their addresses cannot be squeezed into the space available here; however, I have made an attempt to list the names and addresses of some of the companies whose auxiliary publications proved helpful in the writing of this book. I urge you to write to these companies, requesting copies of any catalogs and/or technical bulletins they may have on hand. (Enclose $2.00 with each request, to cover postage and handling costs.)

AC Spark Plug Division
General Motors Corporation
1300 N. Dort Highway
Flint, MI 48556

Alcor, Inc.
P.O. Box 32516
San Antonio, TX 78284

Avco Lycoming
652 Oliver Street
Williamsport, PA 17701

Beech Aircraft Corp.
9709 East Central
Wichita, KS 67201

Bellanca Aircraft Corp.
Alexandria, MN 56308

B. F. Goodrich Co.
Engineered Systems Division
500 South Main Street
Akron, OH 44318

Cessna Service Parts Center
P.O. Box 949
Wichita, KS 67201

Champion Spark Plug Co.
P.O. Box 910
Toledo, OH 43601

Cleveland Wheels & Brakes
1160 Avon Center Road
Avon, OH 44011

Firestone Tire & Rubber Co.
1200 Firestone Parkway
Akron, OH 44317

Goodyear Aerospace Corp.
Aviation Products Division
1144 East Market Street
Akron, OH 44316

Mooney Aircraft Corp.
P.O. Box 72
Kerrville, TX 78028

Piper Aircraft Corp.
Lock Haven, PA 17745

Prestolite/Rebat
Toledo, OH 43694

Teledyne Continental Motors
P.O. Box 90
Mobile, AL 36601

GOVERNMENT PUBLICATIONS

The U.S. Government, via the Federal Aviation Administration, publishes a bewildering variety of handbooks, circulars, and directives bearing on the subject of aircraft maintenance, most of them oriented to professional aircraft mechanics and fleet operators. Some of these publications are (or conceivably could be) of interest to pilots.

The FAA maintenance publications of interest to pilots include various Advisory Circulars, Federal Aviation Regulations, Airworthiness Directives, Parts Manufacturer Approvals, the *Summary of Supplemental Type Certificates*, and (possibly) the *Type Certificate Data Sheets and Specifications* volumes.

The important thing to remember about these publications is that, with the exception of some Advisory Circulars, they all do cost something (there are no free FARs, for instance). With the sole exception of Airworthiness Directives, all "for sale" FAA publications must be ordered through the U.S. Government Printing Office (GPO). In other words, you need to know three addresses.

The address to use when ordering *free* publications is:

U.S. Department of Transportation
Publications Section, M 443.1
Washington, DC 20590

Requests for *Airworthiness Directives* should be directed to:

Federal Aviation Administration
P.O. Box 25461
Attn: ACC-23
Oklahoma City, OK 73125

All *for sale* documents (except Airworthiness Directives) should be ordered from:

Superintendent of Documents
U.S. Government Printing Office
Washington, DC 20402

When ordering publications from the GPO, it is vitally important that you include not only the full title of each publication, but the *stock number* as well. (Do not confuse the AC numbers of Advisory Circulars with their stock numbers, which begin with SN.)

The full titles and (where applicable) stock numbers of some of the more popular and useful government maintenance publications are given below, along with a brief description of each.

AC No. 00-2: *Advisory Circular Checklist.* (Free.)

This triannually updated checklist contains a complete, current listing of all active FAA Advisory Circulars, along with ordering information (not only for the Advisory Circulars themselves, but for Airworthiness Directives, type-certificate data sheets, and various other FAA publications as well). Exceedingly valuable for its up-to-date pricing and ordering information.

AC No. 00-44: *Status of the Federal Aviation Regulations.* (Free.)

The various Parts of the FARs, like the various nonregulatory Advisory Circulars, are constantly undergoing revision and reprinting (which means also that their prices are constantly changing). The purpose of AC No. 00-44 is to set forth the current publication status (i.e., current pricing and ordering data) for all the individually sold Parts of the FARs. If you've ever wondered what all the different Parts are about and how to order them yourself, direct from the government, this advisory circular will tell you.

AC No. 20-106: *Aircraft Inspection for the General Aviation Aircraft Owner.* (SN 050-007-00449-4; $2.75, GPO.)

A simply written primer designed to familiarize owners, pilots, student mechanics, and others with basic inspection procedures.

AC No. 43-3: *Corrosion Control for Aircraft.* (Free.)

An excellent 100-plus-page introduction to the topic, containing much detailed how-to information. Illustrated with line drawings.

AC No. 43-5: *Airworthiness Directives for General Aviation Aircraft.* (Free.)

Explains what Airworthiness Directives are (they're law) and clears up areas of misunderstanding regarding pilots', owners', and mechanics' responsibilities concerning compliance and logbook entries.

AC No. 43-9A: *Maintenance Records: General Aviation Aircraft.* (Free.)

Provides information needed to assist maintenance personnel in fulfilling their responsibilities under FAR 43.9.

AC No. 43-11: *Reciprocating Engine Overhaul Terminology and Standards.* (Free.)

Lays to rest whole hangars full of myths surrounding the meanings of the terms "major overhaul," "top overhaul," "zero-time engine," "remanufactured," "rebuilt," and "factory new" (among others) and makes the FAA's position on engine overhauls (and when they're required) crystal clear.

AC No. 43-12: *Preventive Maintenance.* (Free.)

A brief, not especially helpful bulletin outlining the pilot's responsibilities with regard to (and the legalities surrounding) preventive maintenance.

AC No. 43.13-1A: *Acceptable Methods, Techniques, and Practices: Aircraft Inspection and Repair.* (SN 050-011-00058-5; $4.70, GPO.)

This is the FAA's bible on inspection and repair. It sets forth (in several hundred pages, with the aid of innumerable drawings, charts, and photographs) *the* FAA-approved way of doing things where aircraft maintenance is concerned. An exceedingly informative basic reference manual. Used by all aircraft mechanics.

AC No. 43.13-2A: *Acceptable Methods, Techniques, and Practices: Aircraft Alterations.* (SN 050-007-00407-9; $2.75, GPO.)

A companion volume to AC No. 43.13-1A. Whereas AC No. 43.13-1A discusses widely applicable inspection and repair techniques, this somewhat smaller volume focuses its attention on *alteration* techniques specifically affecting radio, tow-hitch, ski, shoulder-harness, oxygen-system, battery, and cargo-tiedown-device installations. More limited in scope (and usefulness) than AC No. 43.13-1A, but worth having nonetheless.

AC No. 43-16: *General Aviation Airworthiness Alerts.* (Controlled circulation; available through FAA/DOT, P.O. Box 25082, Oklahoma City, OK 73125.)

This circular, which (unlike most Advisory Circulars) is issued monthly, reports on unsafe conditions, unsafe products, and unusual field service difficulties that have come to the FAA's attention through its voluntary malfunction and defect reporting system. Many of the service irregularities reported in AC No. 43-16 later become the focus of factory bulletins and Airworthiness Directives. Unfortunately, the FAA's official policy (as of this writing) is to distribute AC No. 43-16 *only* to certificated repair stations and inspection-authorization-rated (IA) mechanics. Eventually, the FAA may decide to offer it on a subscription basis to all interested parties. In the meantime, if you want to see AC No. 43-16 yourself, you'll have to either borrow a copy from the nearest repair station or IA mechanic or request the circular from the address shown under the Freedom of Information Act.

AC No. 65-9A: *Airframe and Powerplant Mechanics General Handbook.* (SN 050-007-00379-0; $6.75, GPO.)

Designed as a manual for student mechanics, this 549-page volume contains easily understood discussions of aircraft hardware, aircraft drawings, fuel systems, inspection fundamentals, aircraft ground handling, generators and motors, and hand tools, with review chapters on mathematics, physics, and basic electricity.

AC No. 65-12A: *Airframe and Powerplant Mechanics Powerplant Handbook.* (SN 050-007-00373-1; $6.50, GPO.)

Five hundred pages of background material (much of it out of date) on aircraft engines, their design, and their maintenance. Of limited usefulness to the pilot-owner of a modern four- or six-cylinder "flat opposed" piston aircraft engine.

AC No. 65-15A: *Airframe and Powerplant Mechanics Airframe Handbook.* (SN 050-007-00391-9; $6.00, GPO.)

At 601 pages, AC No. 65-15A is the longest (and arguably the most useful) volume in the FAA's trilogy of student-mechanic maintenance handbooks. It covers everything from assembly and rigging to structural repairs, from fabric recovering and painting to mounting and demounting tires. Copiously illustrated with line drawings (and a few photos).

Parts Manufacturer Approvals. (SN 050-007-00444-3; $7.50, GPO.)

This directory (which is not an Advisory Circular) provides the most complete listing in existence of the various replacement and modification parts that the FAA has approved for sale for installation on type-certificated aircraft.

Summary of Airworthiness Directives for Small Aircraft, vol. I. (SN 050-007-00425-7; $21.00, FAA Oklahoma City.)

Relatively few pilots realize that for just $21.00 (made payable to the Federal Aviation Administration), anyone can obtain a 4-in.-thick directory containing *all Airworthiness Directives that have ever been issued,* plus a 2-year subscription to future AD notes (which are issued on a biweekly basis). If you're shopping for planes—or are merely curious about your own airplane's exact AD history—this is a $21.00 investment well worth making. (*Note:* This volume covers AD notes affecting aircraft under 12,500 lb only. Large-aircraft AD notes are contained in volume II of the *Summary,* available separately for $18.00 and again including a 2-year subscription to future directives.)

Summary of Supplemental Type Certificates. (TD 4.36:976; $43.00, GPO.)

This directory lists the names and addresses of all Supplemental Type Certificate (STC) holders in the United States. The list is organized by aircraft model and, in addition to giving names, addresses, and STC numbers, explains in 10 to 20 words what each STC is about. If you've ever wondered whether there's an approved turbocharger kit for your plane's engine (or whether there are an approved heavy-duty brake mod, auxiliary fuel tanks, STOL mods, etc., for your plane) this directory will tell you what you want to know. (*Note:* Quarterly updates are included in the price.)

Type Certificate Data Sheets and Specifications.
  Volume I, *Single-Engine Airplanes.* (TCDS 1; $41.00, GPO.)
  Volume II, *Small Multiengine Airplanes.* (TCDS 2; $34.00, GPO.)
  Volume III, *Large Multiengine Airplanes.* (TCDS 3; $32.00, GPO.)
  Volume IV, *Rotorcraft, Gliders, and Balloons.* (TCDS 4; $29.00, GPO.)
  Volume V, *Aircraft Engines and Propellers.* (TCDS 5; $34.00, GPO.)
  Volume VI, *Aircraft Listing and Aircraft Engine and Propeller Listing.* (SN 050-007-00360-9; $4.15, GPO.)

The Type Certificate Data Sheets are what mechanics and FAA personnel go by to determine whether any given airplane in the field conforms as it should to the basic type design. The data sheets (which are prepared by the FAA from data submitted by the manufacturer) contain information regarding operating limitations, required equipment, special placards, approved engine and propeller combinations, and weight and balance limits established for the make and model aircraft in question. To remain airworthy, every airplane and engine must conform to the specifications listed in the Type Certificate Data Sheets. Period. (Prices for the various volumes include the basic document plus monthly updates for a year except for volume VI, which is a single-sale item.)

Finally, it should be noted that the FAA's Safety Data Branch in Oklahoma City provides a very unique publishing service for pilots and others interested in researching the maintenance history of particular products and accessories: For a relatively small fee, the Safety Data people will provide a detailed computer print-out of service difficulty information pertaining to a particular product (one type of plane, say), as far back as 5 years. The relevant data—based on field reports sent in by mechanics over the years—can be printed out in any numerous formats, depending on what you're interested in. For further information on this unusual service, write to:

Flight Standards National Field Office, FAA
Attn: AFS-580
P.O. Box 25082
Oklahoma City, OK 73125

INDEX